IMAGES
of America

BETHPAGE

ON THE COVER: These "Janes Who Made the Planes" are working on a wing assembly in their coveralls at the Grumman Aeronautical Engineering Company in 1943. (Courtesy of the Central Park Historical Society.)

IMAGES of America
BETHPAGE

John Logerfo

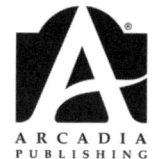

Copyright © 2015 by John Logerfo
ISBN 978-1-4671-2277-1

Published by Arcadia Publishing
Charleston, South Carolina

Printed in the United States of America

Library of Congress Control Number: 2014943868

For all general information, please contact Arcadia Publishing:
Telephone 843-853-2070
Fax 843-853-0044
E-mail sales@arcadiapublishing.com
For customer service and orders:
Toll-Free 1-888-313-2665

Visit us on the Internet at www.arcadiapublishing.com

*To my parents, who shared their guidance and
taught me about strength and perseverance*

*To Nora, Alec, and Jason for being my
compass on this great adventure*

CONTENTS

Acknowledgments		6
Introduction		7
1.	The Bethpage Purchase	11
2.	A Town Takes Root	17
3.	Bethpage to Central Park	23
4.	Road Races and Famous Faces	35
5.	Suburban Expansion	51
6.	Central Park to Bethpage	69
7.	Looking toward the Sky	85
8.	Zorn's: A Taste of History	97
9.	Building a Community	105

ACKNOWLEDGMENTS

This book would not be possible without the cooperation of many people, the generous contribution of materials, and all the support I received during my research. My deepest gratitude goes to the Central Park Historical Society for permitting me access to their extensive collection, with a very special thanks to Ann and Bob Albertson and Leonard Mulqueen for their help, knowledge, and tireless dedication to preserving the history and the story of Bethpage.

Many thanks to those that have shared their enthusiasm, including Howard Kroplick, town historian of North Hempstead; Joyce and Frank Calo for their willingness to share their family history; the Grumman History Center, especially Larry A. Feliu and Ken Spieser; the Nassau County Parks, Recreation and Museums Photo Archives Center, especially Iris Levin; and the Plainedge Public Library, especially library director Marilyn Kappenberg. I wish to acknowledge a very special thanks to Merrill Zorn and the contributions made by Frank DeBobes, Ernie Finamore, Dennis Fleury, Bill Florio, Carol and Kiera Grassi, Brian Nugent, Marie Rusch, Rita Rusch, Mike Tamborrino, and Amanda Laikin, for her editing assistance. Lastly, Rob and Mike Epstein; Bobby and Tara LaValley; Billy Mansfield; Jay and Herb Schneider; my wife, Nora; my sons, Alec and Jason; my parents, Connie and Gus Logerfo; and my brothers, Anthony, Stephen, and Philip. Completing my research has been a fantastic journey, and I wish to thank Arcadia Publishing for the opportunity and my editor, Abby Walker, and title manager, Caitrin Cunningham.

Unless otherwise noted, all images appear courtesy of the Central Park Historical Society.

INTRODUCTION

It is hard to imagine early Bethpage and its surrounding towns as fertile lands with a mix of grassy plains and rolling hills with stands of pine, oak, and chestnut trees, wild berries of all kinds, and ample water sources with abundant deer, quail, and other smaller wild animals. Maybe for a moment, one could stroll through the trails in the Bethpage State Park to catch a little flavor of the time before the development, the railroad, and the building of roads that crisscross the area today.

It was these surroundings that drew Thomas Powell Sr. to make his home here. In 1687, Thomas Powell Sr. bought more than 15 square miles in central Long Island from local Indian tribes. The tract was 3.5 miles east to west and five miles north and south. He purchased it from the three tribes of the area: the Marsapeque (Massapequa), Matinecoc, and Sacatogue. This land purchase included present-day Bethpage, Old Bethpage, Farmingdale, East Farmingdale, South Farmingdale, Plainedge, Plainview, and part of Melville. In 1695, the deed was officially recognized by the Queens County Clerk's Office. In the agreement, the Indians reserved the right to pick berries and hunt on the property sold. This purchased land came to be known as the Bethpage Purchase because the biblical town of Bethphage, meaning "house of figs," was situated between Jericho and Jerusalem in Israel, just as the towns of Jericho and Jerusalem on the island, known today as Wantagh.

For nearly 150 years, this land remained unchanged, as it was the Powell homestead and divided up between his 15 children. His children built homes and raised families. Powell's large family proved helpful in cultivating the vast acreage of his holdings. After Powell's death, the land was divided between his children, but he also gave one third of his lands to a former apprentice named Thomas Whitson. This started the breakup of the family ownership of Bethpage. Land was divided and sold to outsiders who started their own family farms. By 1840, there were a large number of new people settling the land that had previously been unused.

In 1841, a great change occurred when the Central Railroad of Long Island was extended through Bethpage. Land speculators purchased large sections of land near the tracks, which they began building up. As population increased, the needs of the town increased. In 1858, the first school was built, and a local post office was established and a train station constructed. In order to entice more people to settle here, the residents voted to change the name of the local post office to Central Park in 1867. Many businesses opened up around the station, and it soon became the center for settlement and development. The rapid transportation system of the railroad to New York and other communities turned Central Park into a modern town. Central Park grew and expanded with a need for merchants that sold goods. These businesses take away farm help, and the land speculators made the land more valuable than farming it. Homes were being built as well as hotels, blacksmith shops, lumber yards, and butcher shops.

William K. Vanderbilt, heir to a railroad fortune, was a pioneer race car driver and organized America's first international road race. Vanderbilt chartered the construction of a private highway, and he and his associates were careful to position this new and modern highway as a modern convenience to all automobile enthusiasts, praising the virtues of economic development and the efficiency of quickly retreating from the city to the calm and healthful benefits the fresh country air that Long Island had to offer. On June 6, 1908, the motor parkway staged an official groundbreaking ceremony to commemorate the beginning of construction in Central Park. The most distinctive features of the parkway were the reinforced concrete pavement, the elimination of grade crossings, and the banked curves allowing the cars to take them at a maximum speed of 60 miles per hour. In 1908, the race was held over the same course as the Motor Parkway Sweepstakes, and a grandstand with a capacity of 5,000 spectators was built on the Hempstead Plains in today's Levittown. For the first time, America could finally boast of victory in an automobile race against international competition. The crowd that year was estimated at over 200,000 spectators along the 23.46-mile course.

Many famous people came out to Central Park to watch the Vanderbilt Cup Races and stayed at the Beau Sejour Hotel. The finish line of one of the earlier races was not too far from the Beau Sejour, and the participants all came there to celebrate. Other famed and notable people came to dine there as well.

As Central Park started to grow, so did the needs of the community. In April 1910, the Central Park Fire Department was organized. As the population continued to grow, other obligations needed to be met. In 1911, the Powell Avenue School was constructed with four classrooms, which marked the end of the old one-room school and the way of life that went with it. It was soon necessary to add to this building, and eight more rooms were constructed, bringing the total to 12 classrooms. During the course of construction, a two-room wood annex was built, which took care of the overcrowded school until the addition was finished. In 1923, the new structure was completed.

In 1912, Benjamin Franklin Yoakum, a wealthy railroad executive, purchased 1,368 acres of land along the northern edge of Farmingdale extending into what is now Old Bethpage. Yoakum hired Devereux Emmet to design and build an 18-hole golf course on the land. It opened for play in 1923, and Yoakum leased it to the private Lenox Hills Country Club. When Yoakum died in 1929, the Yoakum heirs sold the property, and the Long Island Park Commission took over the lease, operating the Lenox Hills Country Club as a public facility. In 1931, the park commission purchased the Yoakum Estate, the Botto farms, and other area farms to create Bethpage State Park. During this time, the name Central Park created a few problems for the town, and there was a desire to change it. One reason for changing the name was that the mail was always being sent to nearby towns like Central Islip, Center Port, Center Moriches, and even to the actual Central Park in New York City. Some residents felt that the name Central Park had no historical background, and they preferred the name given by the original owner, Thomas Powell. In 1932, Jessie Merritt, the Nassau County historian and a direct descendent of Thomas Powell, proposed naming the properties Bethpage State Park. A petition signed by 435 residents of Central Park was prepared and sent to the US Post Office Department in Washington to change the name of the post office. Letters were written to the Long Island Rail Road (LIRR) for support in changing the name of the train station. Letters were also written to the Long Island State Parks Commission asking for permission to change the name of the village from Central Park to Bethpage. In 1935, the Bethpage State Park, clubhouse, and three of the four 18-hole golf courses were open to the public. On October 1, 1936, the name Bethpage was officially declared by both the post office and the LIRR. The Bethpage State Parkway was opened in 1936 to serve as a parkway connection from the Southern State Parkway to Bethpage State Park, and with its opening, the Bethpage State Park immediately became a popular destination.

In 1935, the Zorn family opened and operated nine poultry farms. The Zorn's Bethpage Farm opened its first retail store on Hempstead Turnpike in 1940. The store remains on 4 of the original 10 acres that opened in 1940. In 1936, Grumman Aircraft Engineering Corporation expanded its operations to Bethpage and soon became the largest employer for Bethpage and Long Island. The company's first ventures into the civilian realm occurred when it developed the G-21 Goose and the G-22 Gulfhawk. Grumman's first major warplane was the innovative F4F Wildcat, a single-seat, single-engine, carrier-based strike fighter equipped with a unique Grumman invention called "sto-wings," which allowed a plane's wings to fold in half for easy storage on cramped aircraft carriers. Grumman's TBF Avenger also contributed significantly to the Allied victory over Japan and Germany. The Avenger was a single-engine, mono-wing torpedo bomber that held a pilot, a turret gunner, and a radioman/bombardier. Grumman soon built one of the classic combat planes of World War II, the F6F Hellcat. Essentially a more sophisticated version of the F4F Wildcat, Grumman engineers specifically designed it to defeat the Japanese Zero. Grumman produced 12,272 Hellcats from June 1942 to November 1945, the largest number of fighters ever made in a single aircraft factory. As World War II was ending, the aviation industry began developing the jet engine. It was a new era of flight, and Grumman engineers worked on perfecting the new technology. By 1949, they had created the F9F Panther, the company's first combat jet and the Navy's primary fighter plane of the Korean War. In 1962, Grumman became the chief contractor on the Apollo Lunar Module that landed men on the moon, and they built 13 lunar modules. The first one landed on the moon on July 1969, during the Apollo 11 mission. In September 1972, the Grumman-designed F-14 Tomcat began replacing the planes used on US aircraft carriers and naval bases. Due to its extreme flexibility, superior weapons system, and the fact that it could travel at Mach 2.5, the F-14 remained the Navy's best all-around fighter for well over 20 years.

With a growing population of young families moving to the area, houses of worship needed to be built for the various religious groups of the community. Schools also needed to be built to accommodate the growing enrollment. In 1955, a complete junior-senior high school program was in operation for the first time. In 1959, Bethpage High School was built on Cherry Avenue, and on June 25, 1961, the first full senior class graduated from the new high school. Previously, students went to neighboring Farmingdale High School. On November 22, 1963, when John F. Kennedy was assassinated in Dallas, Texas, the community of Bethpage came together to have the Bethpage Middle School named to honor President Kennedy. It became the first school in the country to claim this distinction. In 1963, a new library was completed on Powell Avenue.

The roadways of the community were widened, resurfaced, and fitted with storm drains to prevent flooding. The construction of the Seaford–Oyster Bay Expressway was underway, and the Powell Avenue Exit 8 was completed in 1962.

In 1990, a provisional charter was granted to the Central Park Historical Society (CPHS) by the board of regents of the University of the State of New York. The CPHS was founded in 1986, at the suggestion of a committee that assembled to commemorate the 50th anniversary of the name change from Central Park to Bethpage. The purpose of the Central Park Historical Society is to promote and encourage historical research and a greater knowledge and interest in the State of New York, particularly Bethpage and the surrounding area. Its mission is to gather, preserve, display, and make available for study the artifacts, relics, books, manuscripts, papers, photographs, and other records relating to Bethpage.

By the 1980s, most of the available vacant land was occupied by businesses, schools, or homes, and there was no more major development in the area. The town began to focus its efforts on maintenance and improvements. In 1995, the Bethpage Public Library was renovated with the addition of the auditorium. Other improvements were made to the schools. And in 1999, a new post office was built on Hicksville Road.

With the Grumman Corporation on the west side of town preventing expansion westward, and the Bethpage State Park on the east, Bethpage could develop without overdeveloping while still keeping its small-town charm. Today, it remains a quaint, tight-knit community filled with pride.

One

The Bethpage Purchase

Thomas Powell Sr. was born in 1641 in a settlement of Puritans in the New Haven Colony, which was in present-day New Haven, Connecticut. Powell moved and lived for several years in Huntington, New York, and held many positions within the administration of Huntington, including recorder, surveyor, overseer, trustee, and constable. In 1682, Powell declined to serve again as constable, as the job required the officer to swear to levy and collect rates for the Church of England. By then, he had become a Quaker. In 1687, Thomas Powell Sr. bought more than 15 square miles in central Long Island from local Indian tribes in a land transaction know as the Bethpage Purchase. The area is approximately 3.5 miles east to west and five miles north to south. The three tribes were the Marsapeque (Massapequa), Matinecoc, and Sacatogue. This land purchase included present-day Bethpage, Old Bethpage, Farmingdale, East Farmingdale, South Farmingdale, Plainedge, Plainview, and part of Melville. In 1695, the deed that recognized Powell had already been in possession of part of the land for more than seven years was recorded in the Queens County Clerk's Office. Part of the agreement was that the Indians reserved the right to pick berries and hunt on the property sold.

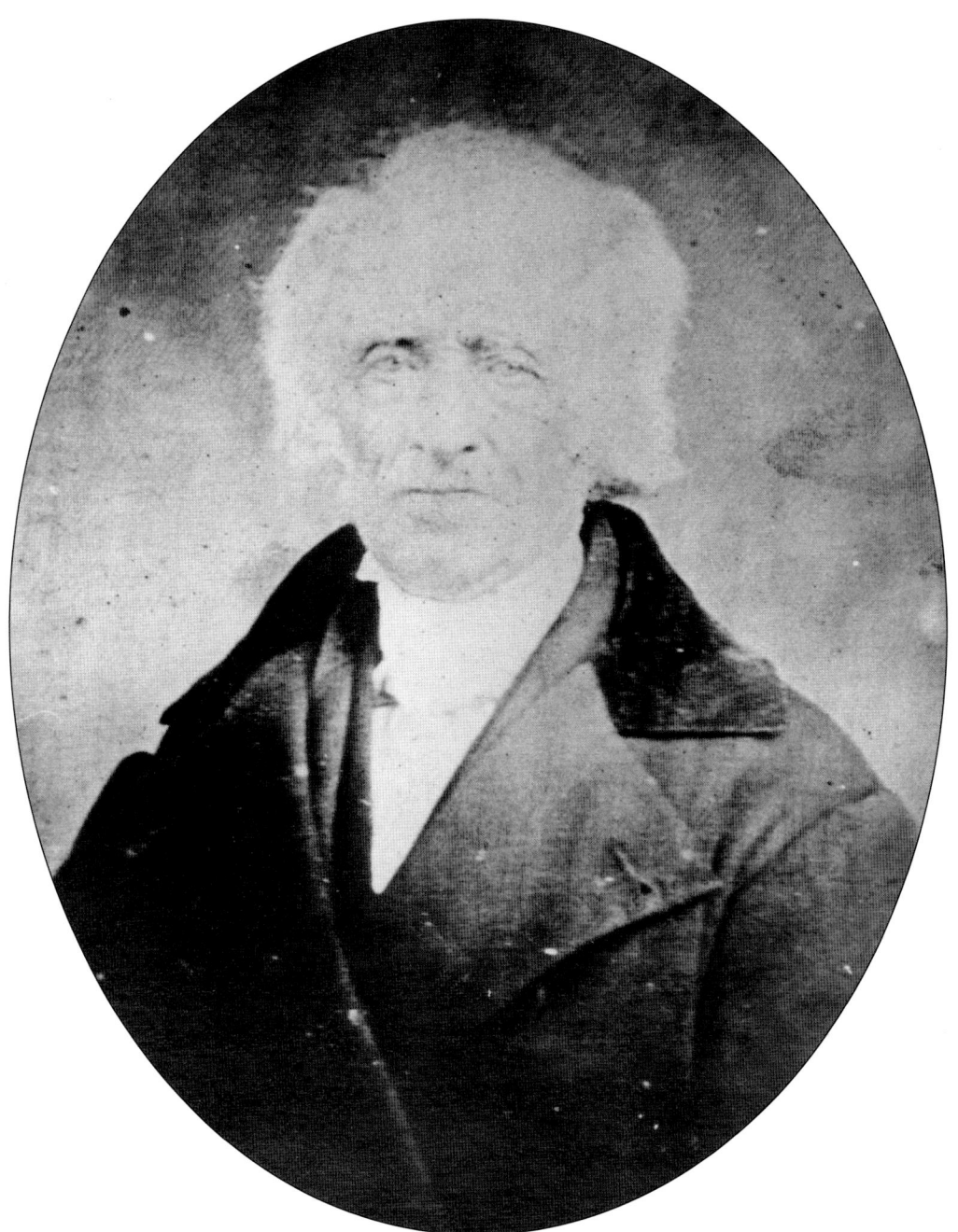

Powell called the land he purchased Bethpage, as it was situated between the towns of Jericho and Jerusalem, just as the biblical town of Bethphage was situated between Jericho and Jerusalem in Israel. Jerusalem was renamed and is now known as Wantagh. In 1699, Powell made a second purchase, the Rim of the Woods Purchase, which includes land to the west of the original Bethpage Purchase, including most of present-day Bethpage and all the land in the northern section of present-day Plainedge (Boundary Avenue, north to Old Motor Parkway, and Hicksville Road east to Cedar Drive). Pictured in 1860 is Joshua Powell, minister at Bethpage Church and a great-great-grandson of Thomas Powell.

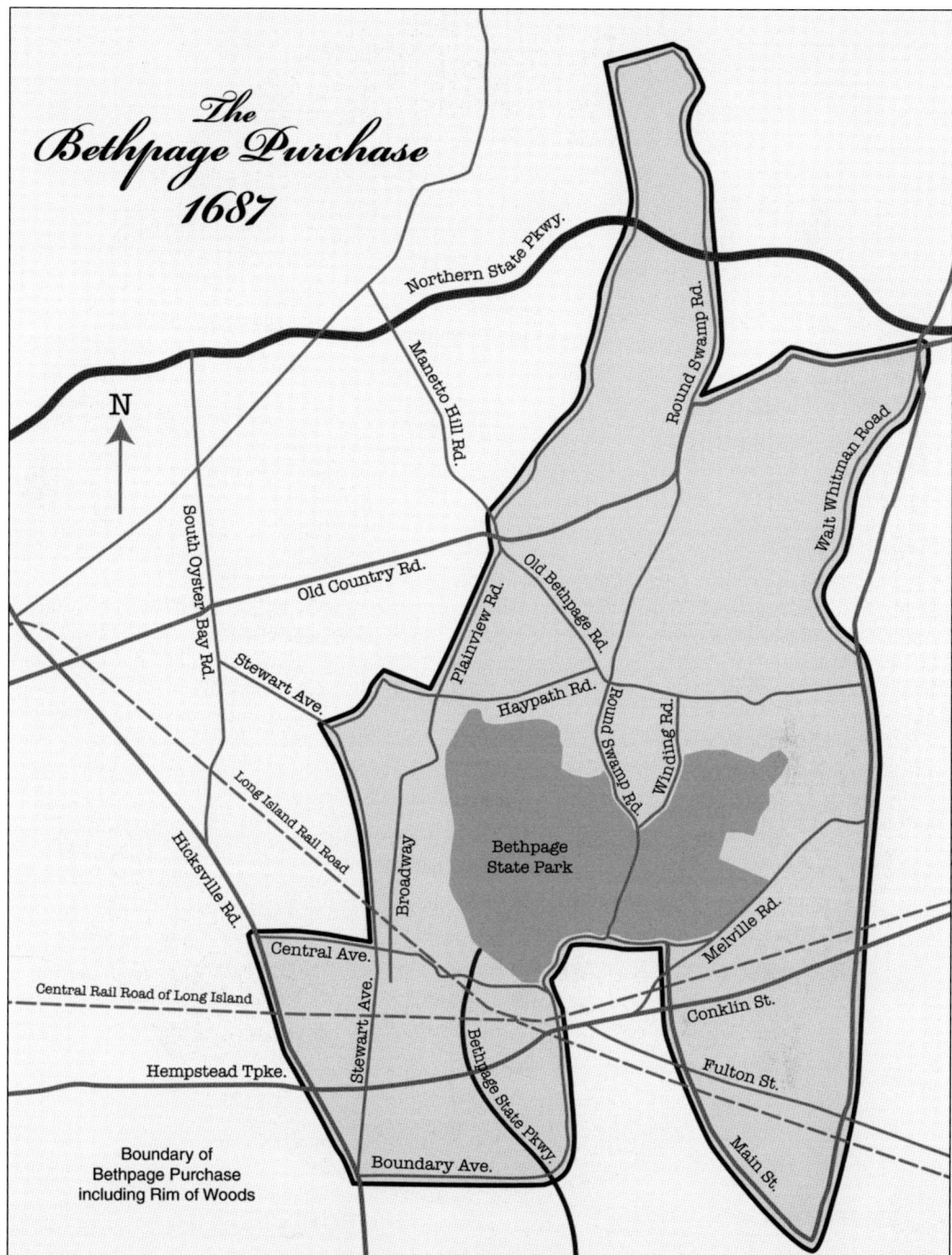

Powell and his first wife had eight children, including another Thomas Powell (1665–1731), the fourth Thomas Powell. His first wife died before 1688 in Westbury, after which Powell married Elizabeth Phillips of Jericho in Westbury in 1690. They had seven children. For years, the Powells prospered in Farmingdale, where Powell built his home. As the family grew and fathers divided land among their sons, the farms began to spread farther away from the Thomas Powell home tract. (Map illustrated by the author.)

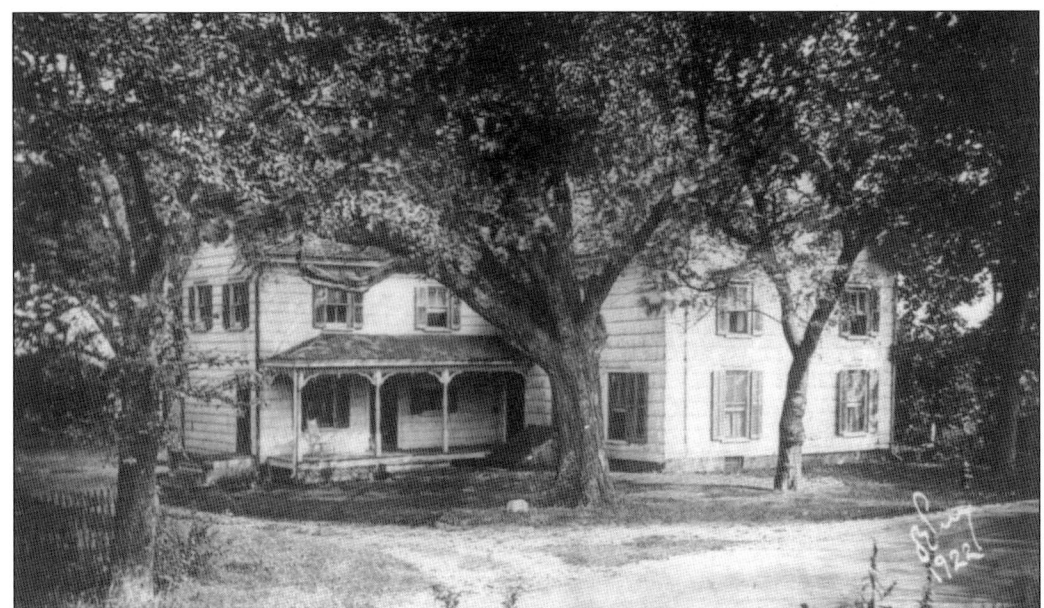

Thomas Powell originally built his house on Hempstead Turnpike. After his 15 children grew up, Powell built himself a new house on Merritt Road in Farmingdale in 1700 and gave his original house to one of his sons. That house was destroyed in 1931. Powell divided up this land between his children, but he also gave one third of his land to a former apprentice, Thomas Whitson. This started the breakup of the family ownership of Bethpage, especially after Powell died, around 1721–1722. For nearly 150 years, the descendants of Powell were the sole inhabitants of the Bethpage Purchase area. Pictured here is the second Powell home in 1922.

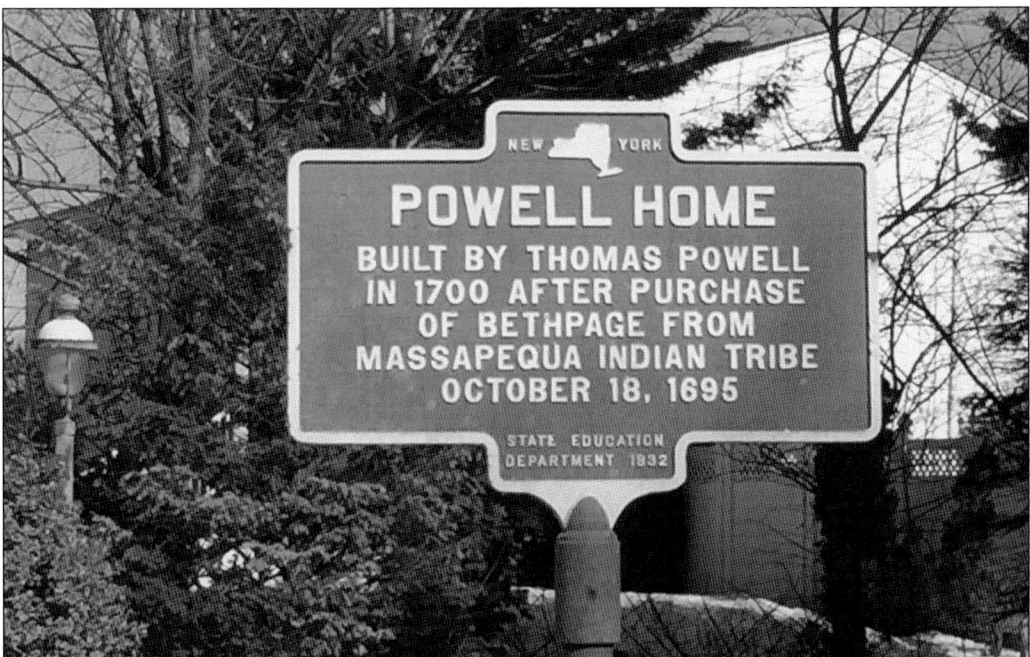

The second home he built is still occupied today and has been granted a marker by the New York State Department of Preservation. (Courtesy John Logerfo.)

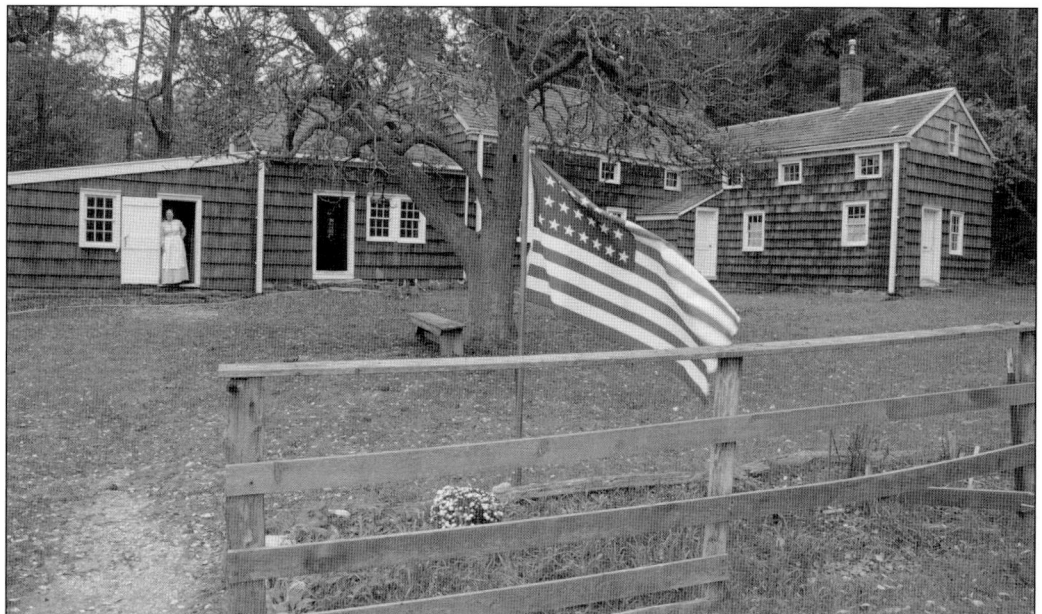

Richard S. Powell (1796–1862) and Sarah Underhill Powell owned and lived in this home on their farm in Old Bethpage. Today, this Powell Farmhouse is the only building that was originally located on land that is now part of the Old Bethpage Village Restoration, a recreated living museum. The village came into existence in 1963, when Nassau County acquired the Powell property, a 165-acre farm located on the Nassau-Suffolk border. (Courtesy of Mike Tamborrino.)

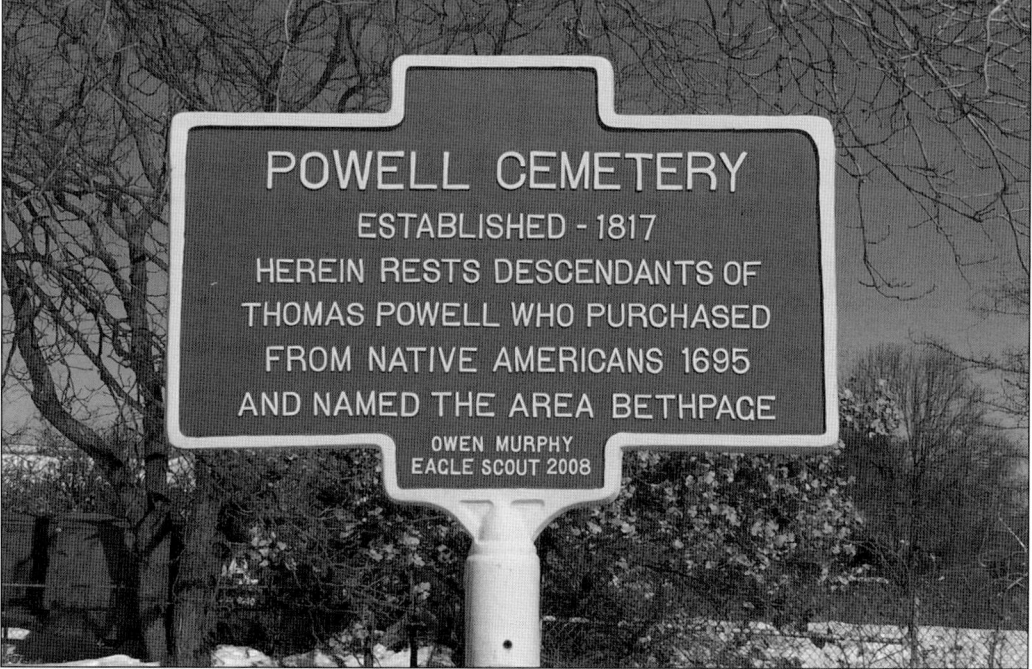

This historic marker identifies the location of the Powell Cemetery on the old Grumman plant property, about a quarter mile west of the Bethpage Community Park. It contains more than 20 Powell family graves. (Photograph by the author.)

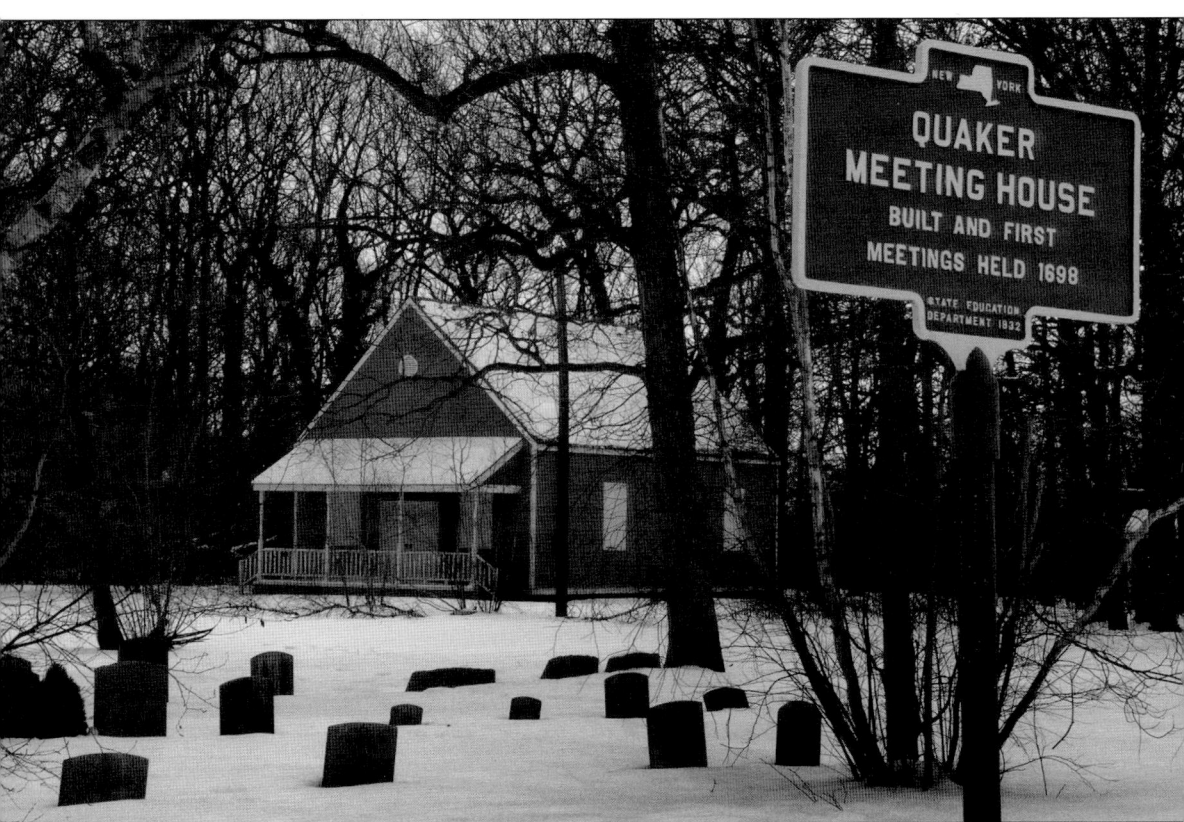

In 1698, Thomas Powell was one of the founders of the area's first faith community, the Bethpage Friends Meeting, when Quakers gathered in each other's homes. The original Bethpage Friends Meeting House was built 20 years after Powell's death on February 28, 1722, and was the first house of worship in the Bethpage Purchase area. It was north of Quaker Meeting House Road in Farmingdale. In 1810, a larger meetinghouse was required, and a second was built with a room for worship and a school room. Unfortunately, it burned down in 1888. The third meetinghouse was built in 1890 on the same site as the earlier two. In 1936, after the Bethpage State Park was established, it was moved to the south side of the road, adjacent to the Friends' Cemetery, Farmingdale's oldest burial ground. In 1990, another fire damaged the meetinghouse, but it was restored and still stands next to the graves of many who worshipped there. (Courtesy of Mike Tamborrino.)

Two

A Town Takes Root

Bethpage was an undeveloped agricultural community and became a small village of farmers and their helpers. There were no stores or retail establishments. Rowland Pearsall was one of the first settlers in the area who bought his farmland from a Powell. The land is located where Plainview Road meets Cherry Avenue, and he lived there from 1748 to his death in 1799. The farm was in his family until the mid-1850s. In addition to the Pearsalls, there were the Bedells, Whitsons, Powells, and Stymuses. William Bedell's family farmed just north of the Pearsalls. By 1790, the 15 Bedell families soon dominated much of the land to the northeast of the community, which came to be referred to as Bedelltown. Nathaniel Whitson had his home just south of the Seaford–Oyster Bay Expressway's Plainview Road exit. He came here in the late 1700s or early 1800s, and his family moved out about 1828. The low area that the expressway traverses there was known at the time as Whitson's Hollow. The makeup of Bedeltown remained basically unchanged for almost 100 years after its initial settlement. In 1836, John Jarvis, a Quaker from Melville, purchased the western end of the Powell estate from John Powell, a son of Thomas IV and his principal heir. The Jarvis home was where the community park is today.

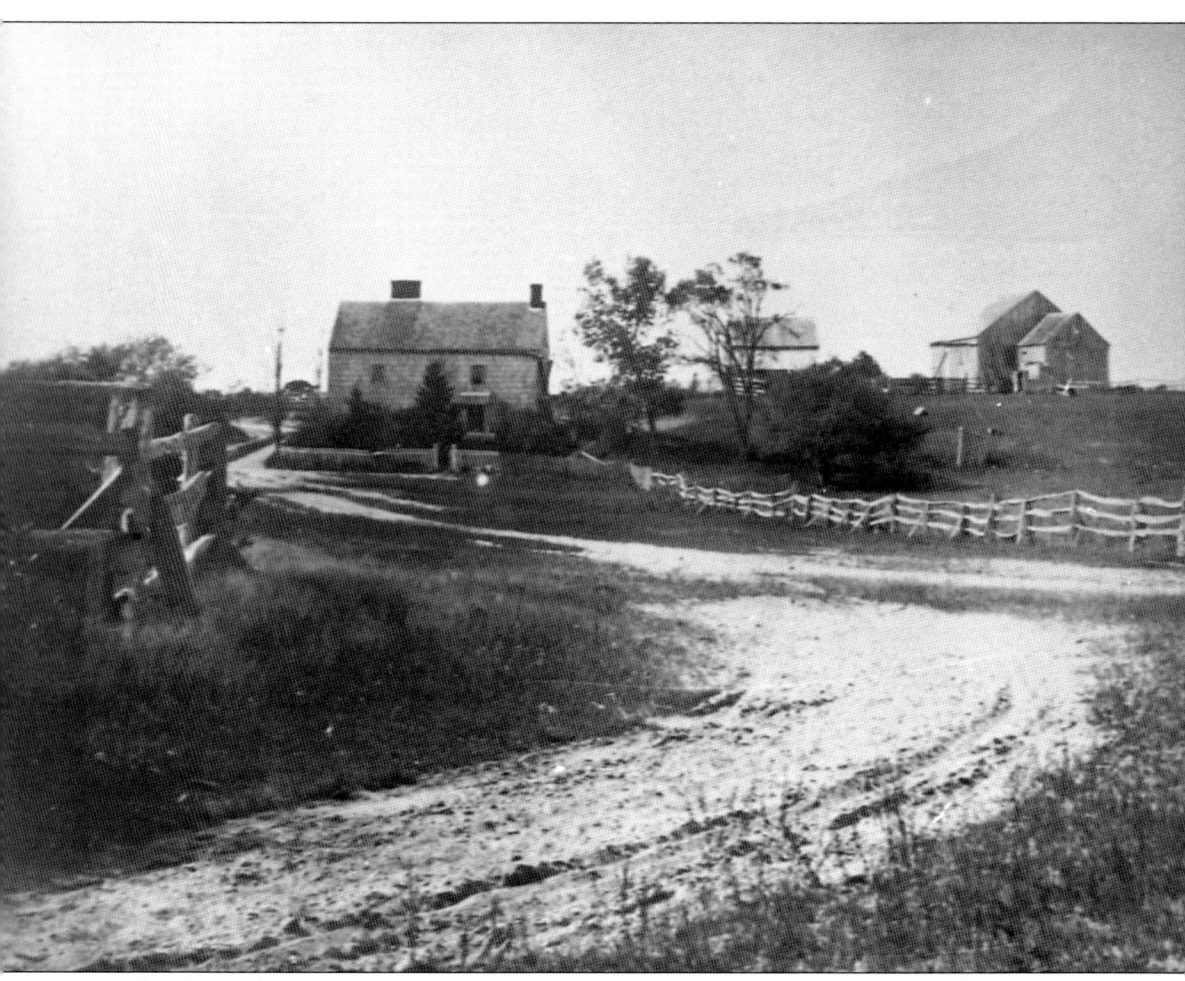

Rowland Pearsall was one of the first settlers in the area, and he lived in a house on the hill where Broadway intersects Plainview Road and Cherry Avenue. This area is where the Bethpage High School athletic track is now located. He married Anna Powell, a daughter of Wait Powell, in 1748. Records indicate that the Rowlands' house had been so solidly built that it had become a landmark for more than 150 years. The first families that settled the area concerned themselves with the welfare of others and often served without pay as public officials. Rowland Pearsall served as highway overseer from 1775 through 1780, and the job entailed rudimentary surveying and commandeering workers for limited repair work after road washouts. Pictured here is the Rowland Pearsall homestead. (Courtesy of Nassau County Parks, Recreation & Museums.)

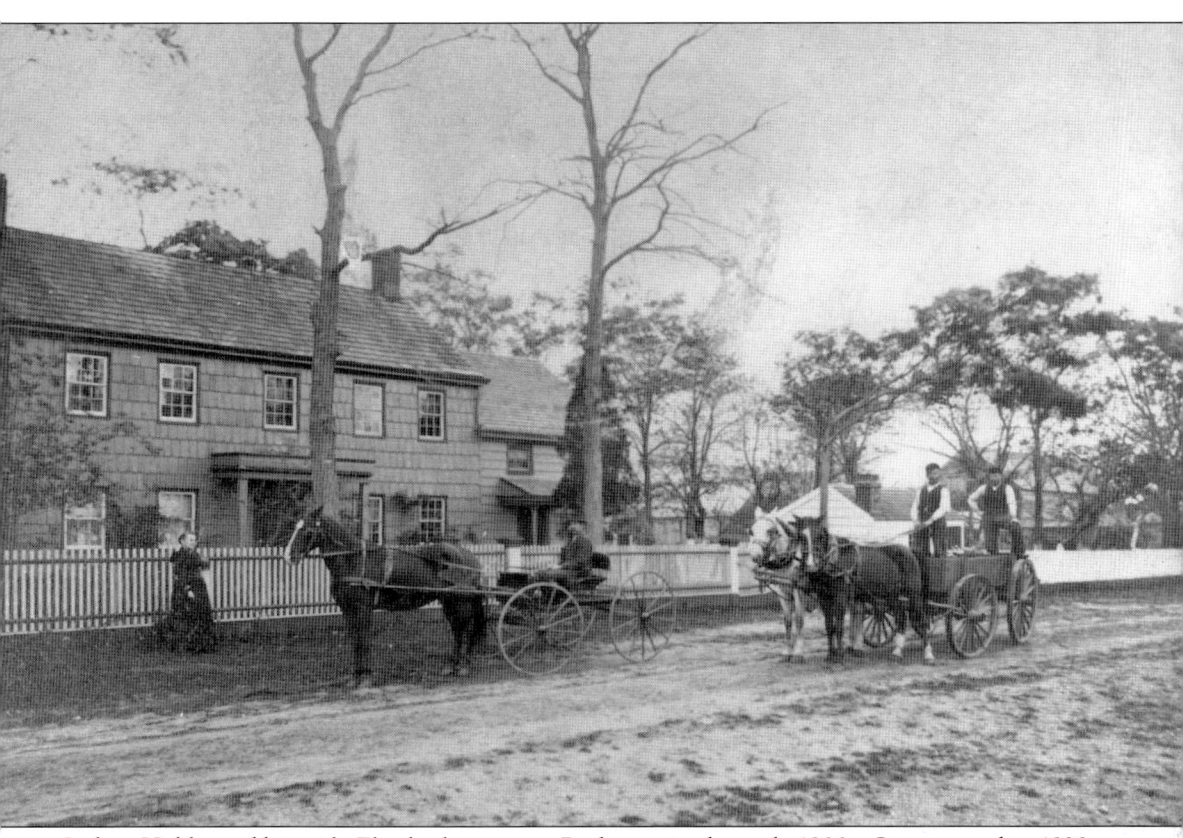

Joshua Hubbs and his wife, Elizabeth, came to Bethpage in the early 1800s. Constructed in 1820, the Federal-style Hubbs House is located at 1 Farmers Avenue, at the corner of Stewart Avenue. Elizabeth Hubbs was the first schoolteacher in 1855, and Joshua Hubbs owned the house from the time it was built until his death late in 1886, when it went to his son George. The Hubbs House is one of the oldest homes in Bethpage, and it is still standing. In 1850, the Dunn family purchased land where Charles Campagne School is today. The Bedells owned their farm until the early 1900s, when Charles Bedell, the last member here, sold it to Osios Karp, who then operated a pickle factory on it. These families were present during the first land boom in the early years of Bethpage.

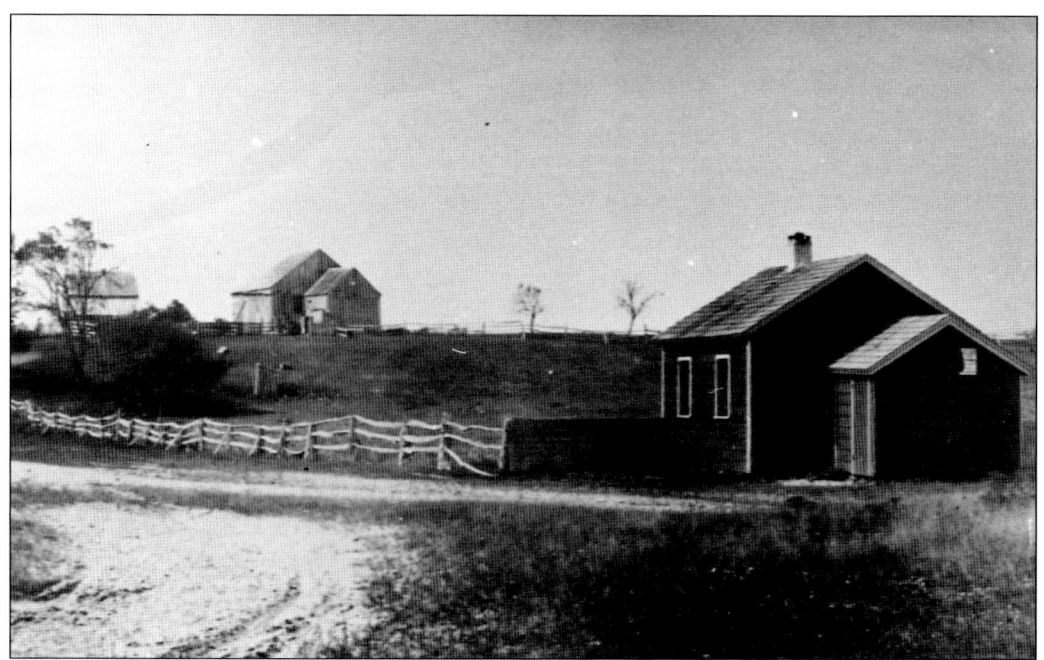

The Bedells are responsible for establishing the district's first school, which was built in 1858 on the grounds of the Pearsall farm. The one-room red schoolhouse was located where Plainview Road and Broadway cross at the bottom of the hill. This school had a wood-burning stove and no lights. Drinking water was carried from a neighbor's house. (Courtesy of Nassau County Parks, Recreation & Museums.)

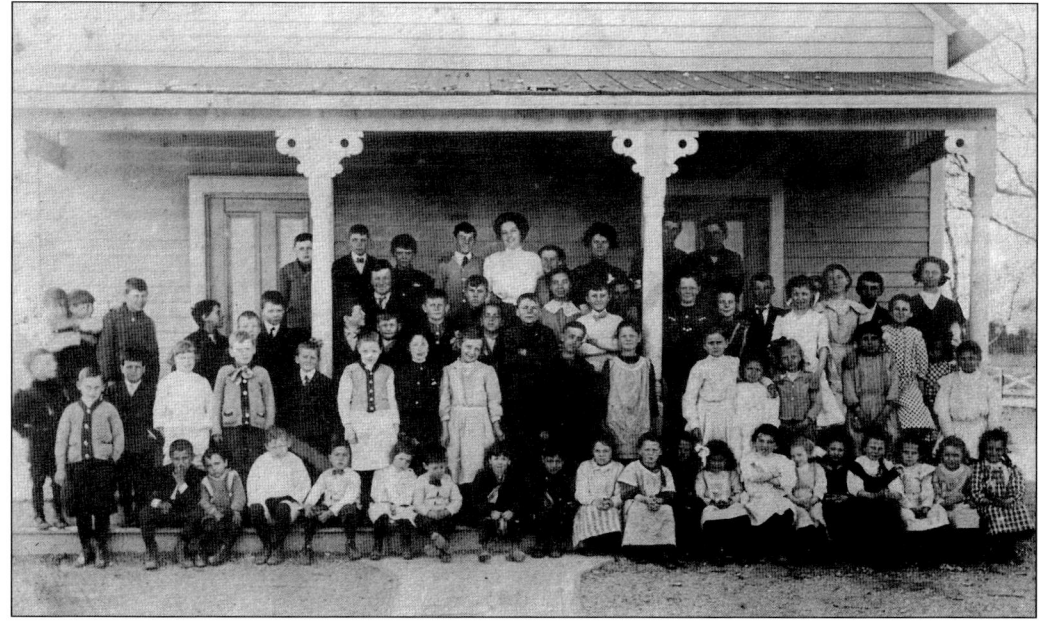

The school's position at the bottom of the hill on Broadway resulted in flooding during rainstorms and thaws. It was abandoned late in the 1890s. The second district school was built at the top of the hill, near the present-day high school football field scoreboard. Pictured here is the Bedell School class of 1910 in front of the second schoolhouse.

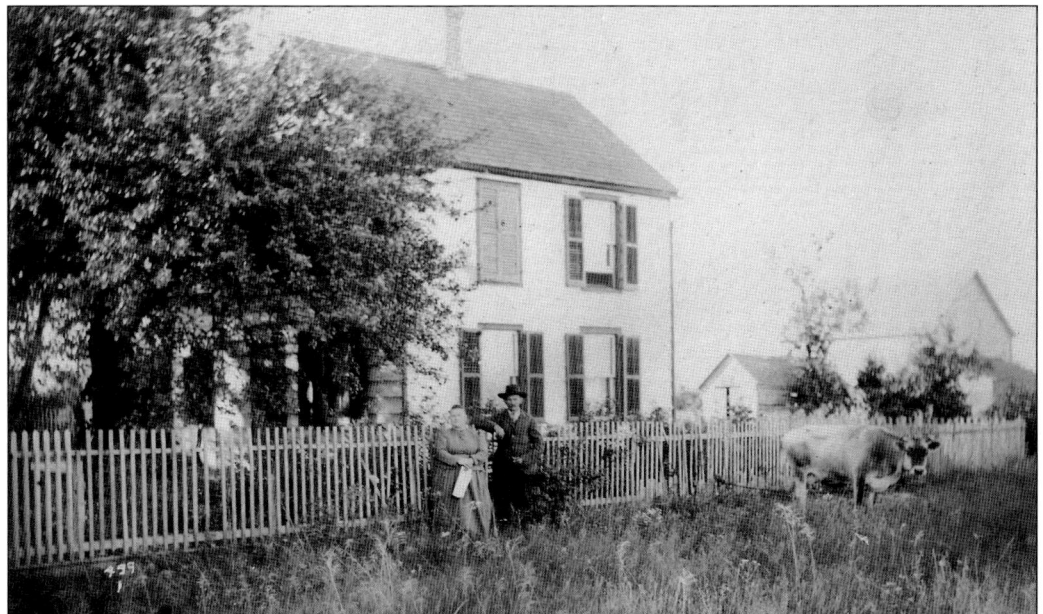

By 1859, there were large numbers of people settling the land that had been unused and the growth continued through the rest of the 19th century. By 1870, Gustafus Witte had moved out of Whitsons' Hollow, selling his farm to Peter Nibbe. John Powell's estate became quite diminished, and it was down to the section that today is the state park. He sold sections to John Jarvis and some to his children. Pictured here is the Nibbe farm.

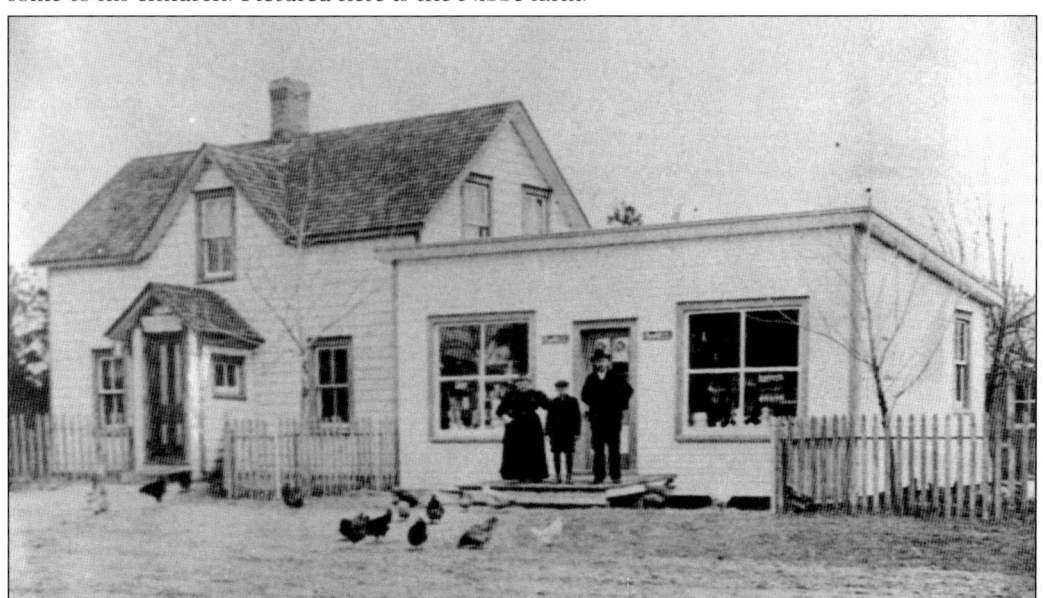

Few people made their living by a profession other than farming. From 1855, there was the one-room schoolhouse where teachers were employed. The first was Elizabeth Hubbs, the wife of Joshua, then Mrs. Grey, a relation of the Stymuses. Early businesses included Carl Damn, a blacksmith, cigar-maker Marcus Schelhammer, railroad worker Louis Klug, and Augustus Freitag, who made silver leaf by pounding lumps of silver into thin sheets. Pictured here is a typical grocery store and house.

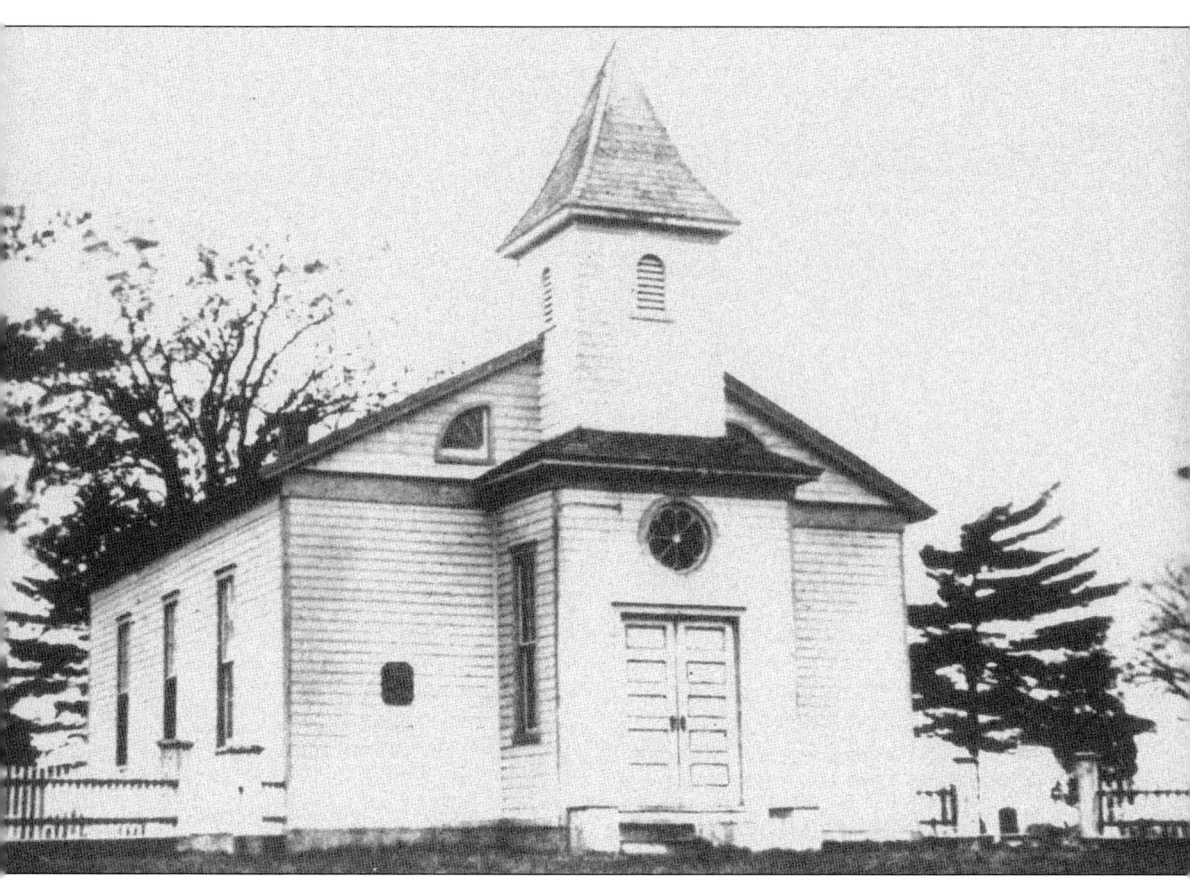

The first house of worship in the original Bethpage Purchase was the Bethpage Friends Meeting House in Farmingdale. The Farmingdale Powells were Quakers, while the Bethpage Powells were Methodists. Therefore, the first house of worship in Bethpage was the Methodist Episcopal church founded in 1835 by Joshua Powell, the great-great-grandson of Thomas Powell. Built on land donated by Joshua Powell, it was called the Plainedge Methodist Church, and Powell was the first minister. This church was located on Hicksville Road in the area of the cemetery at the end of Central Avenue. There was a second Methodist church, on the north side of Hempstead Turnpike between Stewart Avenue and Wantagh Avenue, from 1845 to 1873. Services were discontinued before 1893, and the Lyceum Cemetery is all that remains today. In 1920, the worshippers had the church moved from Hicksville Road to its present location on Broadway, south of Central Avenue. Services have been conducted in this building for almost 180 years.

Three

BETHPAGE TO CENTRAL PARK

The middle of the 19th century was a period of great change. The Central Railroad of Long Island was extended through Bethpage in 1841, and this proved to be one of the most important events in the history of the town. The first railroad station was built near Stewart Avenue, and in 1850 this station was named Jerusalem Station. A local post office opened in 1857 bearing the name Jerusalem Station, with Jeremiah T. Weaver becoming the first postmaster, operating out of his home on Central Avenue. Land speculators purchased large sections of land near the tracks and began building. In order to induce more people to settle here, the land speculators decided to called the town Central Park. In 1867, the residents voted to change the name of the local post office to Central Park. Both the names Central Park and Jerusalem appeared on LIRR schedules until 1884, when the station was named Central Park Station. The railroad brought Central Park to the attention of land buyers. Many businesses opened up around the station in the heart of town, and people began building homes and businesses. Soon it became the center for settlement and development. The rapid transportation system of the railroad, to other communities and to New York, turned Central Park into a modern town.

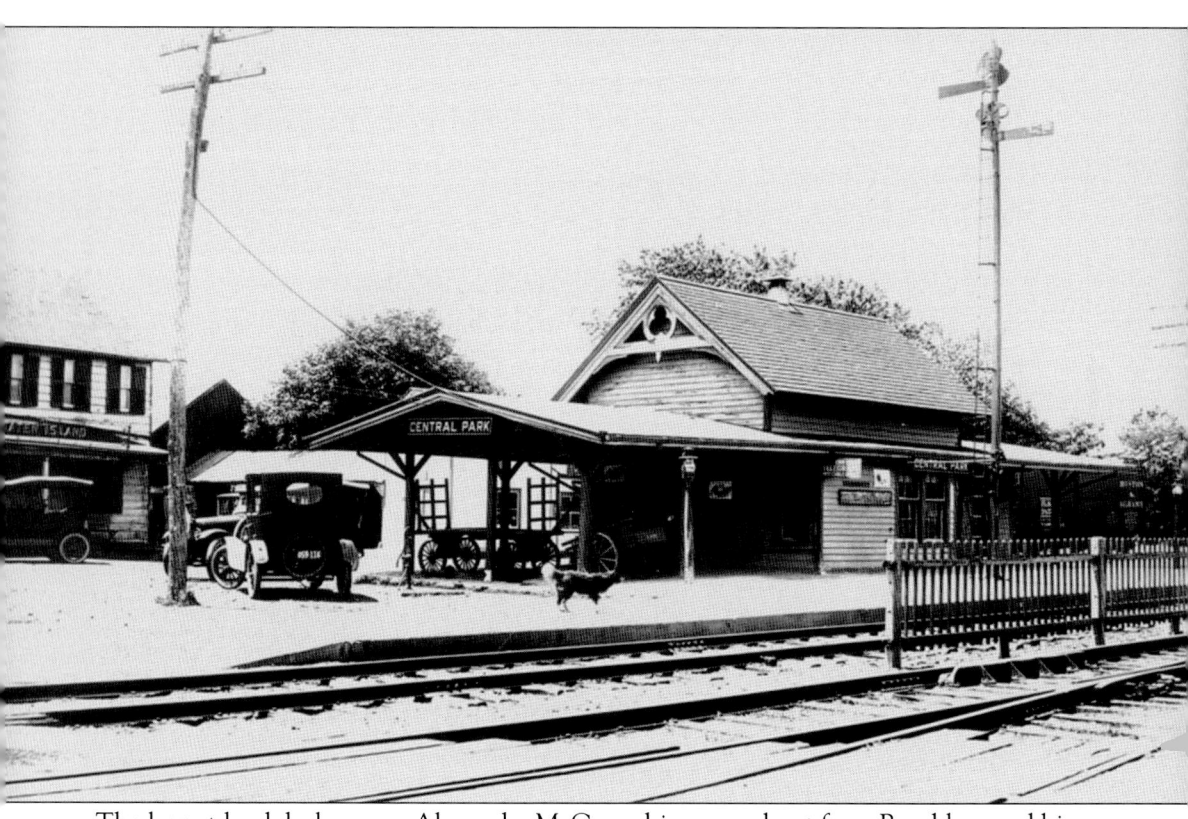

The largest land dealers were Alexander McConochie, a merchant from Brooklyn, and his son-in-law Jeremiah T. Weaver. McConochie first started buying land here in the early 1840s from local people. It was not odd to buy many large tracts of land, and McConochie did. He and the Weavers controlled a good deal of land in Central Park for over 20 years. McConochie, like many well-to-do people, did not live here permanently. He lived in Brooklyn and used his mansion, now known as the Beau Sejour, in the summer. Weaver also lived in the Beau Sejour, as he was married to Adelia McConochie, Alexander's daughter. Weaver owned a home on Central Avenue near Seaman Avenue, and it served as Central Park's first post office, with Weaver as postmaster. Pictured here is the Central Park Railroad Station as it appeared in the early 1900s.

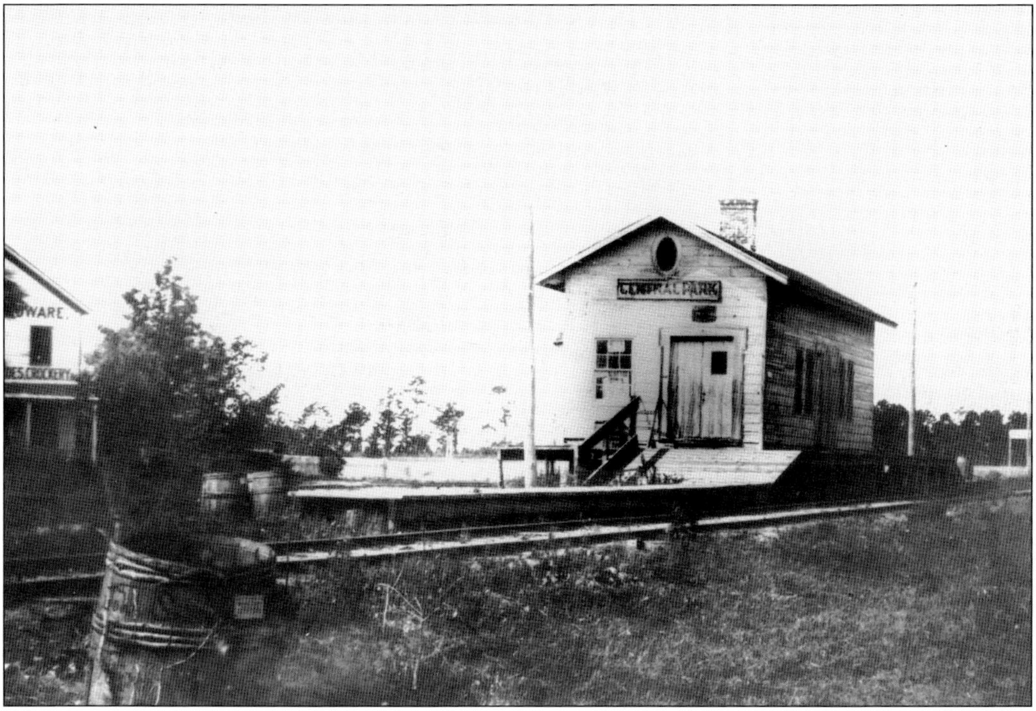

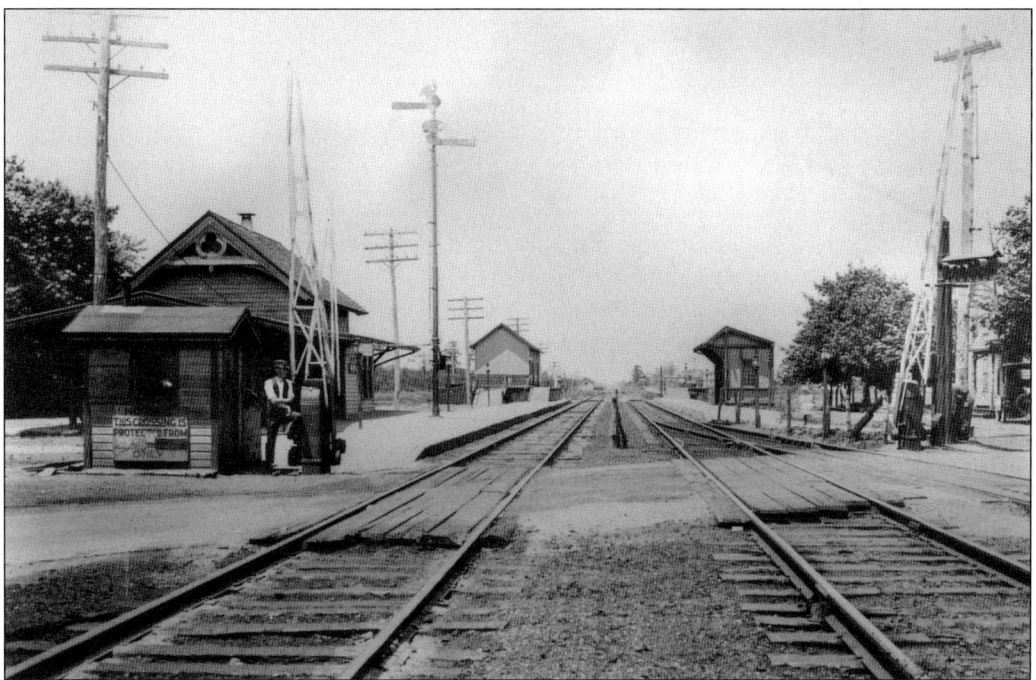

A one-story combination passenger and freight depot was built sometime between 1874 and 1879. In 1882, the railroad station was being listed as Central Park Station.

By 1873, the Central Railroad of Long Island had a regularly scheduled stop, using both the name Central Park and Jerusalem, near Stewart Avenue and Motor Lane, less than a mile south of the present-day Bethpage station. Pictured here is the railroad crossing on Broadway in 1922.

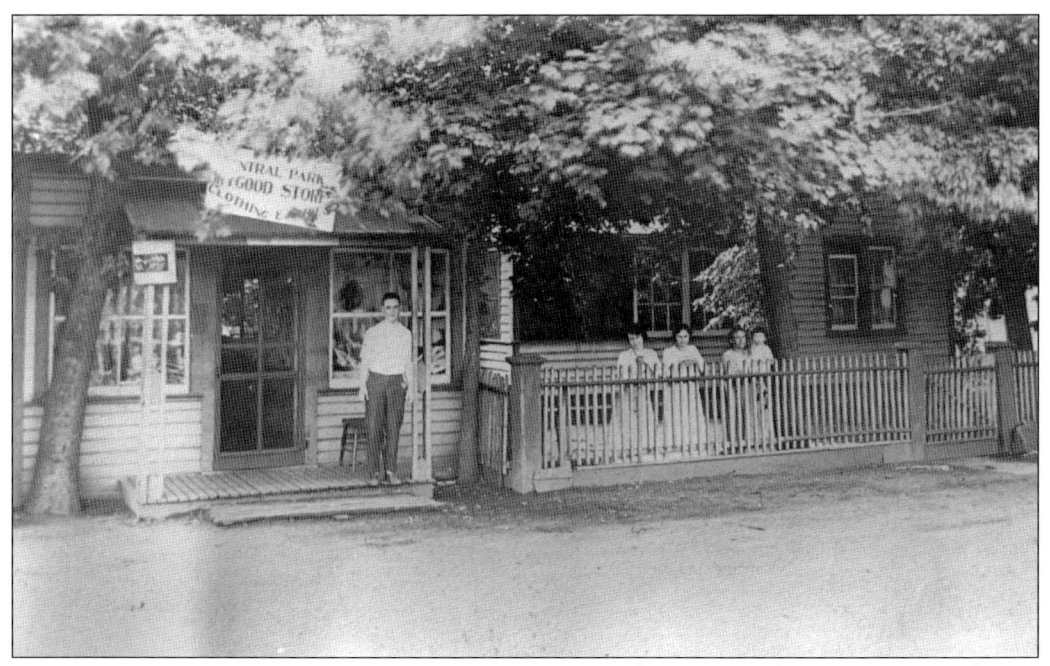

The Dry Goods Store was one of the earliest grocery stores in Central Park, and it was also the home of the Stemple family.

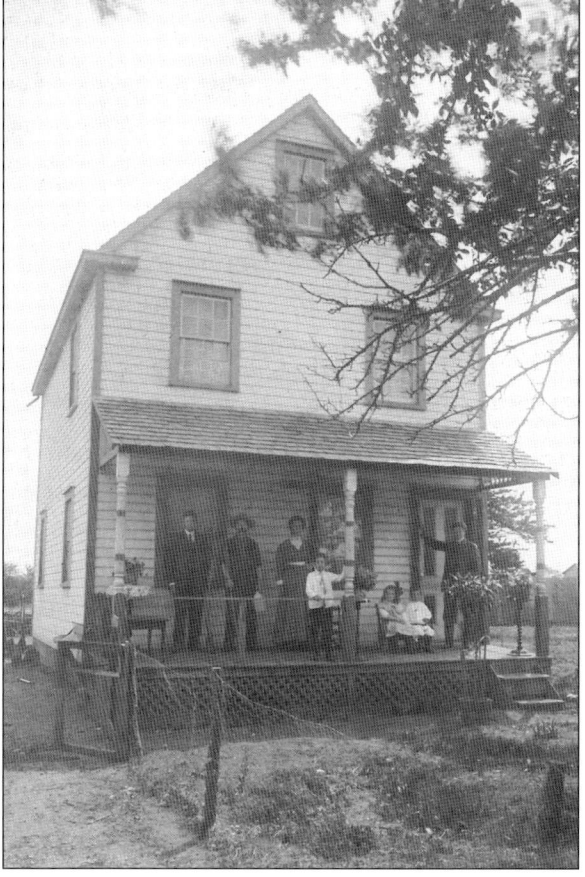

The Miller family farmed land on the north side of Hempstead Turnpike in the early 1900s. Christian and Magdalena (third from the left) are pictured on the porch of their farmhouse on Hempstead Turnpike. (Courtesy of Joyce Calo.)

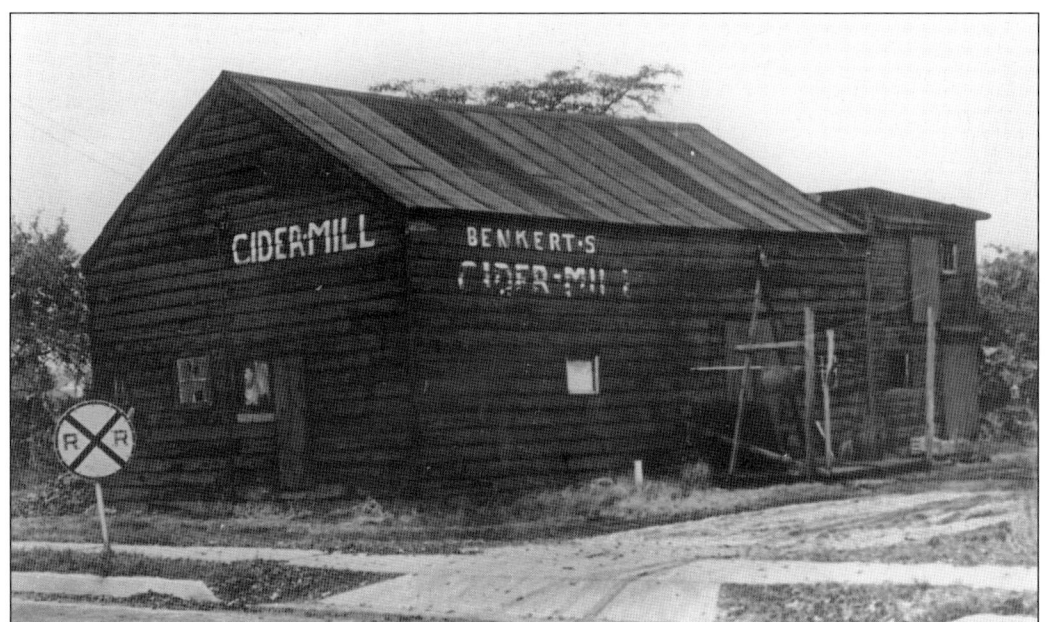

George Benkert, nephew of Albrecht Benkert, inherited the Central Park Cider Mill, which was built in 1888 on Stewart Avenue, just south of the railroad track. This mill pressed apples into cider every autumn until the 1940s. Benkert was a charter member of St. Paul Lutheran Church and his son George Benkert Jr. served in World War I. VFW Post No. 516 in Farmingdale was named in George Jr.'s honor. Pictured here is the cider mill in 1915.

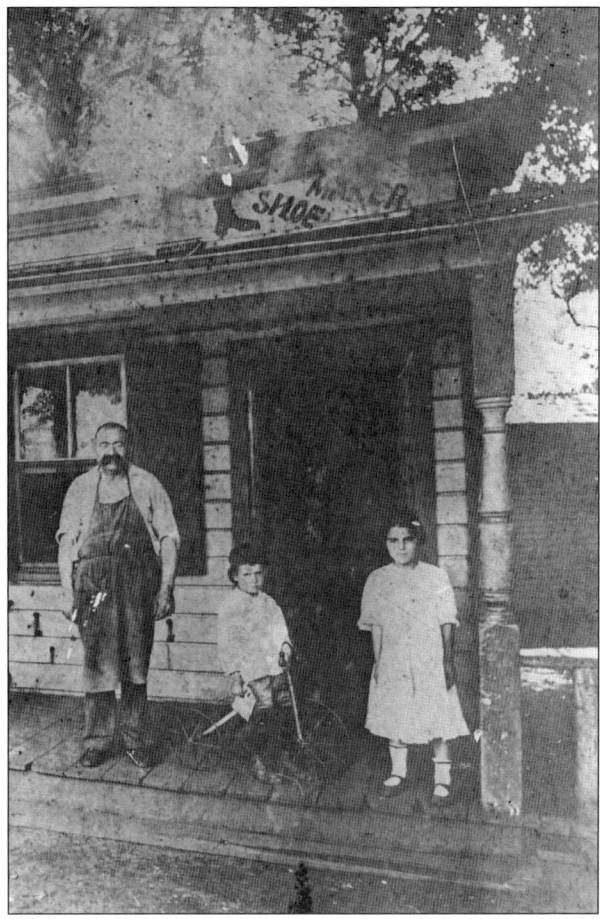

As more and more people settled around the railroad, more businesses became established. Pictured here is Shoemaker Shop at the southwest corner of Broadway and Station Plaza, owned by Andrew Caronia. Pictured from left right in 1915 are Andrew Caronia, son Charles, and daughter Frances.

27

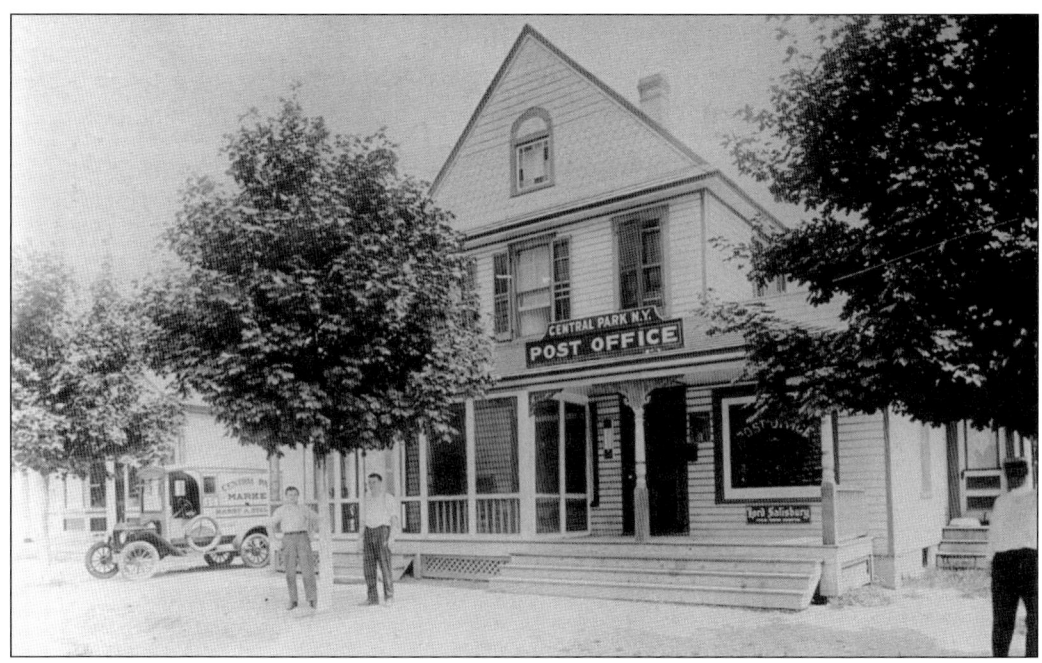

Jeremiah T. Weaver became the first postmaster for the village on January 29, 1857, operating out of his home on the corner of Central Avenue and Seaman Avenue at a salary of $8 a year. Receipts for the year totaled $14. On March 1, 1867, the post office was named Central Park, pictured here in 1914.

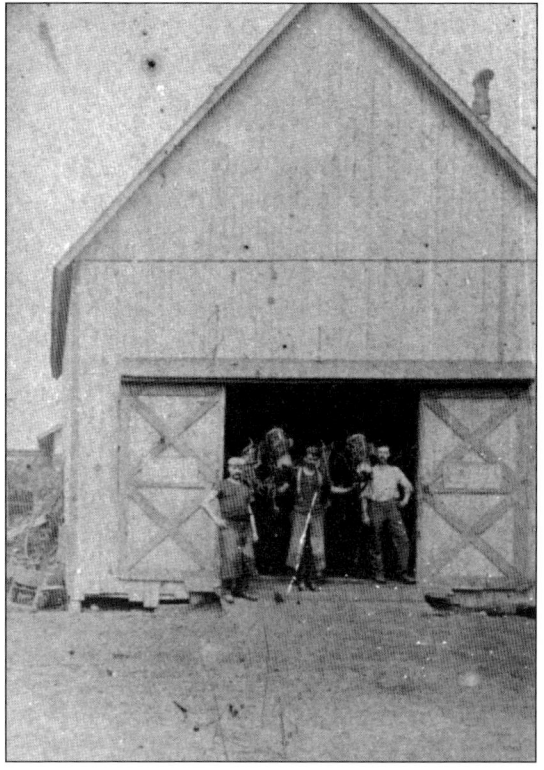

The farmers of the area utilized the services of Harry Seaman's Feed Store, the Benkert's Harness Shop, and Norman F. Godfrey Farm Supply Store. George Baldwin opened his blacksmith shop in 1911, then sold his business to his brother Joseph, who continued until 1924. Pictured here in 1915 is the Baldwin Brothers Blacksmith Shop, on the corner of Stewart Avenue and Baldwin Place.

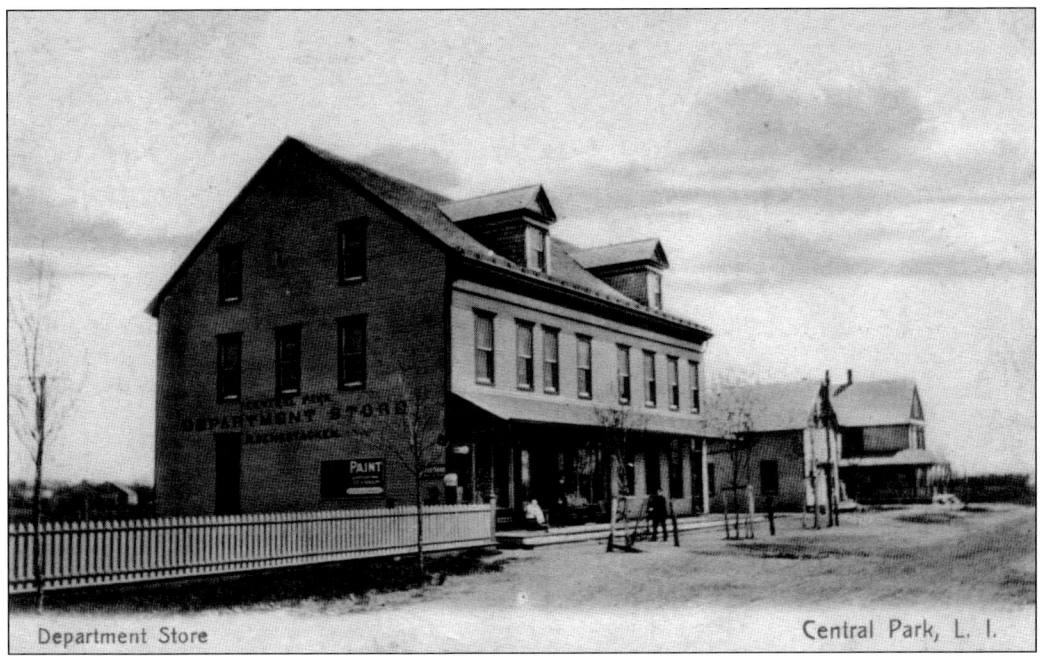

Department Store   Central Park, L. I.

In 1903, Henry Sengstacken built a three-story general store on Broadway just south of the railroad. It was sold to H. Meier and became a department store in 1908. Between 1911 to 1922, it was a general store run by Henry Schaaf. In 1911, one of the first telephones was in this store. Between 1922 to 1936, it operated as a movie theater. In 1936, the store was sold to Burt O'Connor, who operated it as the Colonial. In the 1970s, it was sold to Arthur Hayes and became the Hayes Inn.

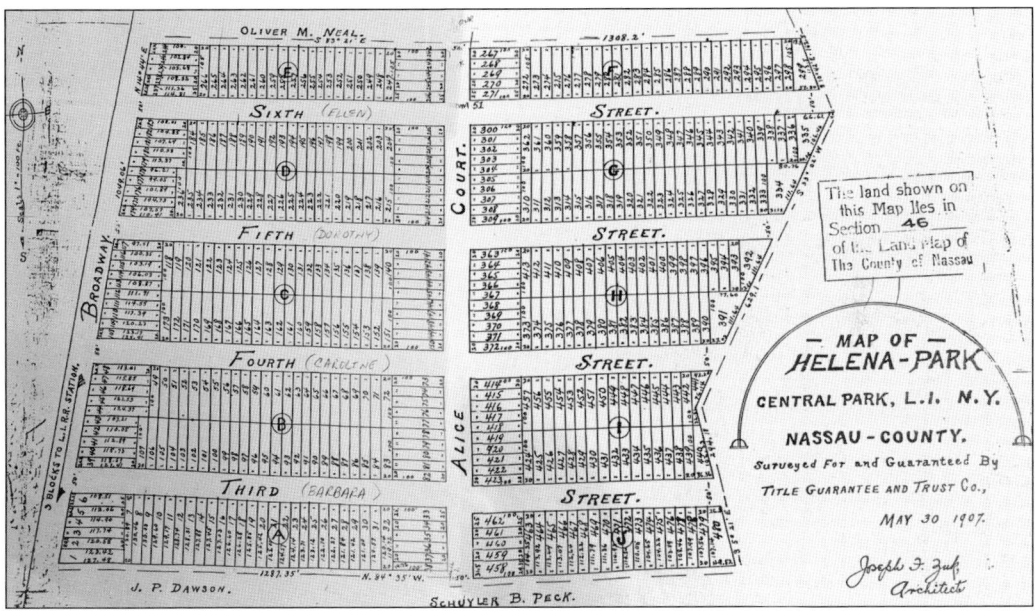

This is a 1907 map of the development of the area east of Broadway and north of present-day Powell Avenue, then known as Helena Park. Barbara Street, Caroline Street, Dorothy Street, and Ellen Street were formerly known as Third, Fourth, Fifth and Sixth Streets, respectively.

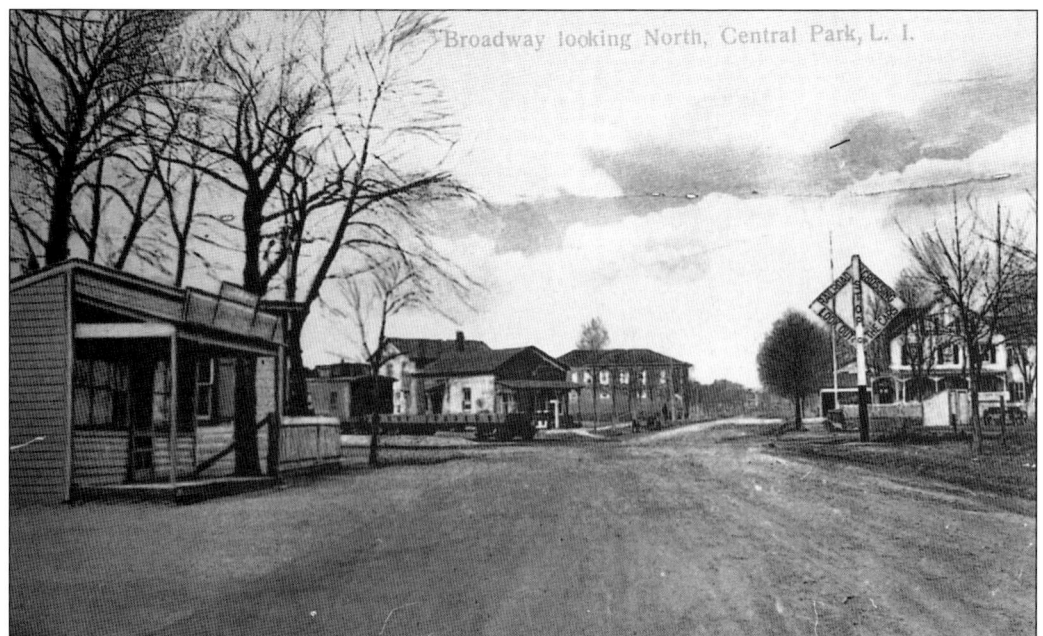

This postcard depicts Broadway just south of the railroad track, looking north from Baldwin Place. On the left is the office of Nobel Heath, who was a real-estate broker, salesman for the Glen Cove Mutual Insurance Company, and Central Park's notary public in 1903. Heath died in 1913. (Courtesy of Nassau County Parks, Recreation & Museums.)

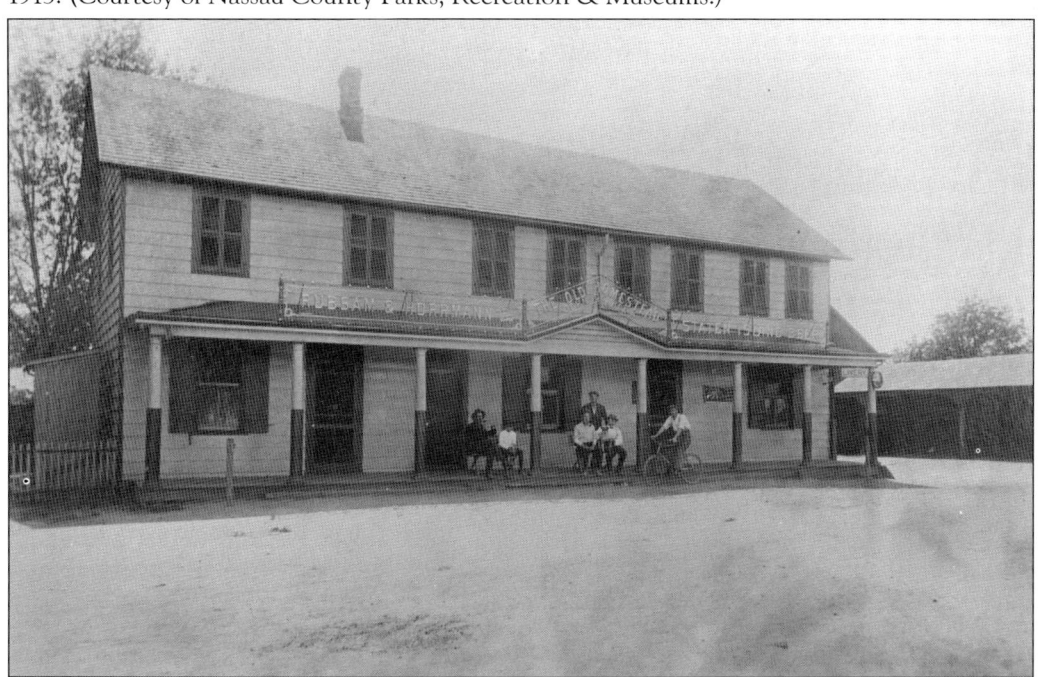

In 1908, John Deubel rented and operated this inn just south of the train station, known as the Old Homestead. Prohibition closed the tavern after World War I, and the building later burned to the ground. In the 1930s, his son Milton opened a new tavern on the northeast corner of Stewart Avenue and Central Avenue. Pictured here is the Old Homestead at Railroad Plaza in 1910.

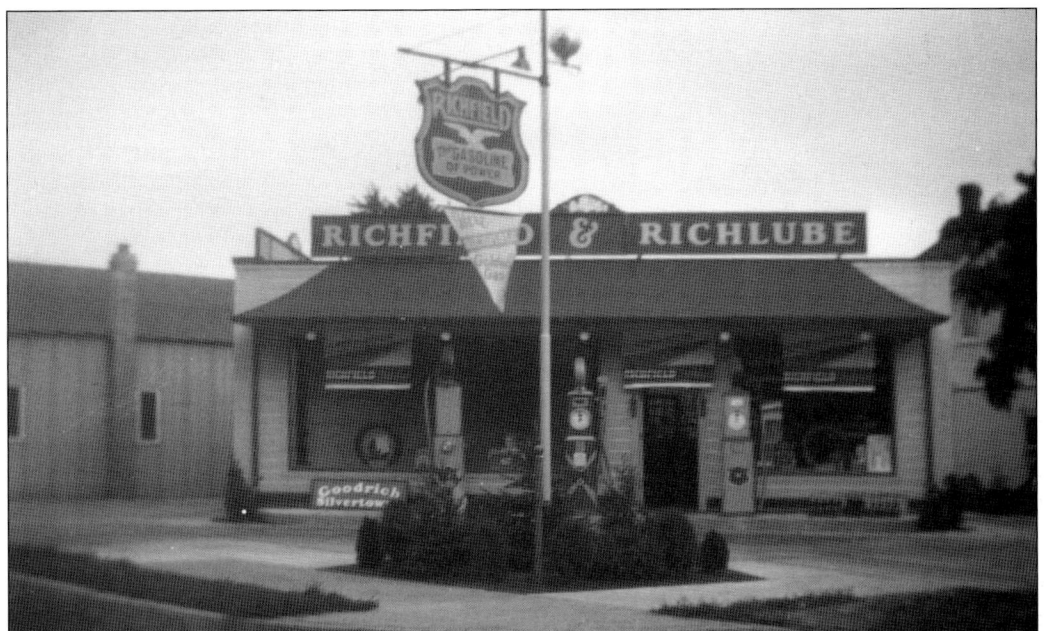

Pictured here is the Richfield and Richlube Service Station on the corner of Baldwin Place and Park Avenue in 1930. (Courtesy of Nassau County Parks, Recreation & Museums.)

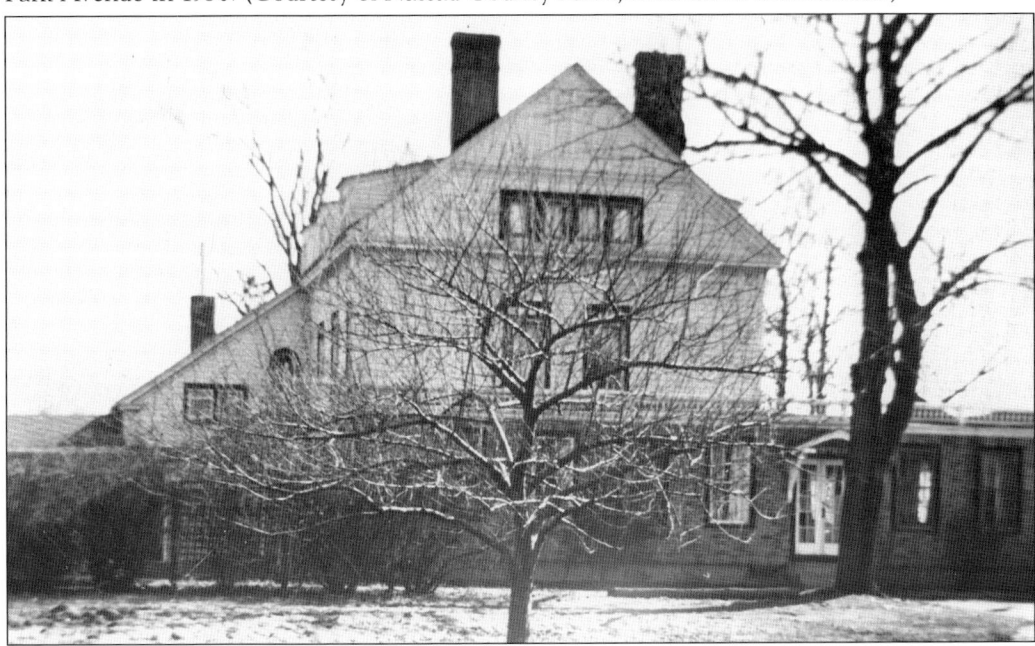

Albert's Inn was owned by Mr. and Mrs. Albert Pirowski from Jericho and located on the northeast corner of Hicksville Road and Hempstead Turnpike on a 5.5-acre site. The house was three stories tall and resembles a castle with a tower. The inn had a stately portico, parquet floors, and each window was topped with stained glass. The restaurant was located on the first floor and opened out to beautiful grounds with its many species of trees. The guests of the inn could enjoy dining al fresco when the weather permitted, but it was sold in 1947. (Courtesy of Plainedge Public Library.)

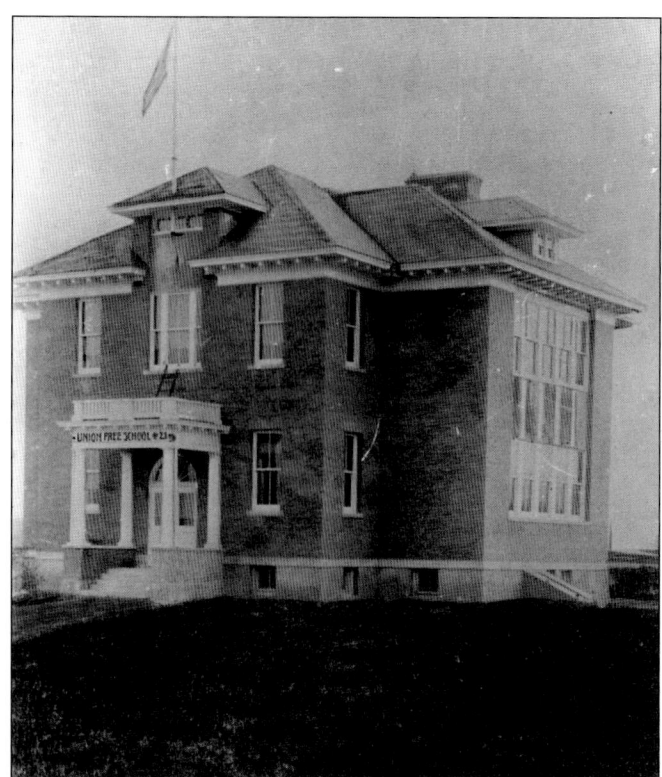

Powell Avenue school was constructed around 1911 on land purchased from Peter Nibbe. It was built on School Street, which is now Powell Avenue. The first building was an eight-room brick structure with central heating. When the population outgrew the school, it was enlarged by an addition for a total of 12 classrooms. The additions were constructed in two sections, the first section in 1915 and the second section in 1923. Later, it was supplemented by a two-room wooden annex.

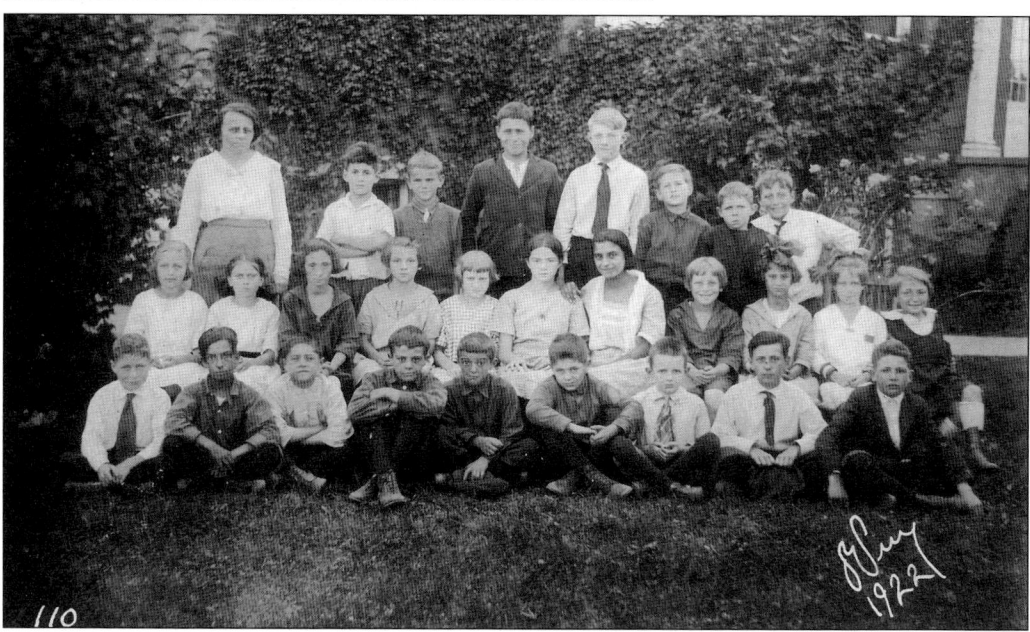

The Powell Avenue School was an elementary school, kindergarten through eighth grade. In the early years, the students went by train to high school in Mineola and later to Hicksville. When Farmingdale put up a new high school, the trustees agreed to accept Bethpage pupils at a lower tuition rate, and transportation was provided by bus in 1931. It served the community through 1960. Pictured here is the Powell School class of 1922. (Courtesy of Joyce Calo.)

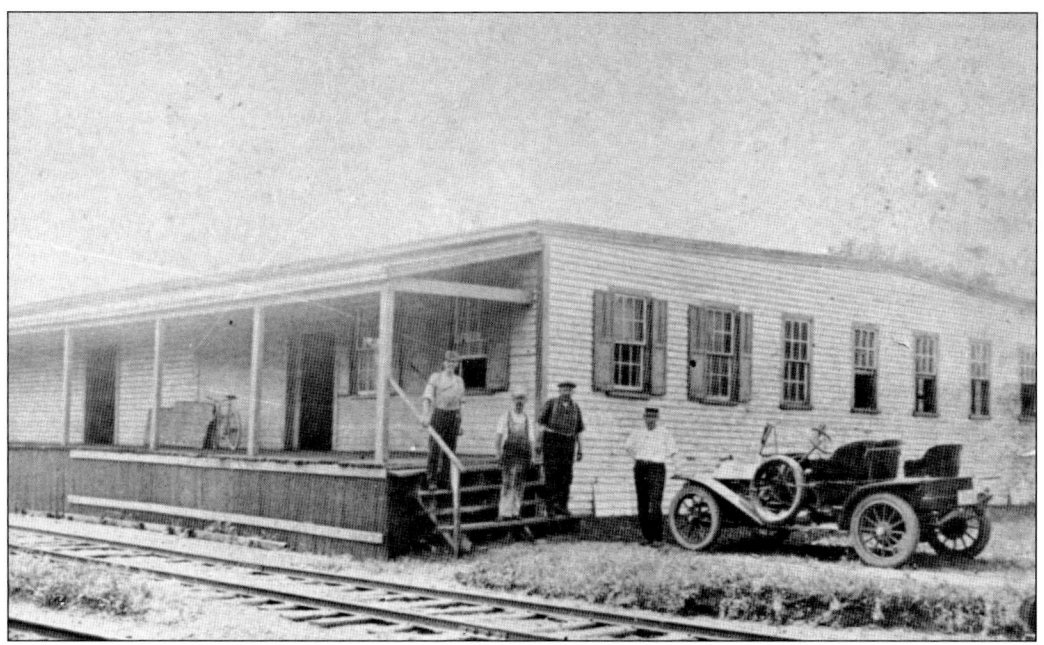

George Feuchsel built the first pickle factory (krautwork) in Central Park around 1880. Built between Broadway and Schneider Lane, it was known as the Central Park Pickle Works. The factory made dill pickles in steam tanks 15 feet in diameter and several feet deep. Pickling took place in the summer and early fall, and the product was allowed to season until it shipped in the winter. The Central Park Pickle Works became the site of the Kessler glass works in 1939.

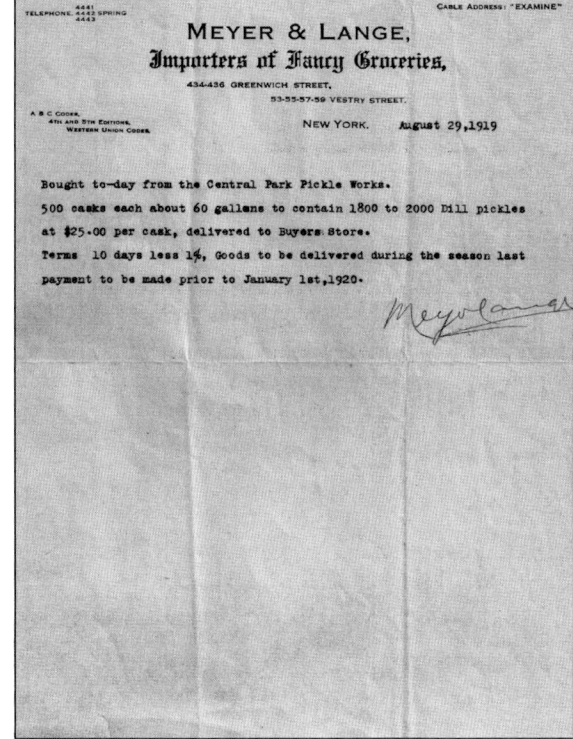

Two other pickle factories were in Central Park. Schneider's was located by the railroad tracks south of Nibbe Lane and Osios Karp's factory was located across from where Charles Campagne School is today. This is a recorded transaction between food importers Meyer & Lange and Feuchsel's Central Park Pickle Works. They purchased 500 casks of dill pickles, each about 60 gallons, in August 1919.

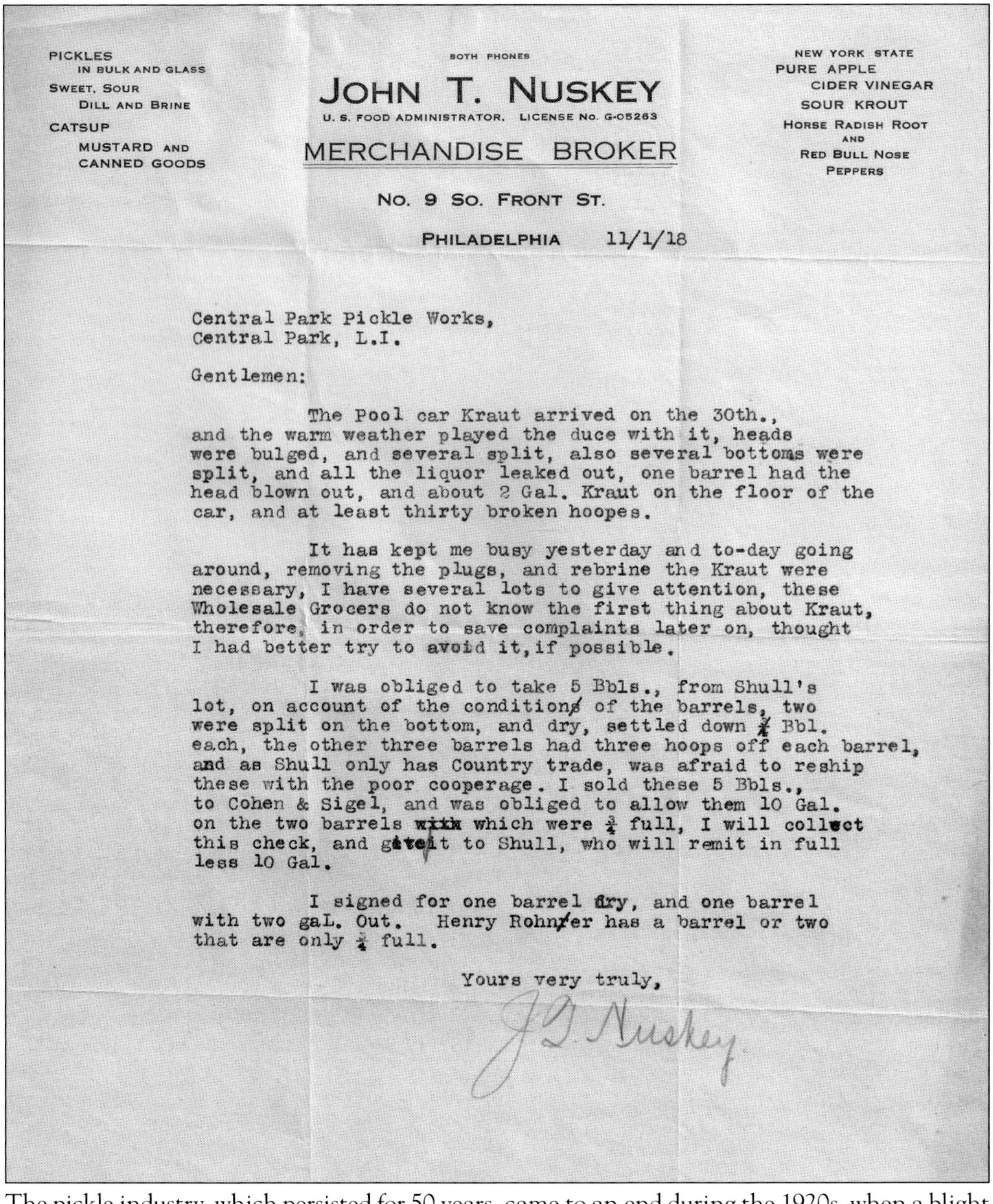

PICKLES IN BULK AND GLASS SWEET, SOUR DILL AND BRINE CATSUP MUSTARD AND CANNED GOODS	BOTH PHONES **JOHN T. NUSKEY** U. S. FOOD ADMINISTRATOR. LICENSE No. G-05263 MERCHANDISE BROKER NO. 9 SO. FRONT ST. PHILADELPHIA 11/1/18	NEW YORK STATE PURE APPLE CIDER VINEGAR SOUR KROUT HORSE RADISH ROOT AND RED BULL NOSE PEPPERS

Central Park Pickle Works,
Central Park, L.I.

Gentlemen:

The Pool car Kraut arrived on the 30th., and the warm weather played the duce with it, heads were bulged, and several split, also several bottoms were split, and all the liquor leaked out, one barrel had the head blown out, and about 2 Gal. Kraut on the floor of the car, and at least thirty broken hoopes.

It has kept me busy yesterday and to-day going around, removing the plugs, and rebrine the Kraut were necessary, I have several lots to give attention, these Wholesale Grocers do not know the first thing about Kraut, therefore, in order to save complaints later on, thought I had better try to avoid it, if possible.

I was obliged to take 5 Bbls., from Shull's lot, on account of the conditions of the barrels, two were split on the bottom, and dry, settled down ¼ Bbl. each, the other three barrels had three hoops off each barrel, and as Shull only has Country trade, was afraid to reship these with the poor cooperage. I sold these 5 Bbls., to Cohen & Sigel, and was obliged to allow them 10 Gal. on the two barrels which were ¾ full, I will collect this check, and give it to Shull, who will remit in full less 10 Gal.

I signed for one barrel dry, and one barrel with two gaL. Out. Henry Rohnfer has a barrel or two that are only ¼ full.

Yours very truly,

J. D. Nuskey

The pickle industry, which persisted for 50 years, came to an end during the 1920s, when a blight made raising cucumbers unprofitable. Most farmers turned to truck farming and growing potatoes, as truck farming brought markets within easy reach. Later, these potato farmers found their crops preyed upon by the golden nematode, a parasite brought in from Europe on tulip bulbs. By 1950, land had a new value as homesites, and most farmers sold to developers. Pictured here is a letter from merchandise broker John Nuskey to Feuchsel's Central Park Pickle Works complaining about the condition of shipping barrels and the arrival of product that fell short of expectations in November 1918.

Four

ROAD RACES AND FAMOUS FACES

William K. Vanderbilt, heir to a railroad fortune and a pioneer race car driver, organized America's first international road race. The first William K. Vanderbilt Jr. Cup Race was held in 1904 over 30 miles of public roads in central Long Island. By 1906, fans from all over the country swarmed to Long Island to witness the battle of automobiles from the United States, France, Germany, and Italy. Some 250,000 spectators surged onto the narrow dirt roads to view their favorite drivers. During the 1906 race, a reckless spectator was fatally struck by a race car, and it nearly brought the classic to a premature demise. The marvel was that only one spectator had been killed in the three races that had been held by that time. Demonstrating vision again, Vanderbilt chartered the construction of a private highway. His dream was for a safe, smooth, police-free road without speed limits and a place to conduct his beloved international race without spectators running onto the course. Vanderbilt and his associates were careful to position this new, modern highway as a convenience to all automobile enthusiasts and not primarily as a speedway for race cars. They extolled the virtues of economic development and the benefits of quickly retreating from the city to the calm and the fresh country air that Long Island had to offer.

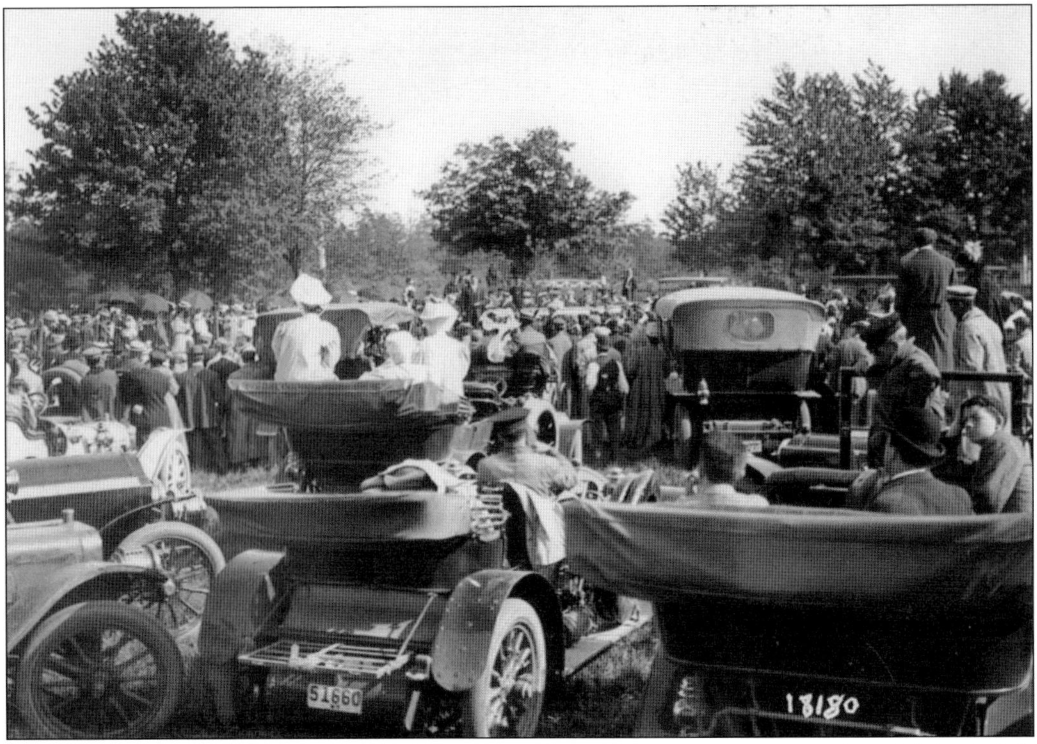

On December 3, 1906, the Long Island Motor Parkway Inc. was incorporated, with Vanderbilt as president. The other officers were vice president Harry Payne Whitney and treasurer Jefferson De Mont Thompson. Second vice president, and eventually general manager, was Vanderbilt's good friend, A.R. Pardington. Other notable directors included Henry Ford, August Belmont, Frederick Bourne, Mortimer Schiff, John Jacob Astor, and Clarence Mackay. Pictured here is the ground-breaking ceremony on June 6, 1908. Today, this site is Stewart Avenue and Albergo Court. (Courtesy of Howard Kroplick.)

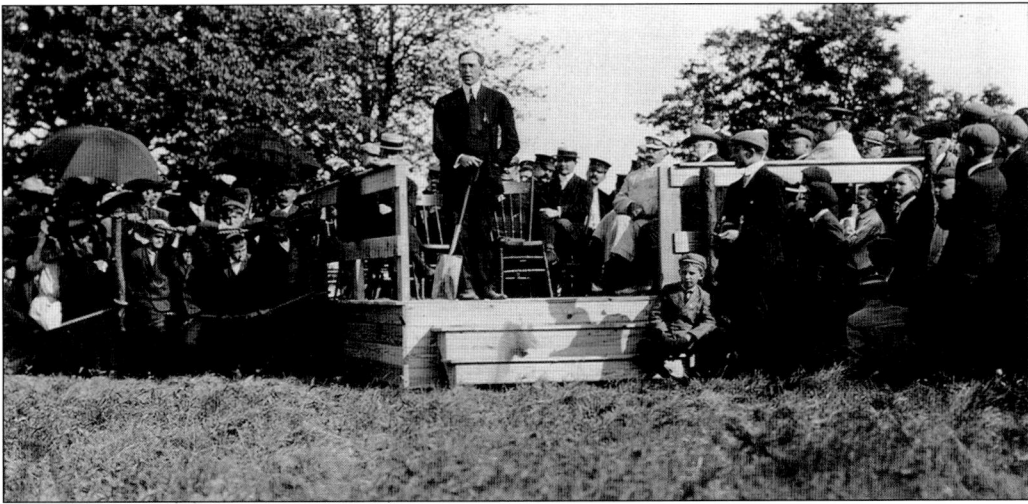

Pictured here is A.R. Pardington filling in and reading from remarks Vanderbilt had written to mark the occasion. His comments praised the impact and potential of the automobile and reflected on the unforeseen obstacles that impeded the parkway's progress. (Courtesy of Howard Kroplick.)

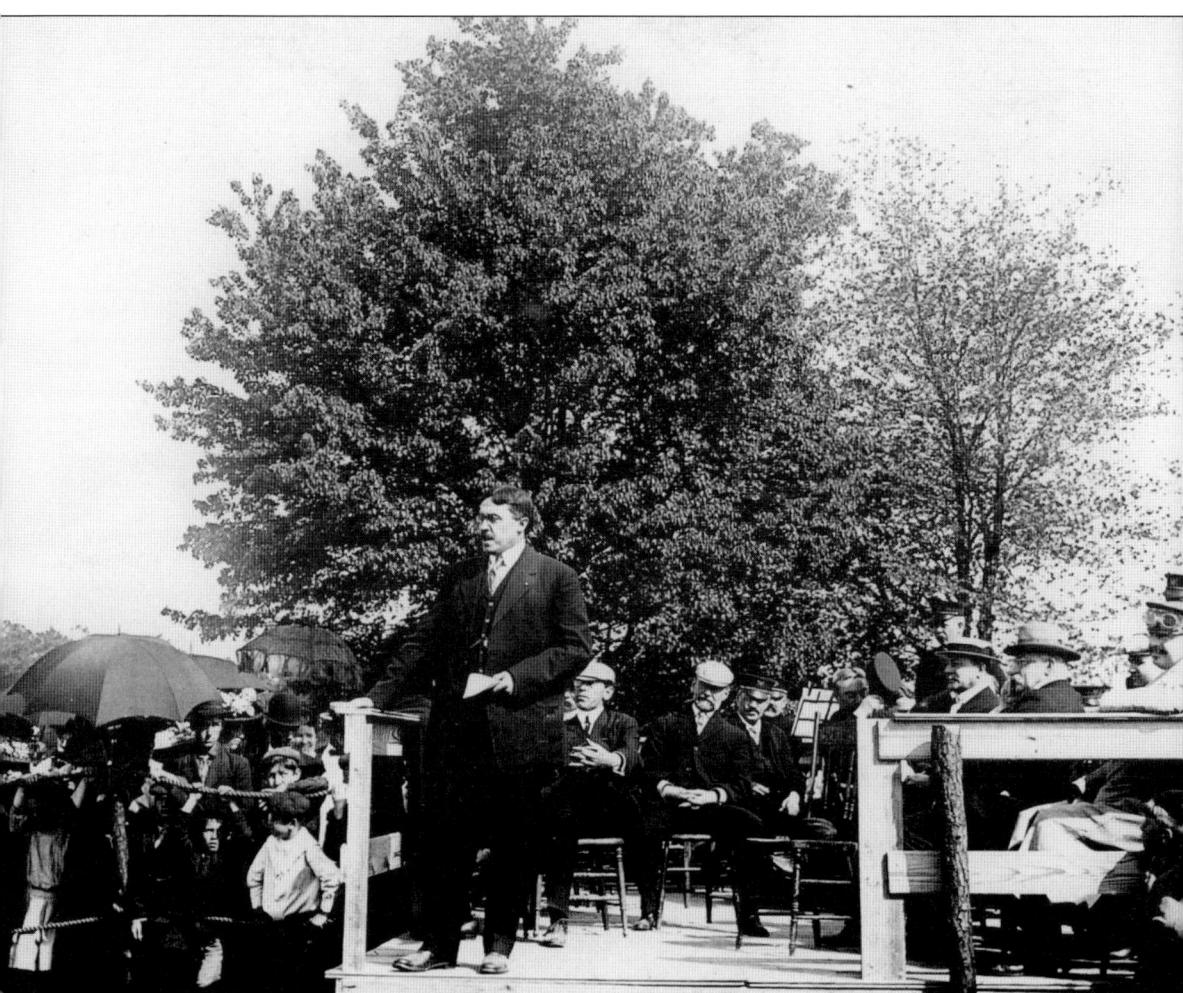

Vanderbilt voiced his goals with the Parkway: "It has been the dream of every motorist to own a perfect car and to have a road without speed limit . . . Grade crossings for both railways and highways are to be eliminated by bridges and tunnels and the entire distance to be fenced. Access and egress will be obtained at toll gates at intervals of about five miles. The surface of the road will be maintained in first class order so that the motorist can enjoy a ride without dust, without bumps, and with no interference from the authorities." Pictured here is Judge William H. Hotchkiss, president of the American Automobile Association, expressing how automobile ownership would be within the reach of the everyday working man. (Courtesy of Howard Kroplick.)

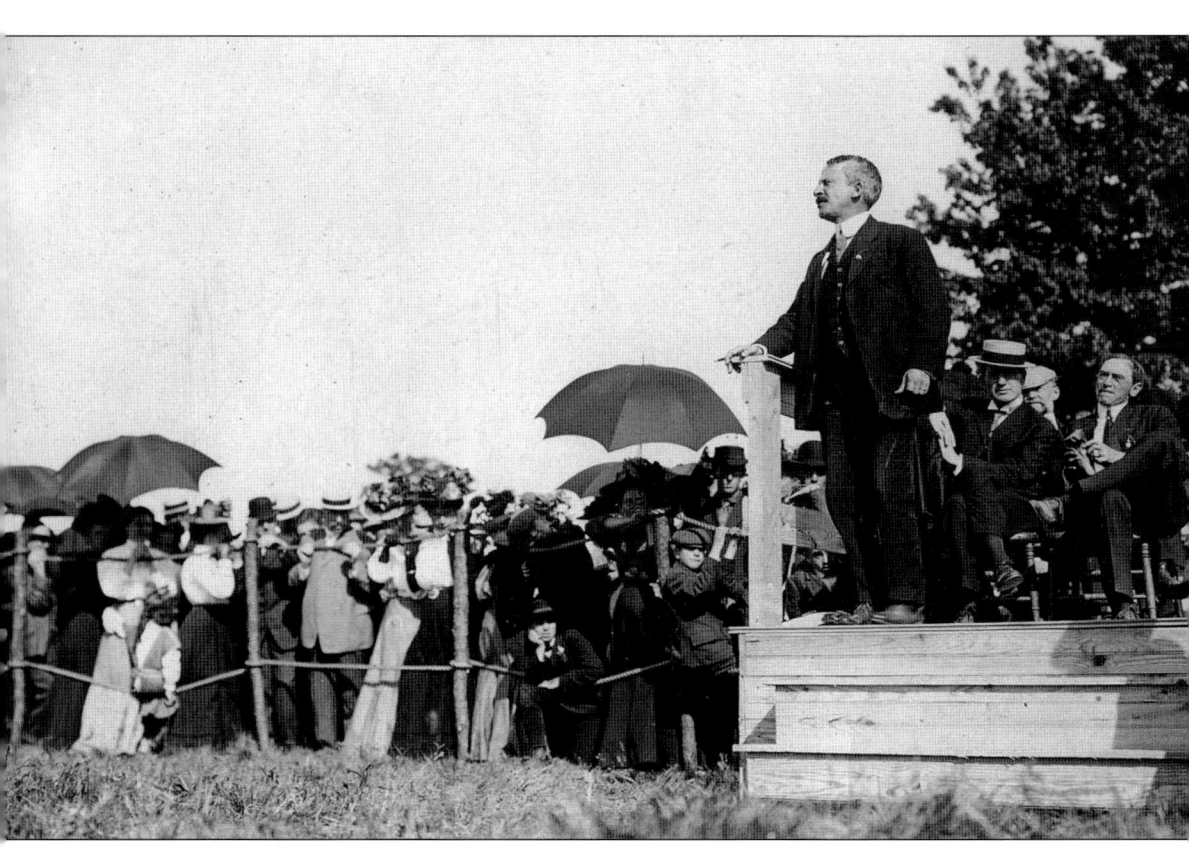

A series of setbacks in obtaining rights-of-way to privately owned property resulted in a steady series of missed project milestones. The Vanderbilt Cup Race Commission was eventually forced to cancel the 1907 race, and construction of the motor parkway was delayed until 1908. Throughout 1907 and the first half of 1908, Pardington, the parkway's general manager, worked hard to successfully obtain the right-of-way from Queens to Lake Ronkonkoma. On June 6, 1908, the parkway staged an official ground-breaking ceremony to commemorate the beginning of construction in Central Park, now Bethpage. With several hundred people in attendance, the original plan was for William K. Vanderbilt Jr. to make the keynote speech. But the sudden and grave illness of his stepfather, Oliver Hazard Perry Belmont, kept him away. Pictured here is John C. Wetmore, considered the dean of New York automobile writers, who took the podium. He lavishly praised Vanderbilt and the other parkway organizers for their vision and foresight in conceiving the motor parkway and bringing it to fruition. (Courtesy of Howard Kroplick.)

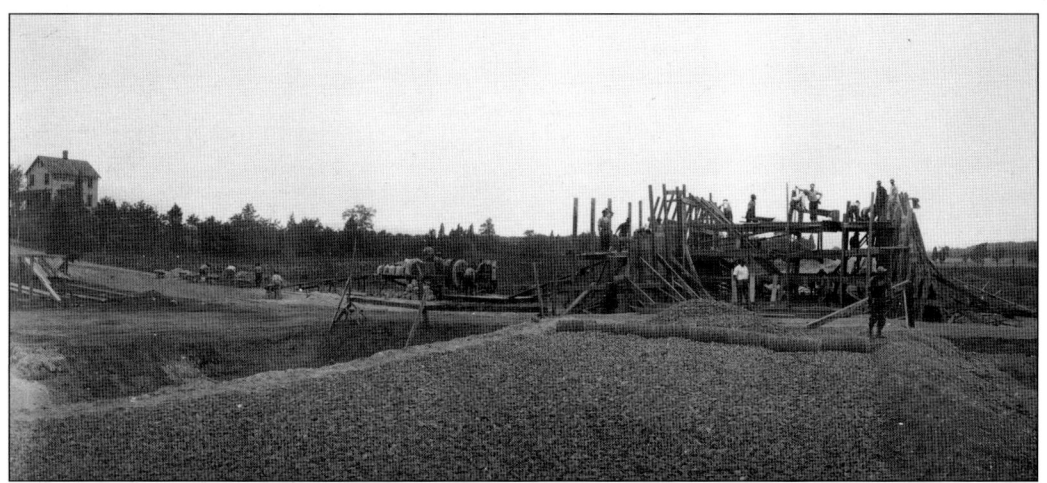

Construction of the parkway began between Westbury and Bethpage with a little more than nine miles of the planned 50-mile road completed in 1908. Pictured here is one of the bridges under construction for the motor parkway. One can see the wooden molds, the mixing machines for the cement and stones, and the wire netting that goes between the layers of stones for reinforcement. (Courtesy of Howard Kroplick.)

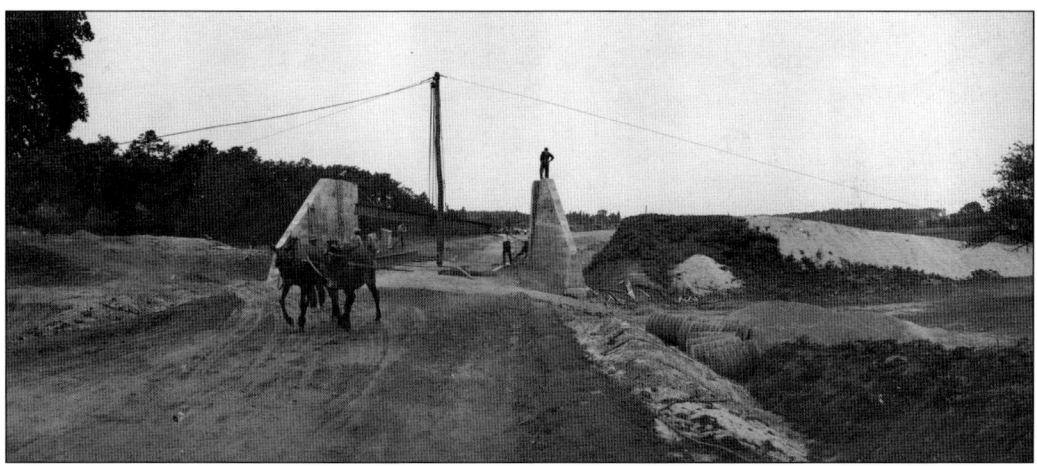

The most distinctive features of the parkway were the reinforced concrete pavement and the elimination of grade crossings. Another innovation was the banked curves, "allowing the cars to take them at a maximum speed of 60 miles per hour." Pictured here is the raising of the first steel beam for the construction of the bridges in Central Park in 1908. (Courtesy of Howard Kroplick.)

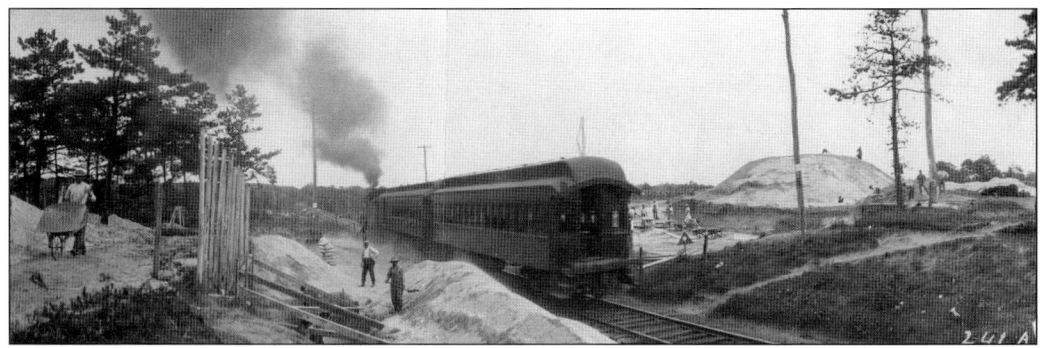

On September 10, 1908, plans were announced to christen the parkway with the Motor Parkway Sweepstakes, an event held a month later. The purpose was to create an opportunity to test the new parkway and the course for the 1908 Vanderbilt Cup Race on October 24. The circuit for the sweepstakes and the Vanderbilt Cup Race included the finished portion of the parkway and 14.45 miles of public roads. Pictured above is the construction of the bridge over the Long Island Rail Road and Central Avenue in Central Park in August 1908. (Courtesy of Howard Kroplick.)

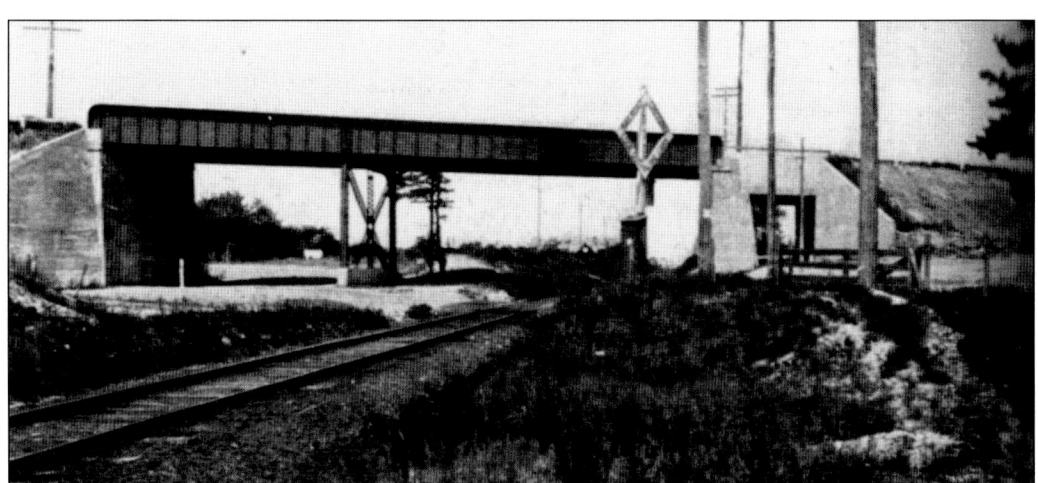

Pictured is the completed bridge, the longest bridge built by the motor parkway and the only one that crosses a railroad track and a road. It is classified as a parkway bridge, since the motor parkway went on top of the bridge. The steel trestle construction, rather than concrete, was mandated by the railroad. (Courtesy of Howard Kroplick.)

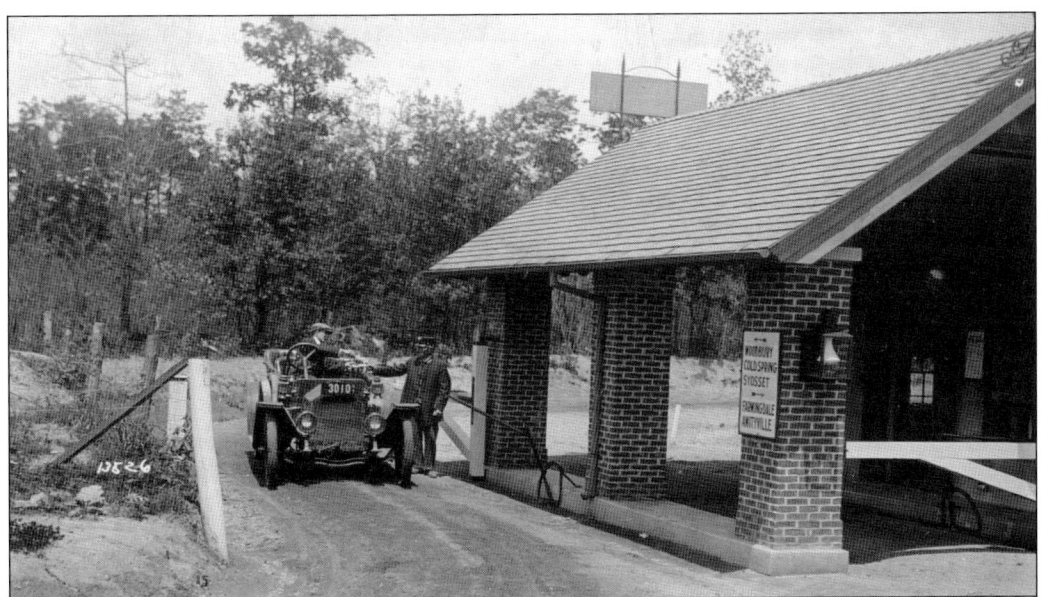

The Long Island Motor Parkway officially opened on October 10, 1908, in conjunction with the five sweepstakes races. Cars entered the course through the three toll lodges that had been constructed that year. These were the Meadow Brook Lodge (Merrick Avenue, Westbury), the Massapequa Lodge (Massapequa-Hicksville Road, Plainedge), and the Bethpage Lodge (Round Swamp Road, Old Bethpage). Pictured here is toll collector Thomas Grafenstein at the Bethpage Toll Lodge, near Round Swamp Road. (Courtesy of Howard Kroplick.)

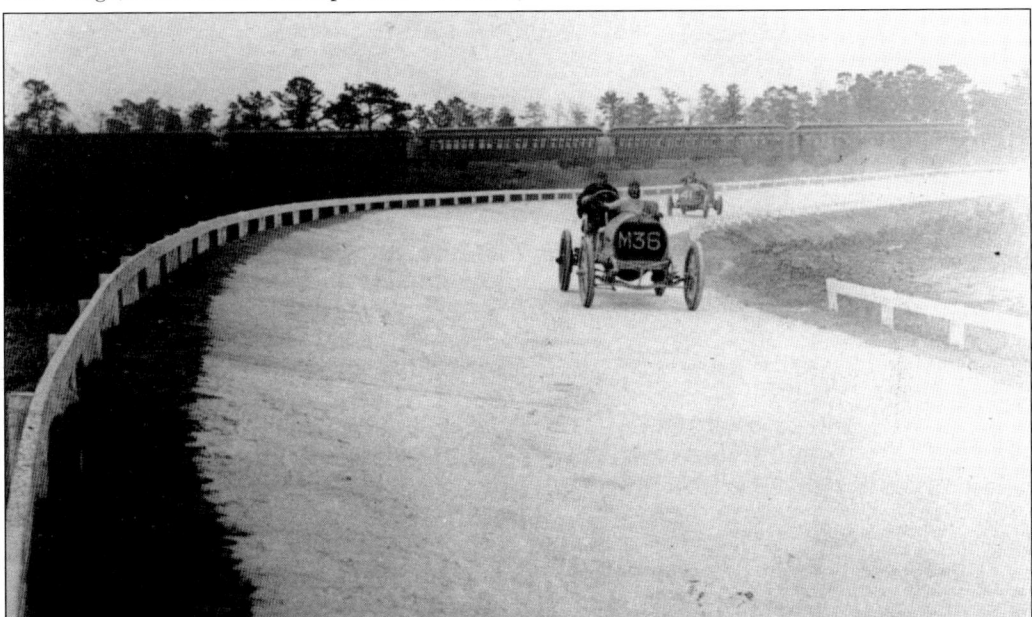

The motor parkway received excellent reviews from the public, newspapers, and automobile journals. In their October 15, 1908 editorial titled "First of the Motorways is Opened," *Automobile* magazine predicted the impact of the parkway and the place of William K. Vanderbilt Jr. in automobile history. They called it "an epoch in motor-driven land transportation." Pictured here is Deadman's Curve, which is near present-day North Herman Avenue. (Courtesy of Howard Kroplick.)

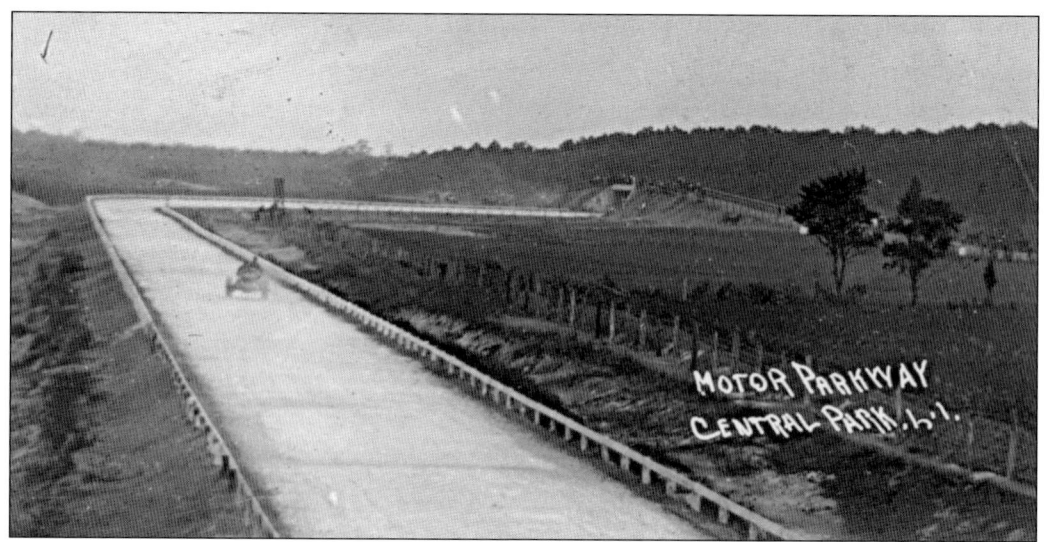

The 1908 race was held over the same course as the Motor Parkway Sweepstakes. With the construction of the parkway, a grandstand with a capacity of 5,000 spectators was built on the Hempstead Plains in today's Levittown. It was won by an American, George Robertson, driving a Connecticut-made Locomobile. For the first time, America could finally boast of victory in a race against international competition. The crowd that year was estimated at over 200,000 spectators along the 23.46-mile course. Pictured here is the Long Island Motor Parkway in 1908. Today, this location is the wooded median on the Seaford–Oyster Bay Expressway between Powell Avenue and Plainview Road, looking north. (Courtesy of Howard Kroplick.)

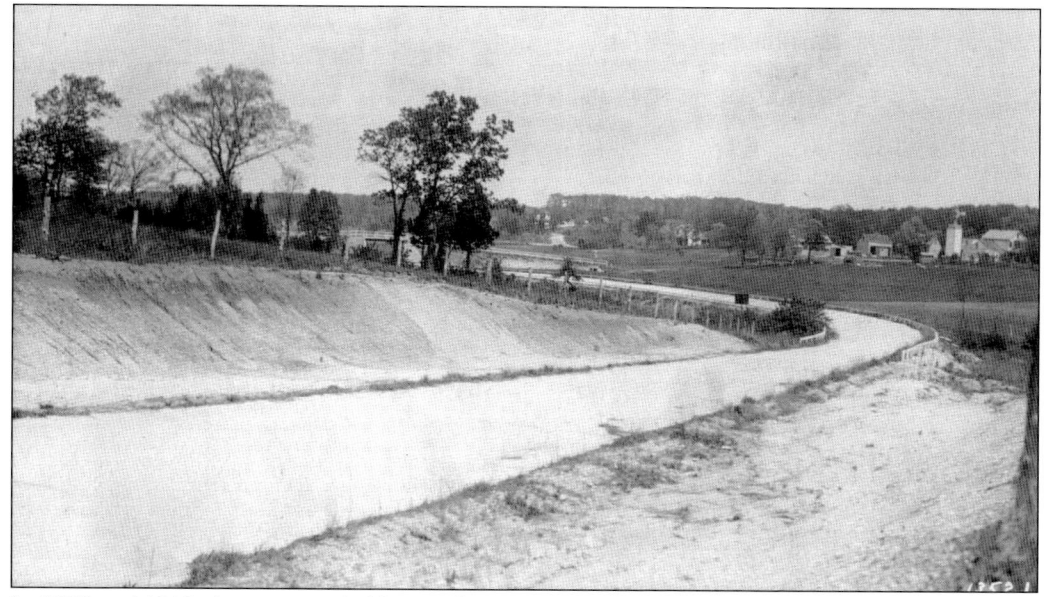

In 1909 and 1910, the race was held on a shorter course than any previous Vanderbilt Cup Race, with the motor parkway making up only 5.51 miles of the total 12.64-mile distance. Organizers believed the shorter circuit would decrease the intervals of time between the appearances of cars and provide more exciting entertainment for spectators. Driver Harry Grant and his driving mechanic, Frank Lee, won both races in an American-built ALCO. Pictured here is the completed Long Island Motor Parkway west of Stymus Farm. (Courtesy of Howard Kroplick.)

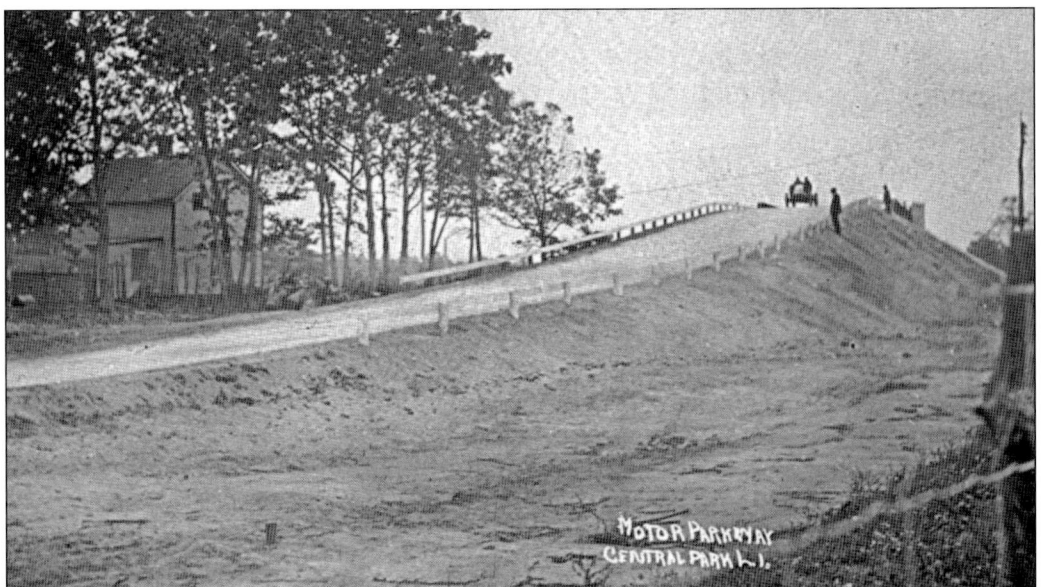

In 1909, the parkway was extended westward from Merrick Avenue in Westbury to Jericho Turnpike in Mineola and eastward from Bethpage to Dix Hills. Where the previously constructed roadway was 22 feet wide, the new extensions had a width of only 16 feet. By June 1912, the parkway measured 40 miles from Rocky Hill Road (Springfield Boulevard) in Queens to Lake Ronkonkoma. Pictured above is the Central Avenue Motor Parkway Bridge. (Courtesy of Howard Kroplick.)

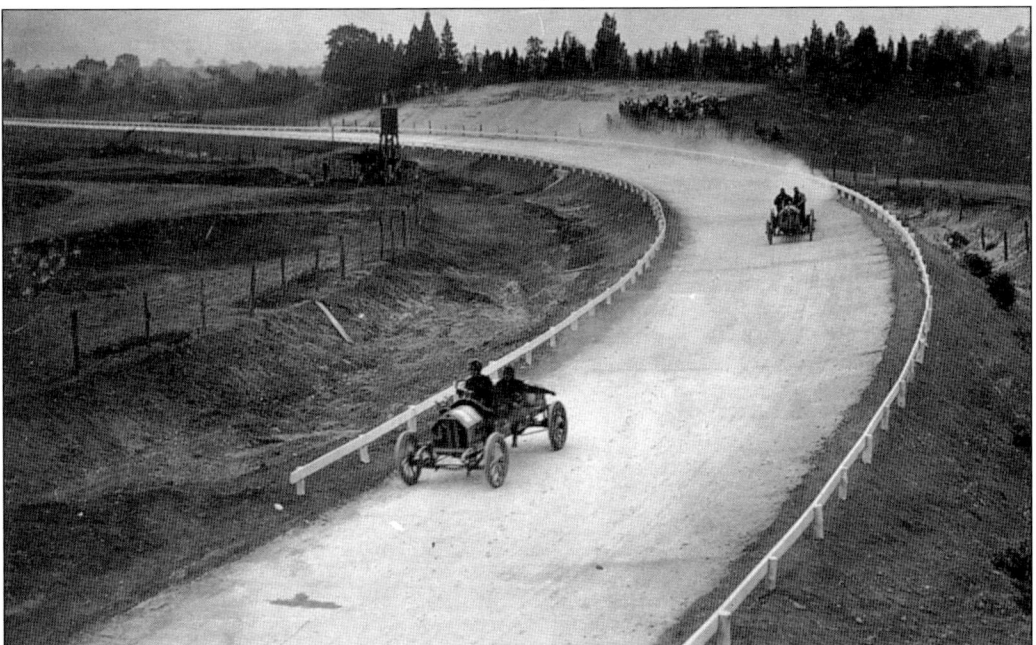

Initially, there were plans for inns and automobile-service facilities to be constructed along the length of the parkway for the travelers. Due to financial considerations, these features were eliminated. Another casualty was the shortening of the projected length of the parkway. The eastern terminus would be on the western shore of Lake Ronkonkoma and never reach Riverhead. Below is a view from the Plainview Road Bridge looking west. (Courtesy of Howard Kroplick.)

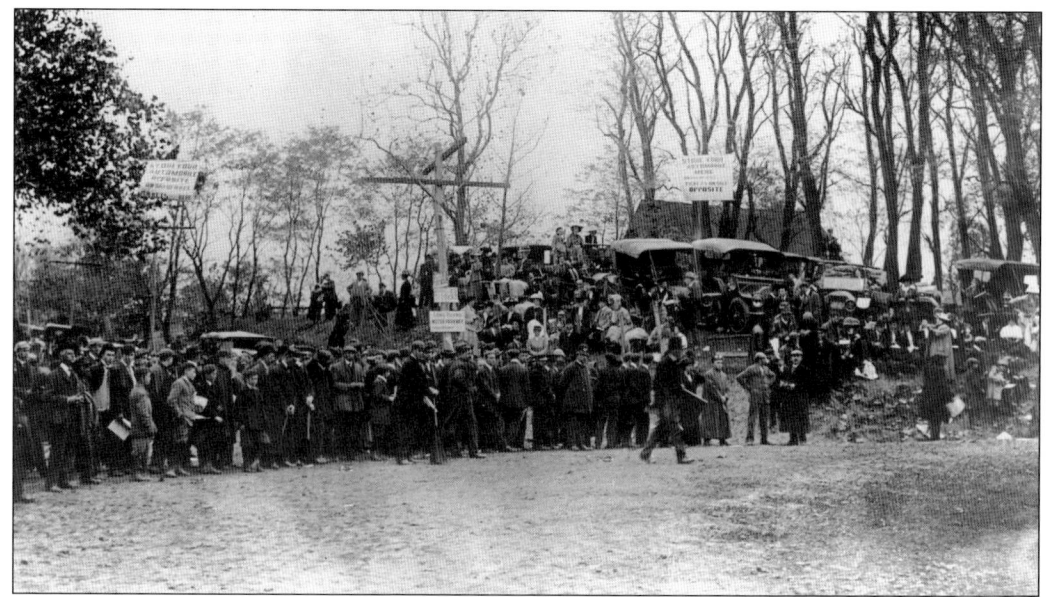

During the 1910 race, two driving mechanics were killed, and several spectators were injured. Newspapers and trade journals harshly criticized the race organizers for the fatalities and injuries, citing crowd control as nonexistent. It was clear that after six years of controversy that accompanied each race, the sport had outgrown the venue. The two deaths from the 1910 contest put an end to road racing on Long Island. Pictured above are spectators enjoying the race on Round Swamp Road. (Courtesy of Howard Kroplick.)

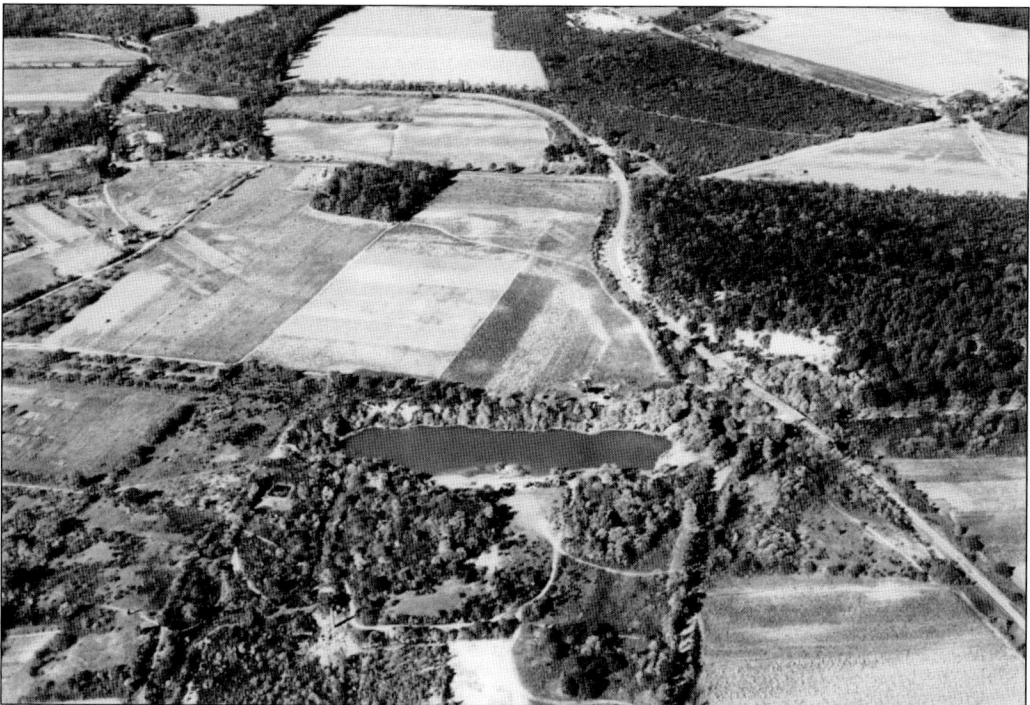

This aerial view of the Long Island Motor Parkway in Central Park was photographed in 1935. (Courtesy of Howard Kroplick.)

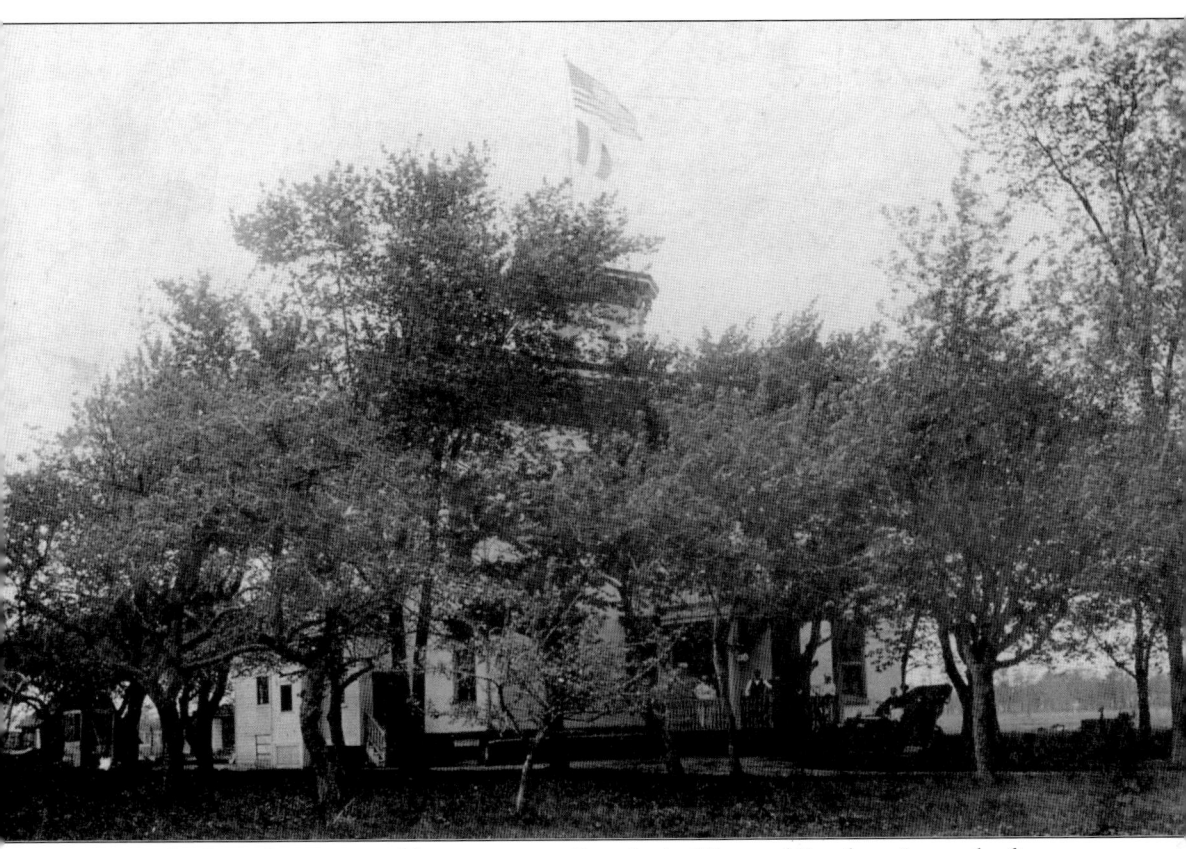

In 1908, the Beau Sejour was sold to prominent French chef Bernard Pouchon. It was the first stop off of Hempstead Turnpike that offered facilities needed by the carriage traveler for an overnight stay. When the Long Island Motor Parkway was built, the finish line of one of the earlier races was not too far from the Beau Sejour. The race participants and spectators came there to celebrate and stayed at the hotel. Eventually, the carriage trade gave way to the "horseless buggy." Pictured here is the Beau Sejour in 1908.

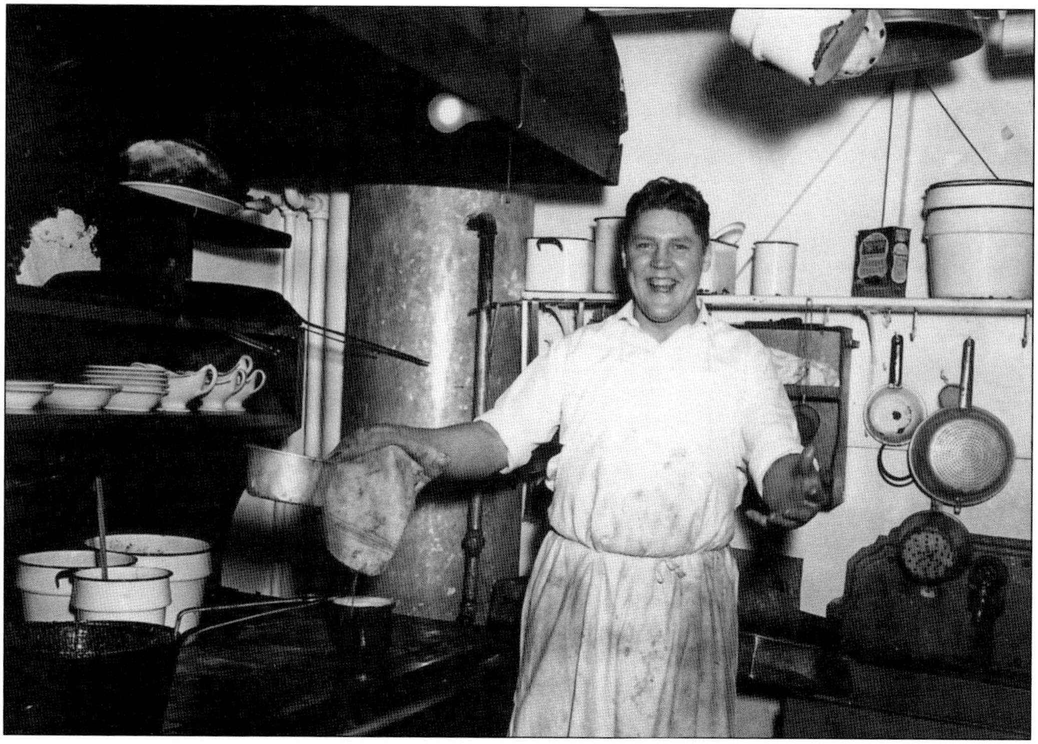

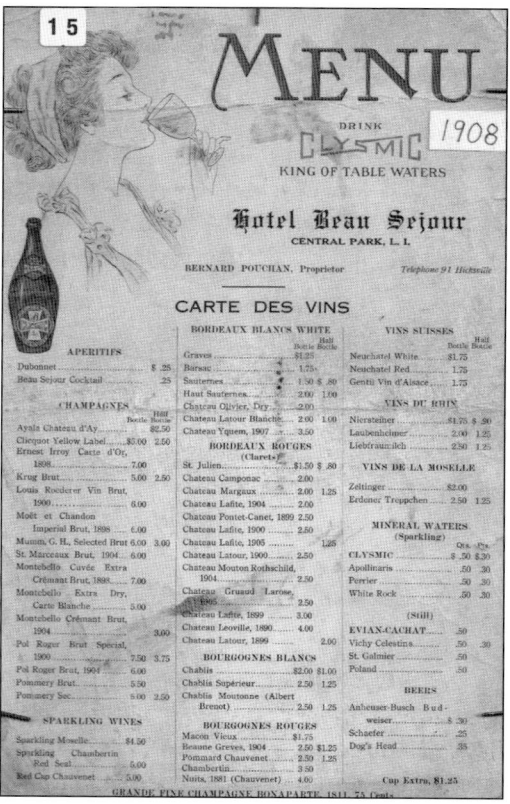

In 1918, Bernard Pouchon sold the Beau Sejour to Harry G. Wilson, and three generations of the Wilson family worked in the restaurant. The Beau had a reputation for very fine dining, and the Wilsons entertained the rich and famous. As they grew, they catered to the aircraft industry, especially the Grumman Aircraft Engineering Corporation, which held corporate functions and luncheons there. Pictured here in 1940 is Paul Wilson cooking in the world-famous Beau Sejour restaurant.

This is an original beverage menu from the Hotel Beau Sejour in 1908. While patrons could purchase a Budweiser beer for 30¢, the average bottle of champagne went for around $6.

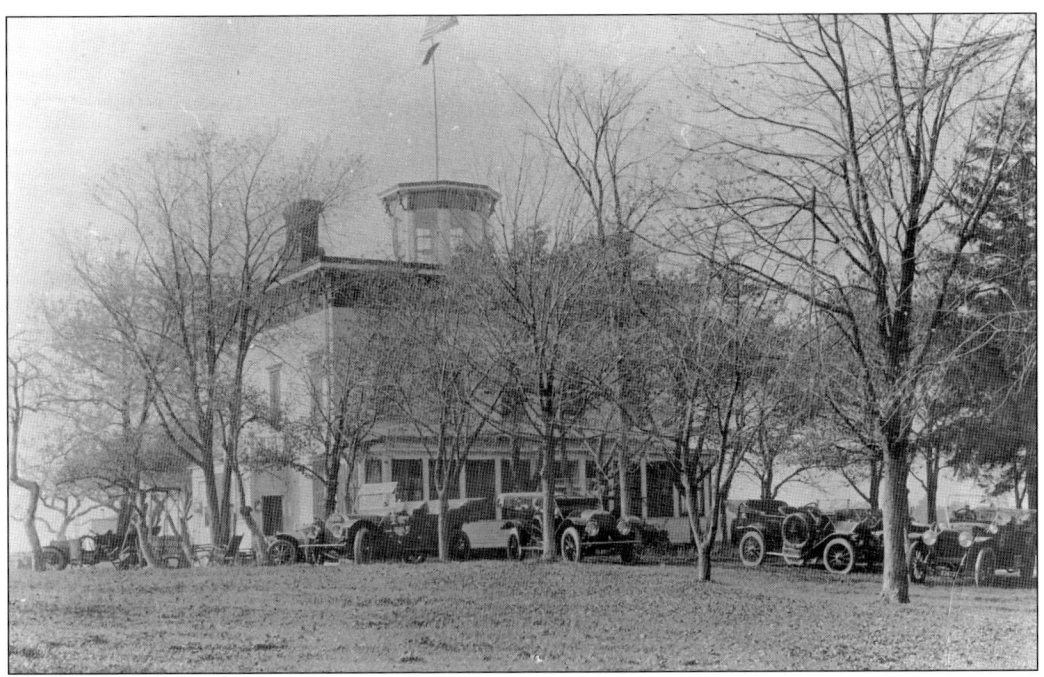

Among the most memorable and regular customers from 1937 through 1973 were the executives from Grumman and their guests. The Beau Sejour continued catering to its customers under the hands of Edward and Paul Wilson until its closing in 1974.

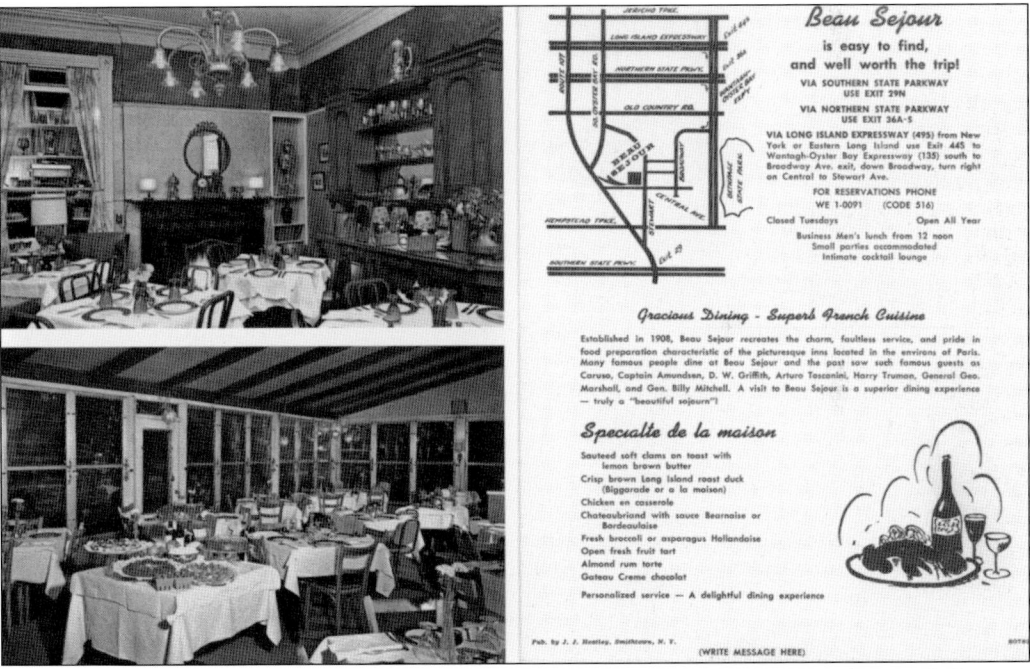

This 1960s postcard from the Beau Sejour announces "Gracious Dining—Superb French Cuisine . . . recreates the charm, faultless service and pride, and pride in food preparation characteristic of the picturesque inns located in the environs of Paris . . . A visit to Beau Sejour is a superior dining experience—truly a beautiful sojourn!"

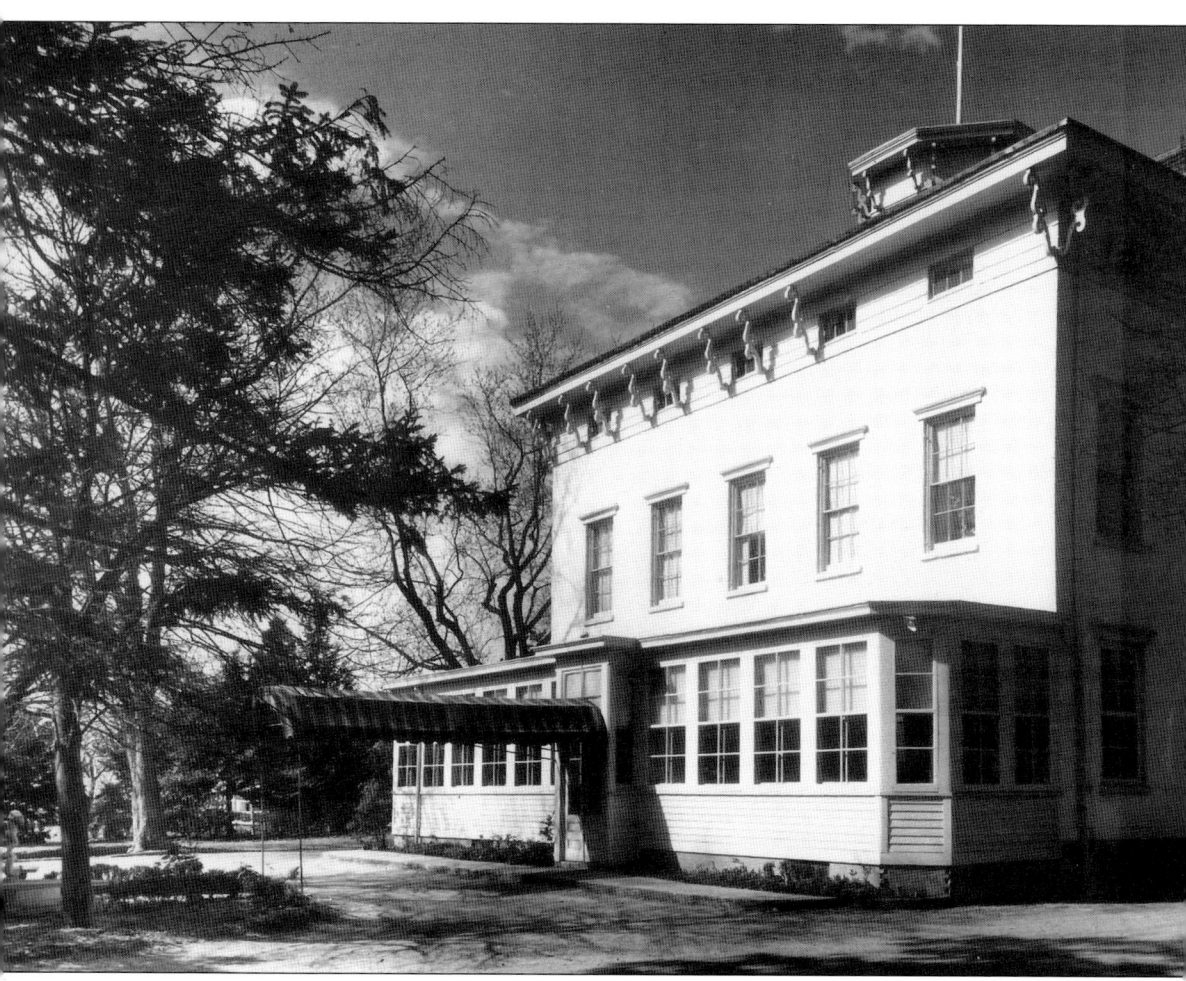

Other famed and notable people who dined at the Beau were Elizabeth Arden (cosmetic empire), Lord Beaverbrook (lord of London), Ralph Bellamy (American actor), Betsy Bloomingdale (American socialite and philanthropist), George Burns and Gracie Allen (American actors and comedians), Scott Carpenter (American astronaut and test pilot), Enrico Caruso (Italian operatic tenor), Antonine Chapal (New York City furrier), John Crews (Brooklyn commissioner), Donahue (of Woolworth's retail chain), Farouk I (prince of Egypt), Arthur Godfrey (American radio and television broadcaster and entertainer), Leroy Grumman (American aeronautical engineer, test pilot, and cofounder of Grumman Aeronautical Engineering Co.), Hammacher & Schlemmer (catalogue distributor), Sir Cedric Hardwicke (English stage and film actor), Frida Hempel (German soprano), Sonja Henie (world skating champion and film star), Hohner (manufacturer of musical instruments especially harmonicas), Johnston (Long Island judge, Hempstead), Peggy Cass (American actress and comedian), and the Kennedy family (American politics, government, and business). Pictured here is the Beau Sejour in 1950.

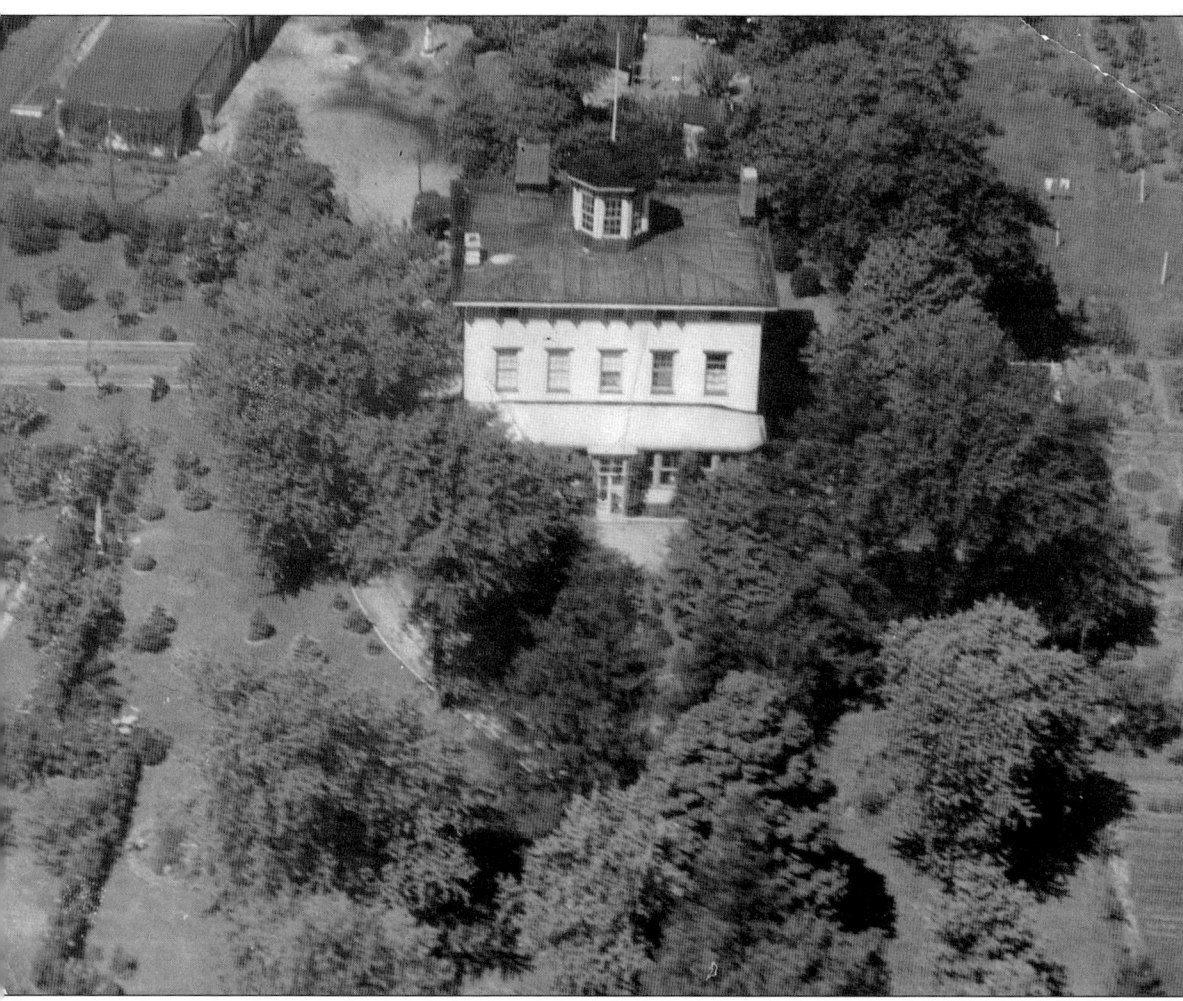

The list of famous patrons is extensive: Alan King (American actor), Myrna Loy (American actress), Robert Moses (NYS Parks commissioner) Walter and Katherine O'Malley (owners of the Brooklyn Dodgers), A. Holly Patterson (county executive of Nassau County), Cole Porter (American composer), Rainier (prince of Monte Carlo), Bill Shea (founder of the Continental League and Shea Stadium), Shubert (New York theatre producers), Prince Edward (prince of Wales) Leon "Jake" Swirbul (cofounder of Grumman Aircraft), Arturo Toscanini (director of the Metropolitan Opera), Helen Traubel (American opera singer), Harry Truman (senator and later president), Gene Tunny (American world heavyweight champion boxer), Donald Voorhees (American composer and conductor), Robert Wagner (US senator from New York), Jimmy Walker (mayor of New York City), Barbara Walters (American journalist), and Ziegfeld (the Ziegfeld Follies theatrical productions).

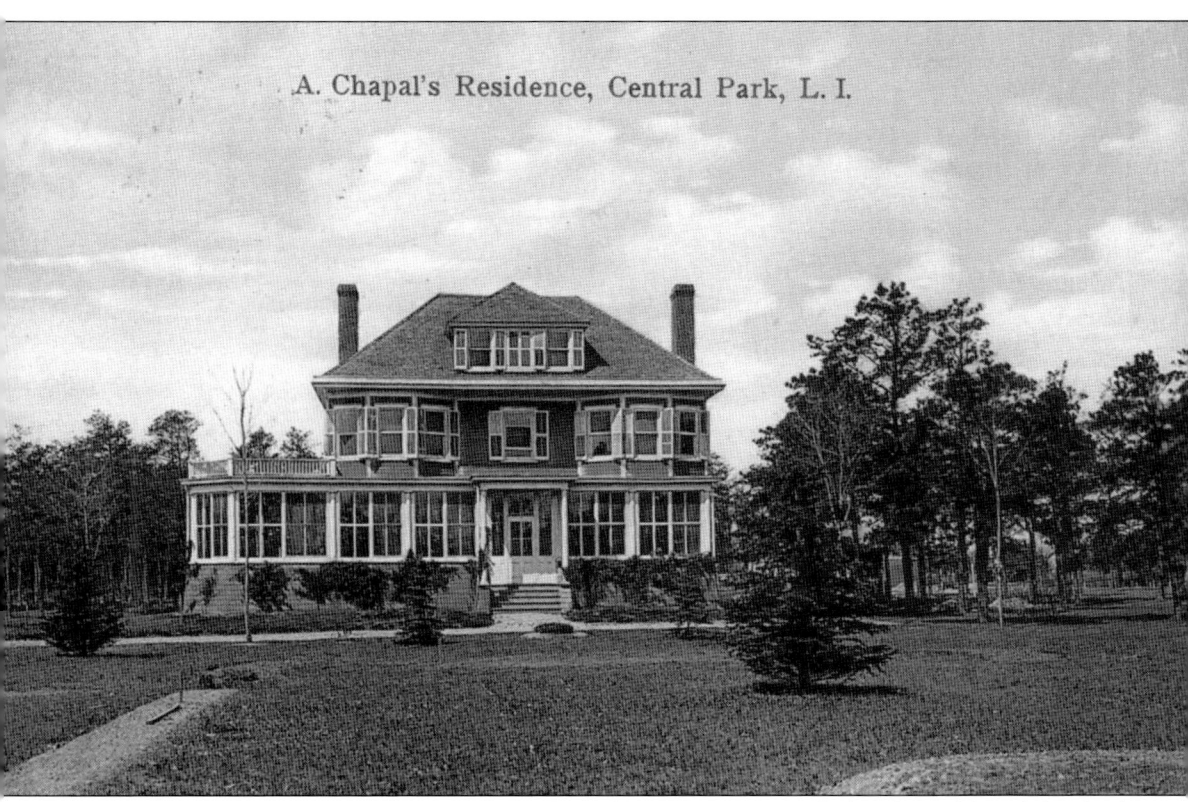

A. Chapal's Residence, Central Park, L. I.

Antonin Chapal settled in Bethpage around World War I. He married Blanche Field, and they had a son, Robert Irving, and a daughter, Francoise. Antonin Chapal was well known in New York, Paris, and London through his furrier business and as owner of Chapal Freres of Fifth Avenue in New York City. Blanche Chapal was well known for her philanthropic work and willingness to assist those in distress. At Christmastime, she distributed food, and throughout the year she helped those in need with food, shoes, and clothing. She was active in the American Red Cross and was cited by the government after World War I. The French government presented her with a medal for services rendered to the soldiers of that nation during the war. They also maintained lands and vineyards over in France. Their home was called Villa Bel Air, pictured here in 1910. This estate was located on Broadway across from the present-day JFK Middle School.

Five

SUBURBAN EXPANSION

As Central Park started to grow, so did the needs of the community. There was no fire department prior to 1910, so a board of trade fire committee was formed, and $852 was collected from 60 interested residents. These funds provided for the formation of a fire district of about 10 square miles. In April 1910, the Central Park Fire Department was organized and incorporated under the name of Central Park Fire Company in May 1911. The original firehouse stood on the east side of Stewart Avenue at the corner of Baldwin Place, on land donated by Henry Sengstacken. The dues to belong to this first fire department was one four-foot by eight-foot sheet of sheet rock, which one had to install in the new firehouse. The total cost for the building, engine, supplies, and equipment amounted to $821.96. The balance of $30.04 was turned over to the fire company. The first piece of fire equipment used by local firemen was a hand-drawn chemical engine, which was sometimes hitched to Johann Gutenburger's horse and wagon. By 1915, William Burnham's automobile had been commandeered to tow the apparatus. In 1920, Charles Romscho Sr. was elected the first fire chief, and by 1923 the department had a motorized pumper truck. In January 1924, it was reorganized as a department consisting of two companies, to be known as Company No. 1 and Company No. 2.

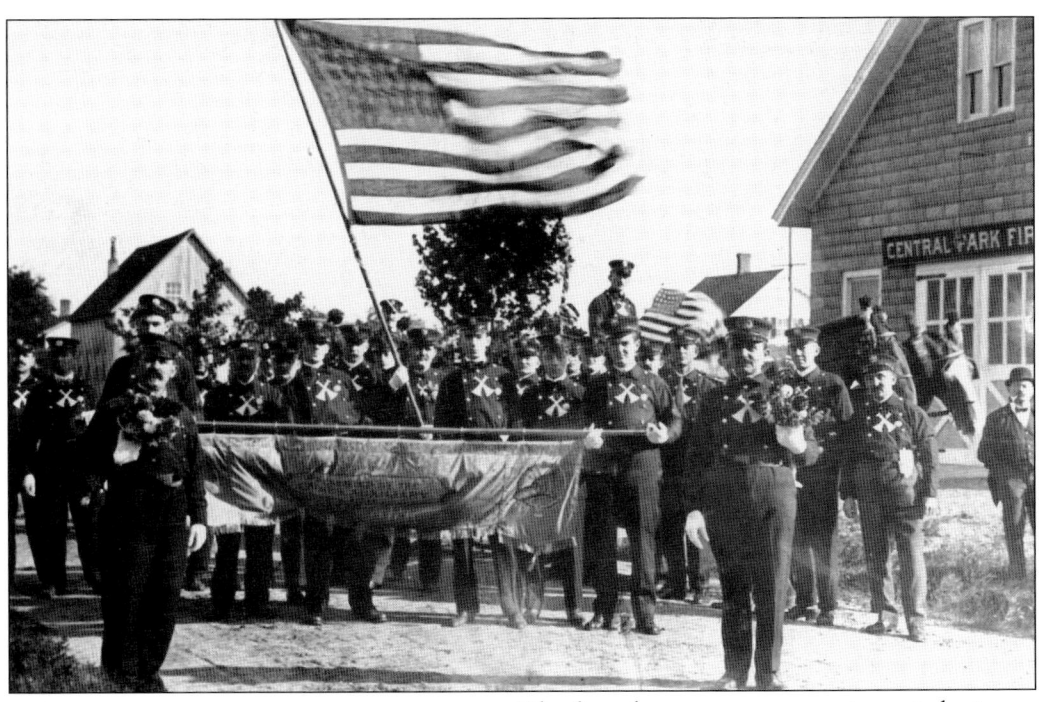

The first alarm system was an iron circle ring at the corner of Central Avenue and Peach Streets The next improved alarm system was at Dr. Louis A. Luttge's Broadway home. Luttge was department surgeon and first deputy chief. When he received the fire call at his home, he sounded the alarm on top of the firehouse by an attachment on his telephone. Firemen would call the doctor to learn where the fire was. He was on duty 24 hours a day. Pictured here are early members of the Central Park Fire Department in 1912. In the background, the Baldwin brothers' blacksmith shop is visible.

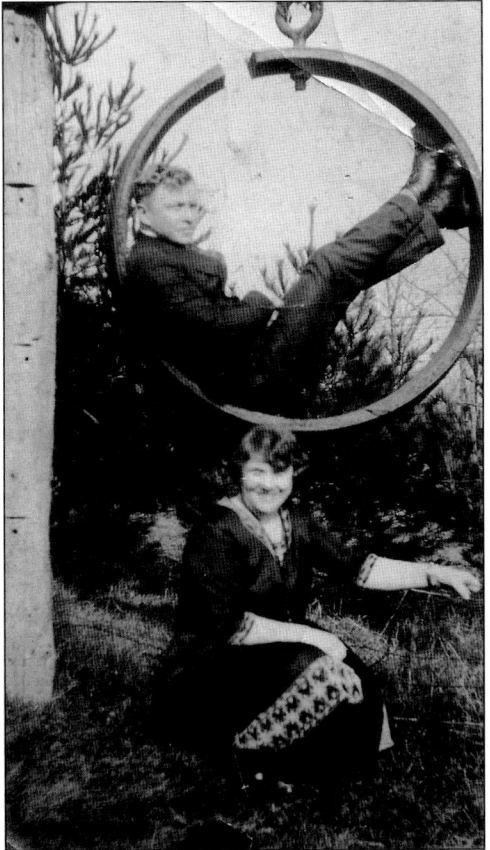

Ragna Kranz and Willie Englebert pose here with the fire ring used to alert firemen on the corner of Peach Street and Central Avenue in 1921. It had to be struck with a hammer to sound the alarm calling the volunteers to a fire. (Courtesy of Joyce Calo.)

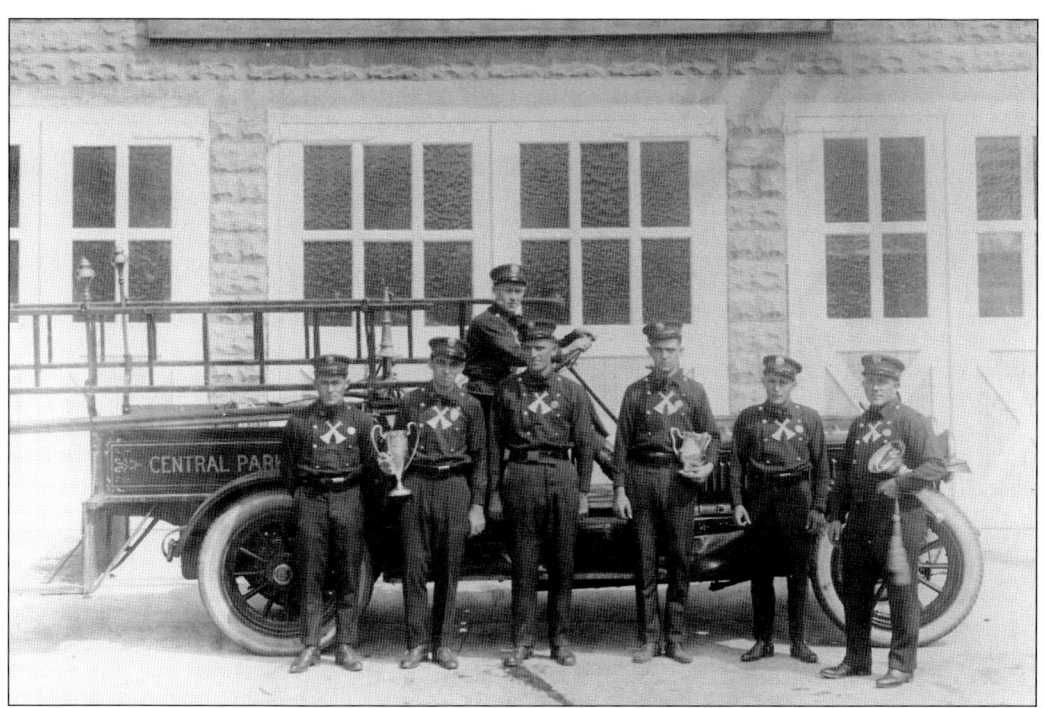

As time passed, the hand-drawn engine was replaced by a horse-drawn wagon. In 1915, Fireman Bill Burnham purchased an automobile to be used to pull the wagon while the other firemen ran alongside. Pictured here from left to right are members of the Central Park Fire Company: Henry Moesch, Hans Benkert, Fritz Miller, Fred Benkert, Chick Moesch, Charles Romscho Sr., and driver Otto Romscho in 1920.

The first fundraising activity was a card party held at the firehouse that raised $125. Pictured here is the membership application for the Central Park Fire Department dated August 1911.

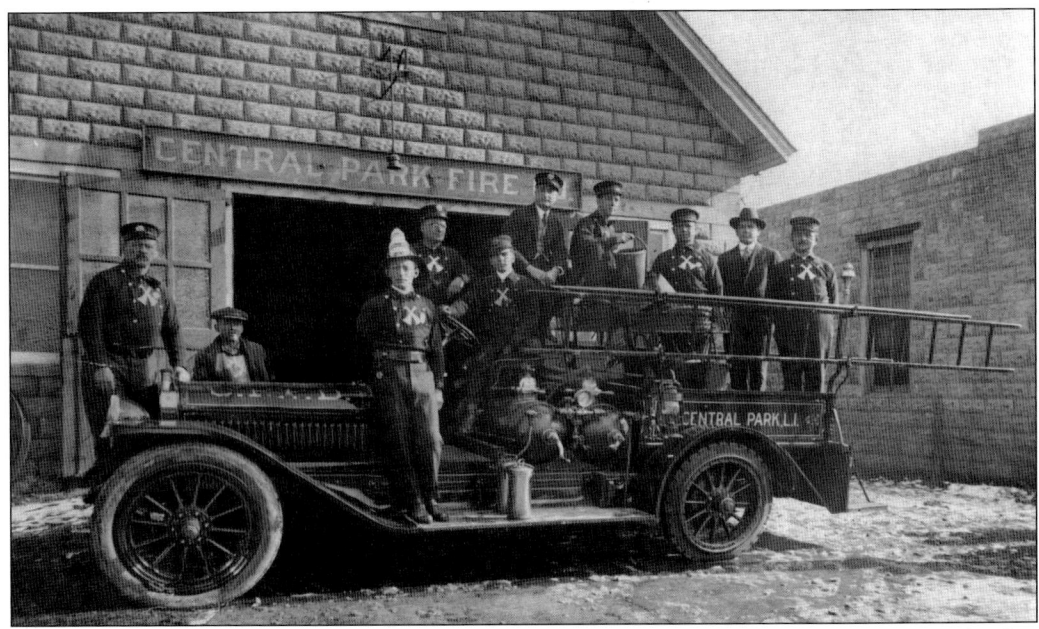

On August 5, 1941, a group of ladies whose husbands or brothers were members of the fire department met at the original firehouse on Stewart Avenue and formed a ladies' auxiliary to the Bethpage Fire Department. There were 34 charter members. The first officers were Mae Benkert (president), Rose Seitz (vice president), Marita Looney (secretary), and Lillian Keuchler (treasurer). Pictured above is the Central Park Fire Department and their motorized ladder truck.

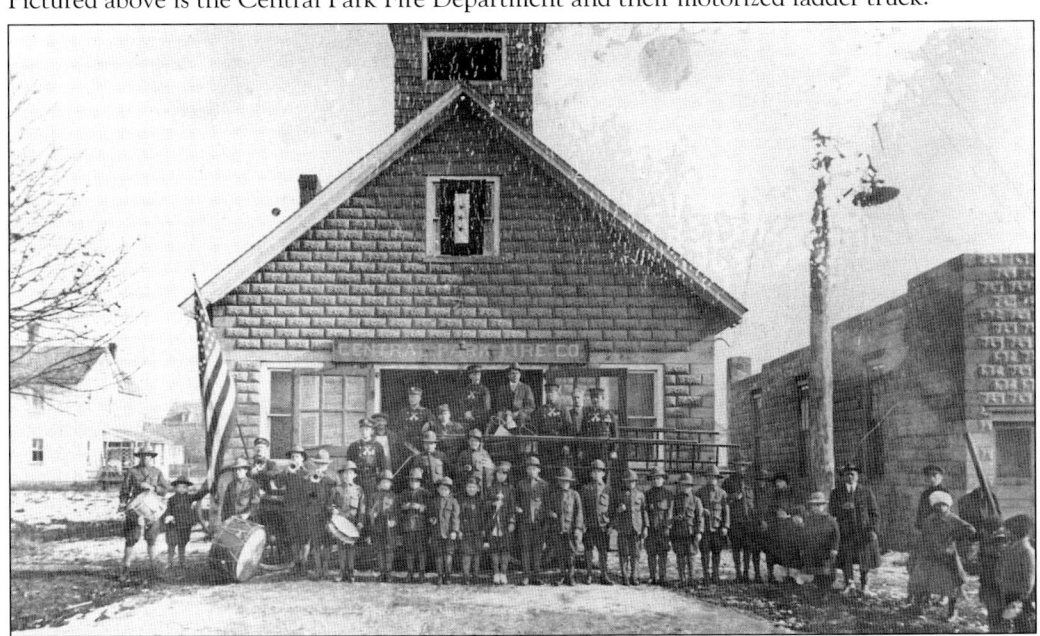

In 1942, the Comfort Committee was organized to raise money to help the servicemen of World War II from Bethpage. Various items like candy, books, cookies, and so forth were regularly sent to the servicemen. The first annual dinner was held on August 8, 1942, at the Colonial Inn, located on the east side of Broadway. The cost was 75¢ per meal. Pictured here is the Fife and Drum Corps of Central Park in 1917.

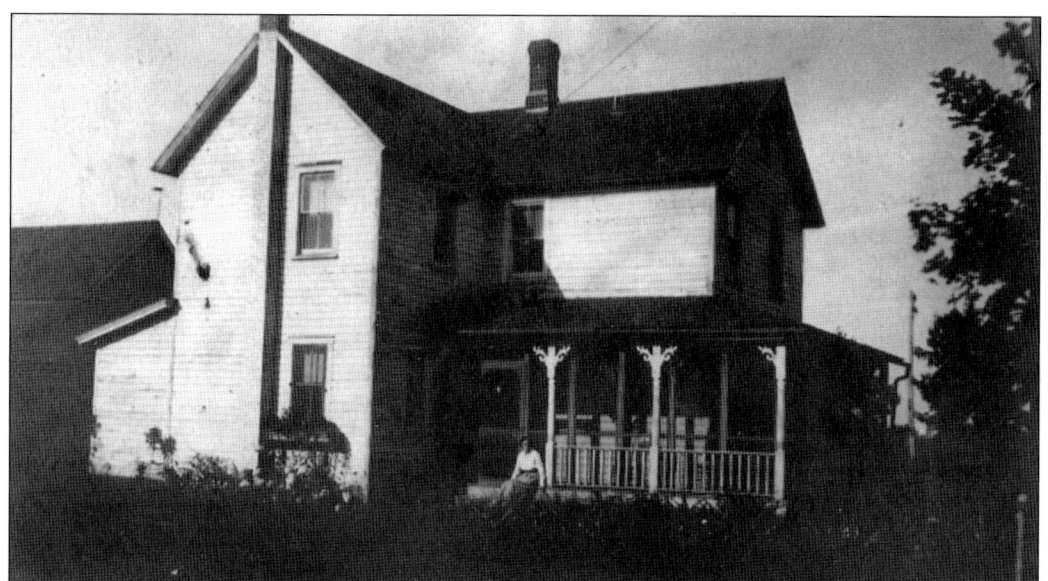

In 1917, Gustave and Gerda Anderson bought a small greenhouse on Park Avenue behind the firehouse on Baldwin Place. Anderson's Florist grew flowers that were sold locally and shipped to New York City. In 1924, Gustave built a house and three greenhouses on five acres located at Central Avenue to the north and Edward Street to the south. Their sons Raymond and Harold were involved in the business. Gustave and his first son, Raymond, built Raymond's home on Edward Street. In 1952, Harold had a home built on Central Avenue. Gustave died in 1952, leaving Gerda and her sons to run the business, who eventually renamed it Anderson Brother's Florist. Pictured here is Gerda Anderson on the porch on Baldwin Place around 1920.

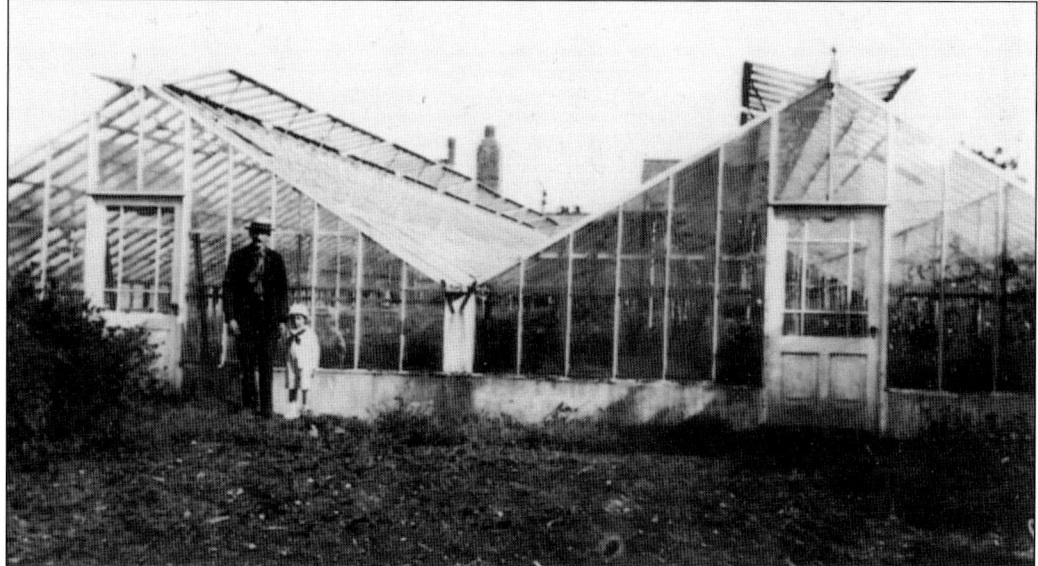

In the early 1960s, land south of their greenhouses was sold, and the subdivision on Lynn Place was built. In 1968, Harold left the business, and with demand for cut flowers waning, the business closed in 1972. The property sold in 1975, and the subdivision Monika Court was built. Anderson Street, named after the family, is located across from the old florist shop's entrance. Pictured here is Gustave Anderson and his son Harold with their greenhouses in 1924.

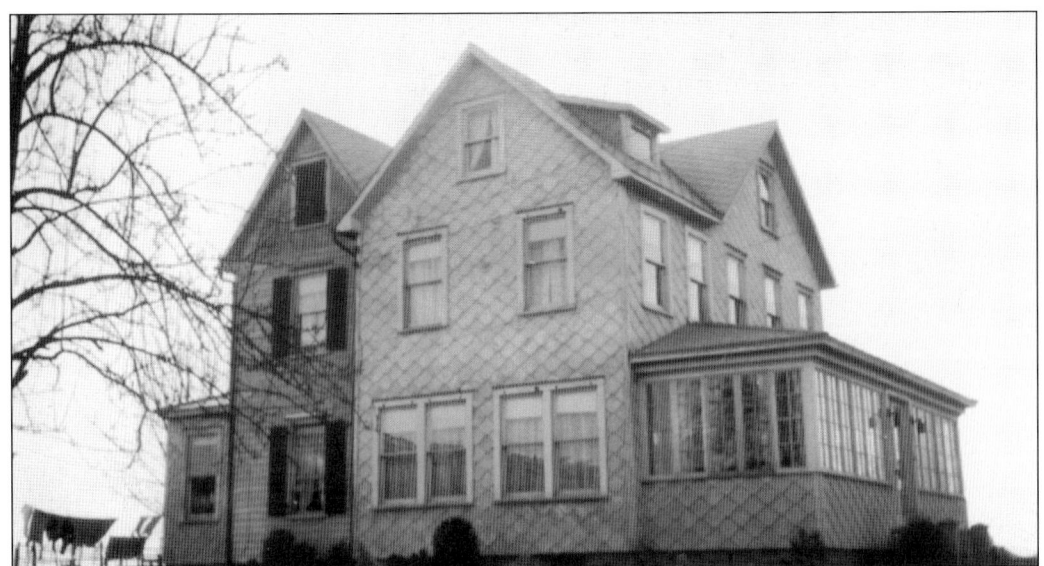

Charles Schwartz came to Central Park as a boy in 1909, and his family operated a florist shop on Central Avenue. During World War I, he served with the 87th Division. Schwartz's boyhood friend Archie McCord did not return from the war, and Schwartz helped found the Archie McCord Post of the American Legion and served as its commander. In McCord's honor, he arranged the Memorial Day parade for over 50 years. In 1936, he was one of the prime movers in changing the name of Central Park to Bethpage. And at the height of the Great Depression, he worked tirelessly to convince the Grumman Corporation to locate in Bethpage. This provided needed employment for the residents. Schwartz served as a fire commissioner and has been closely associated with the fire department for most of his life. He served as president on the Bethpage Board of Education for 12 years and laid the groundwork to build six schools. Pictured here in 1931 is Schwartz Florist, located on Central Avenue, now the site of the former Knights of Columbus.

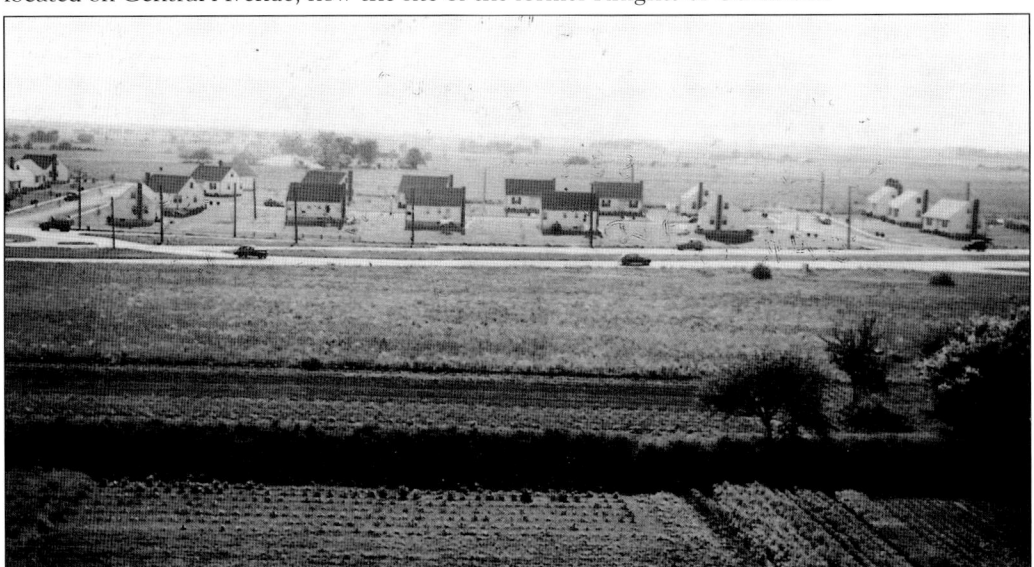

Many florists were situated around Central Avenue in Central Park. Pictured here is the view from the roof of Anderson's Florist. Looking west, one can see Hicksville Road and Wantagh Avenue between 1946 and 1950.

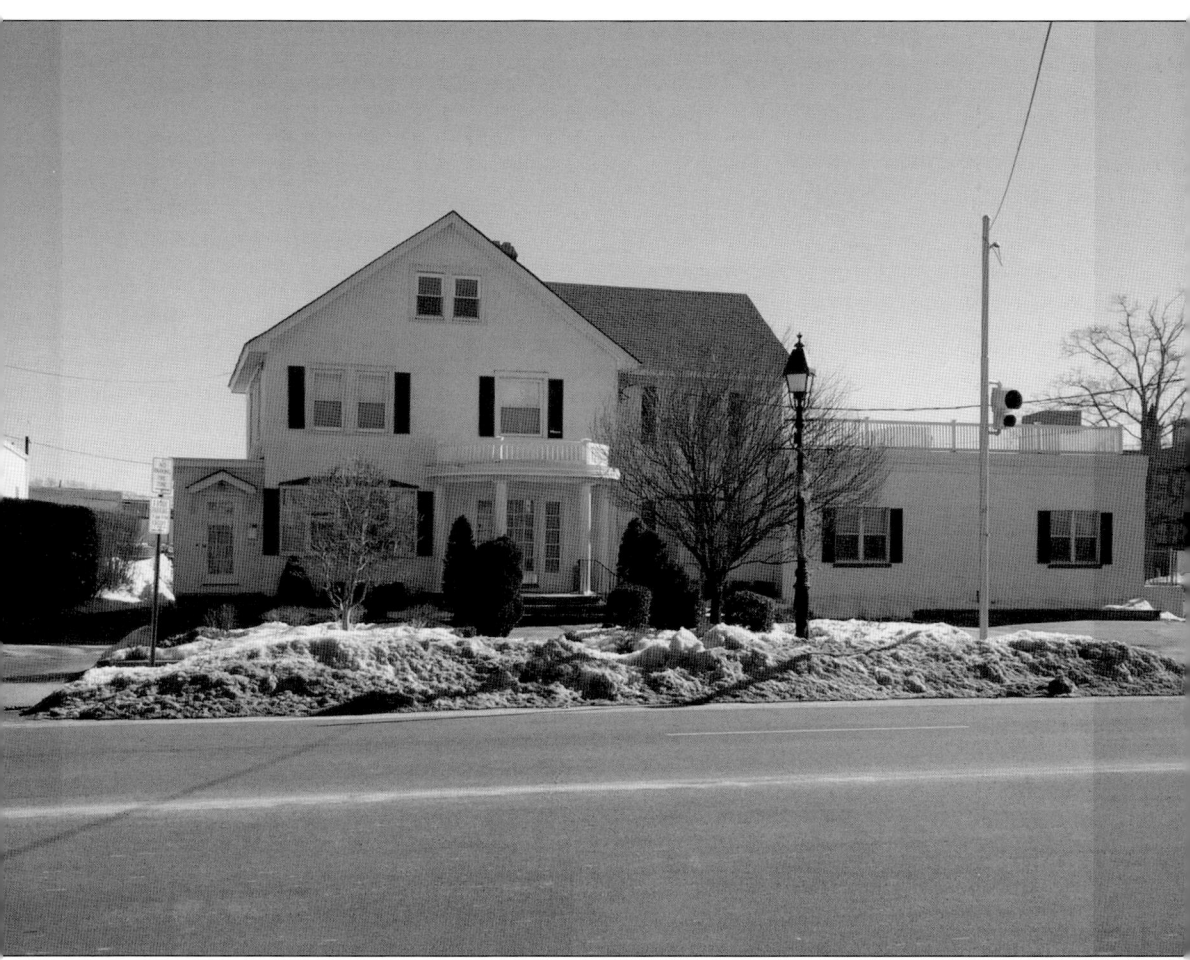

Al and Kate Guerin moved to Central Park from Brooklyn in 1910 and purchased 2.5 acres from William and Emma Stymus on Central Avenue. It was part of a parcel that had been in the Stymus family for generations. Al built two houses; one home is now known as White's Funeral Home on Broadway. The two houses are still there and are opposite the old Gerhard Neuman property. The biggest part of the property now belongs to Bethpage Park. Guerin was the original organizer of the Central Park Fife and Drum Corps, around 1917, and he was active in the Central Park Fire Department. He was singly responsible for securing a bond for the fire company when it marched in the Hicksville Invitational Parade. Pictured here is the Guerin House, which is now Arthur F. White's Funeral Home on Broadway.

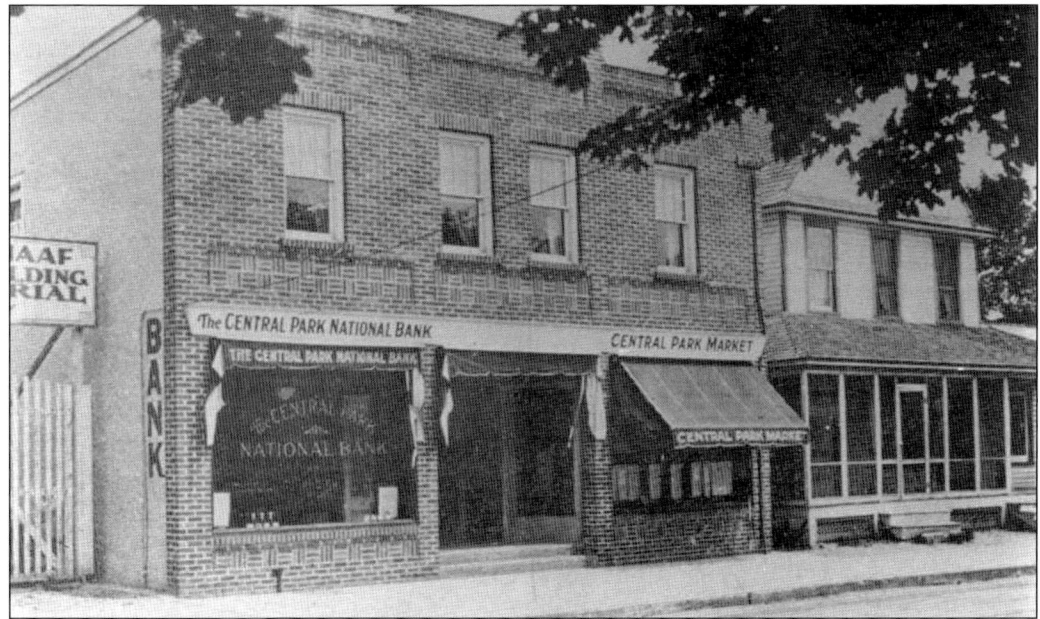

Harry A. Stolz lived in Central Park on the corner of Broadway and Seaman Avenue. The post office was inside the Stolz home, and he was postmaster from 1914 to 1920. He also owned the building next to his home where he operated a butcher shop known as the Central Park Meat Market. He had a Model T Ford truck used for making deliveries and obtaining supplies.

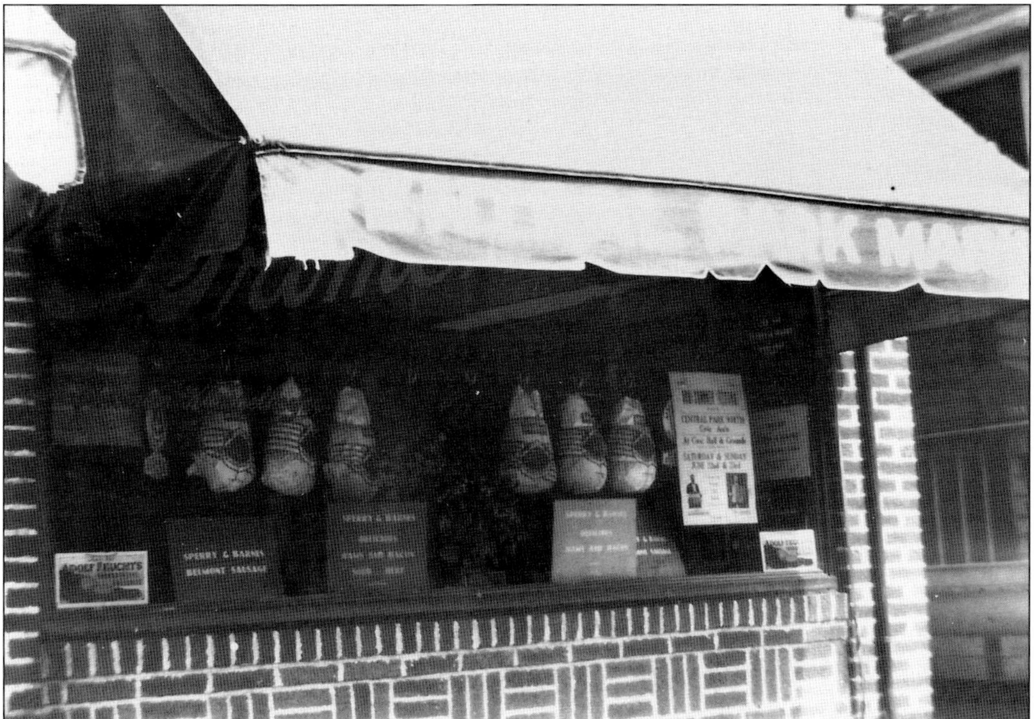

Pictured here in 1932 is the Central Park Meat Market on Broadway, when it was sold to owner Herman Klingelhoefer. Today, it is the former Bethpage Hardware Store.

Located next door to the Central Park Meat Market was the Central Park National Bank. Officers of the bank were Stephen J. Madden (president), William J. Ahern (vice president), and Edward C. Dienst (cashier). Directors were William J. Ahern, Frank Dupuis, Oscar Jacobs, Stephen J. Madden, Jeremiah W. Robinson, Harry V. Walton, Harry A. Stolz, Harry G. Wilson, and Frank Zuk. The Central Park Bank closed its doors during the Great Depression and never reopened.

This is a cancelled check from the Central Park National Bank made out to Jacob Schaaf, who sold fire and automobile insurance. The check was written by Harry G. Wilson, owner of the Beau Sejour and one of the directors of the Central Park National Bank in 1928.

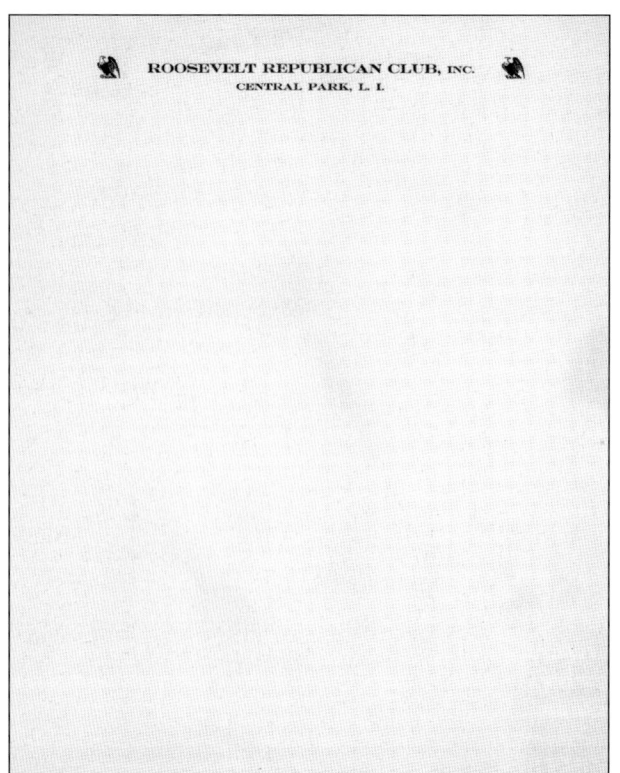

The Theodore Roosevelt Republican Club of Bethpage was formed in 1920; however, its roots go back further. The Farmer's Republican Club held its first meeting in 1891, and the Lincoln Republican Club formed in 1918. In the 1930s, an Italian-American Republican Club was formed and later absorbed by the Theodore Roosevelt Republican Club. The present meeting hall, the American Legion Hall, was purchased from the government and used as its headquarters. It was sold to the Archie McCord American Legion Post No. 86 in 1949 with a proviso that the Republican club be permitted use of the building.

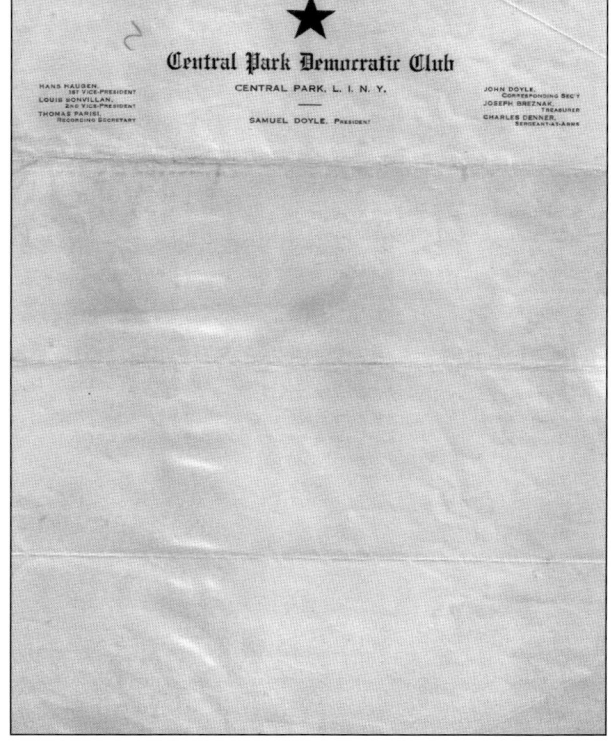

The Central Park Democratic Club was founded in 1914. About 70 members attended the meeting. Speakers included James Amendola, Joseph Ellinger, and Albert Guerin. The committeemen reported that they had been successful in having the Town of Oyster Bay hire all married men in Central Park for relief work. Dances and other entertainment was planned so that those profits would be used in employing single men in the village one day a month.

World War I veterans are listed on the Memorial Boulder Honor Roll in the Bethpage Community Park on Stewart Avenue. This memorial used to stand in front of the Powell Avenue School. It features the following names: Amendola, Raphael; Bourguignon, Lewis; Benkert, George Jr. (second local boy killed in action in World War I); Brandt, Herman; Bartovitch, Benjamin (killed in action); Campagna, Frank; Deubel, Milton J. (son of the proprietor of Duebel's Restaurant); Garrett, John (whose family owned Garrett Garage); Gloeckler, Gustave; Hoebel, Louis; Henn, Edwin; Howell, Jason; Jackson, Townsend; Jackson, Clarence; Koehler, Henry; Kranz, William (brother of George Kranz); Klug, Frank (a carpenter); Laumann, Fred; Liandier, Jacques; Leslie, Milton; Leslie, Sidney; Leslie, Walter; Margot, William; McCord, Arthur (a builder, brother of Archie McCord); McCord, Archibald (first local boy killed in World War I); Miller, Jacob (brother of Henry Miller); Nardi, Edward; Niemczyk, Joseph; Ott, Herman (street named for this family); Olsen, John V.; Possenti, Humbert; Ruggiero, Domenick (brother of Stella (Ruggiero) Finamore, US Army); Stevens, Edwin; Schwartz, Carl (owned a greenhouse business on Central Avenue); Stumpel, Henry (concrete contractor); Seaman, Henry (ran local feed store); Vogtlander, William; Wagner, Henry A.; Walsh, Valentin; Zuk, Joseph (farmer north of Powell Avenue); Zwickert, Alfred (brother of William Zwickert); Zwickert, William. (Photograph by the author.)

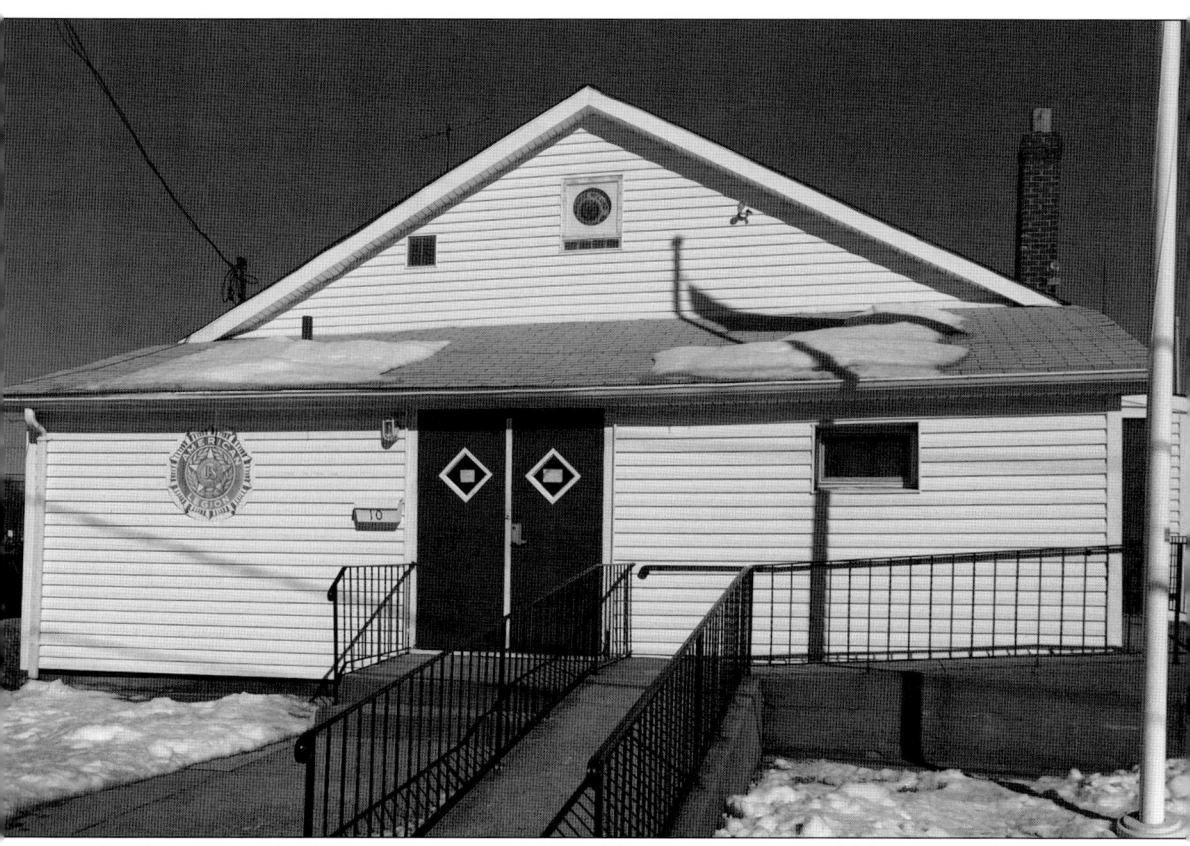

In the spring of 1927, seven veterans of World War I met in an old house on the corner of Broadway and Railroad Avenue. They formed a committee and decided to apply to American Legion Headquarters in Indianapolis, Indiana, for a charter to form a post in Central Park. The rules for granting a charter required that a name must be one of a veteran who had served in World War I and died while in service. Two names of men that qualified were submitted to be voted on. They were Archie McCord and George Benkert. Archie died in service on October 5, 1918, and George Benkert Jr. died shortly after being shipped overseas. The vote for the name of Archie McCord was unanimously approved by the charter from Indianapolis on March 24, 1927. The name of George Benkert was approved for the VFW post in Farmingdale. (Photograph by the author.)

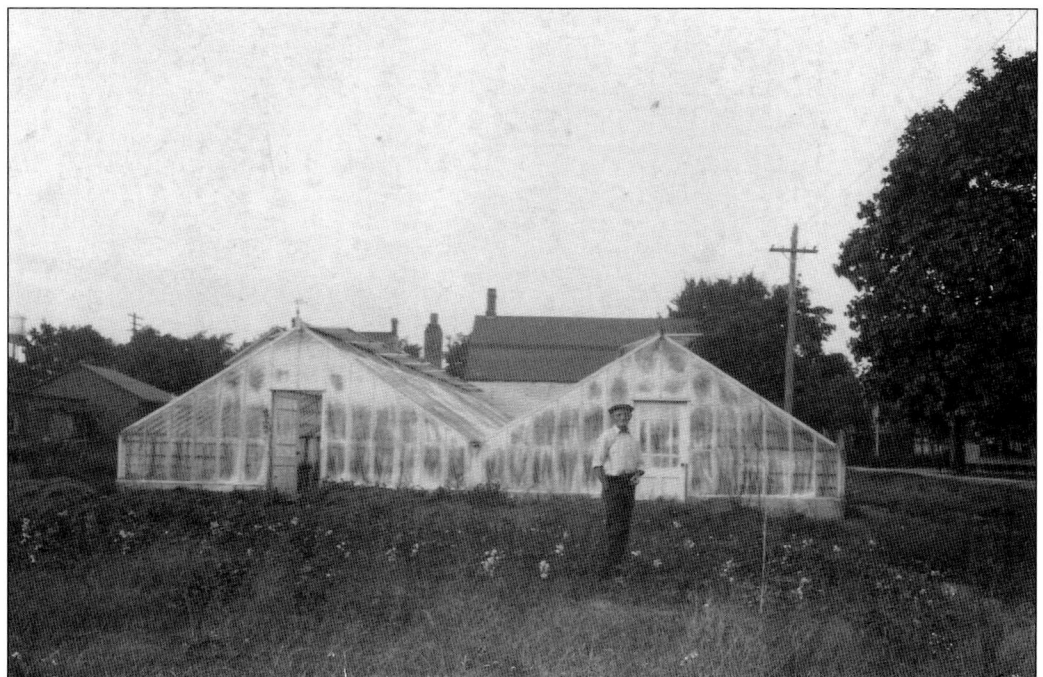

In 1896, John Klug was born on Broadway, where the JFK Middle School is located. He was orphaned and raised by Mr. and Mrs. Ulrich Friedrich, who lived on Sherman Avenue, which is now known as Park Avenue, right behind the firehouse on Broadway. In the 1920s, he operated the Broadway Garage in the building behind his Park Avenue home. The business closed during the Great Depression. Pictured are Anderson's Greenhouses on Park Avenue, on the west side looking north from John Klug's house in 1925.

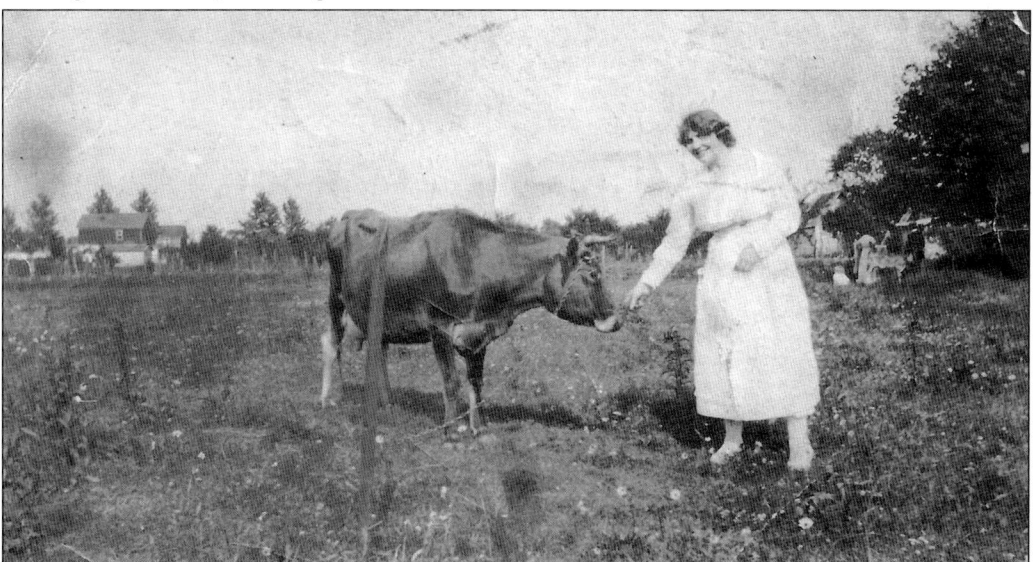

Ragna Kranz is pictured here feeding a cow on Central Avenue, now Carriere Street, in 1925. Gertrude Kranz, along with a few others, sold potatoes and other farm produce to start the building of the Central Park Assembly of God Church in 1922, which is now the Bethpage Assembly of God Church. (Courtesy of Joyce Calo.)

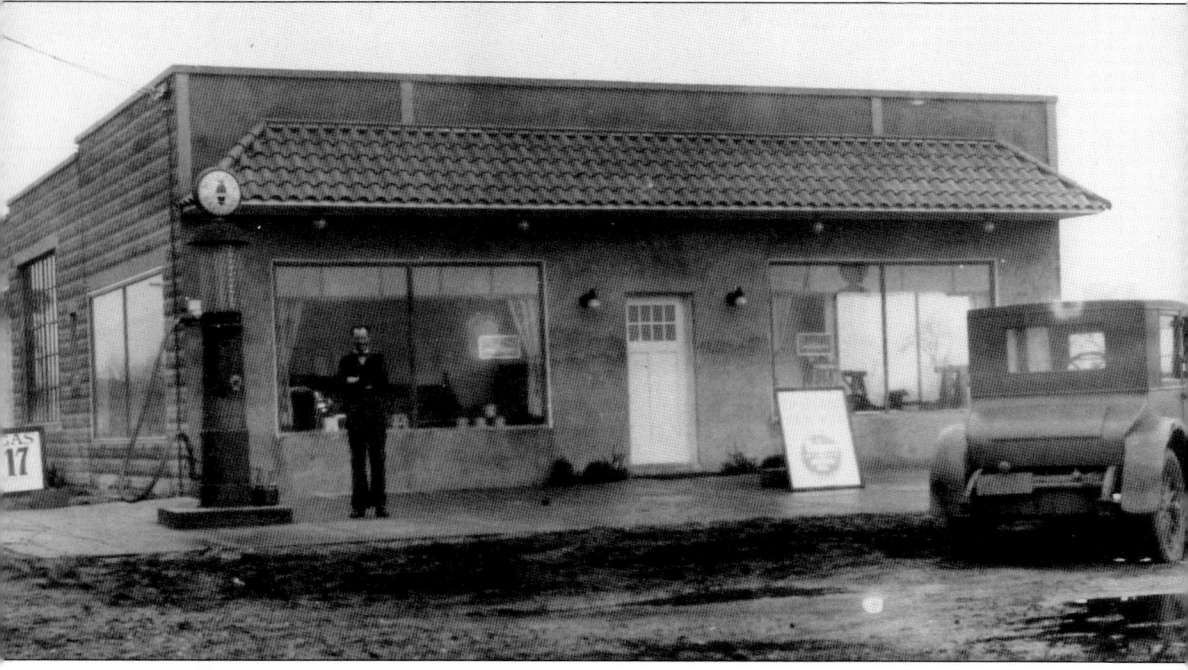

Frog Hollow Garage was opened in 1927 by owner Ben Reinke on property at the intersection of Hicksville Road and Stewart Avenue. Gasoline was 17¢ a gallon. Reinke was born in 1895 and raised on a farm on Seamen's Neck Road in Wantagh. In the early 1920s, Reinke ventured into the business world when he purchased the first tractor in the area and did contract plowing for local farmers. A tractor-drawn plow could turn over the soil five to six inches deeper than a horse-drawn plow and was in demand because crop yield and quality was increased. By plowing that extra depth, hundreds of arrowheads turned up. Reinke's collection has been displayed throughout Long Island. In 1923, he married Emily Decker from North Bellmore. In 1925, their son Duke was born, and that same year Ben and Emily bought property in Central Park at the intersection of Hicksville Road and Nibbe Avenue, which is now Stewart Avenue. Pictured here is owner Ben Reinke in front of Frog Hollow Garage in 1927.

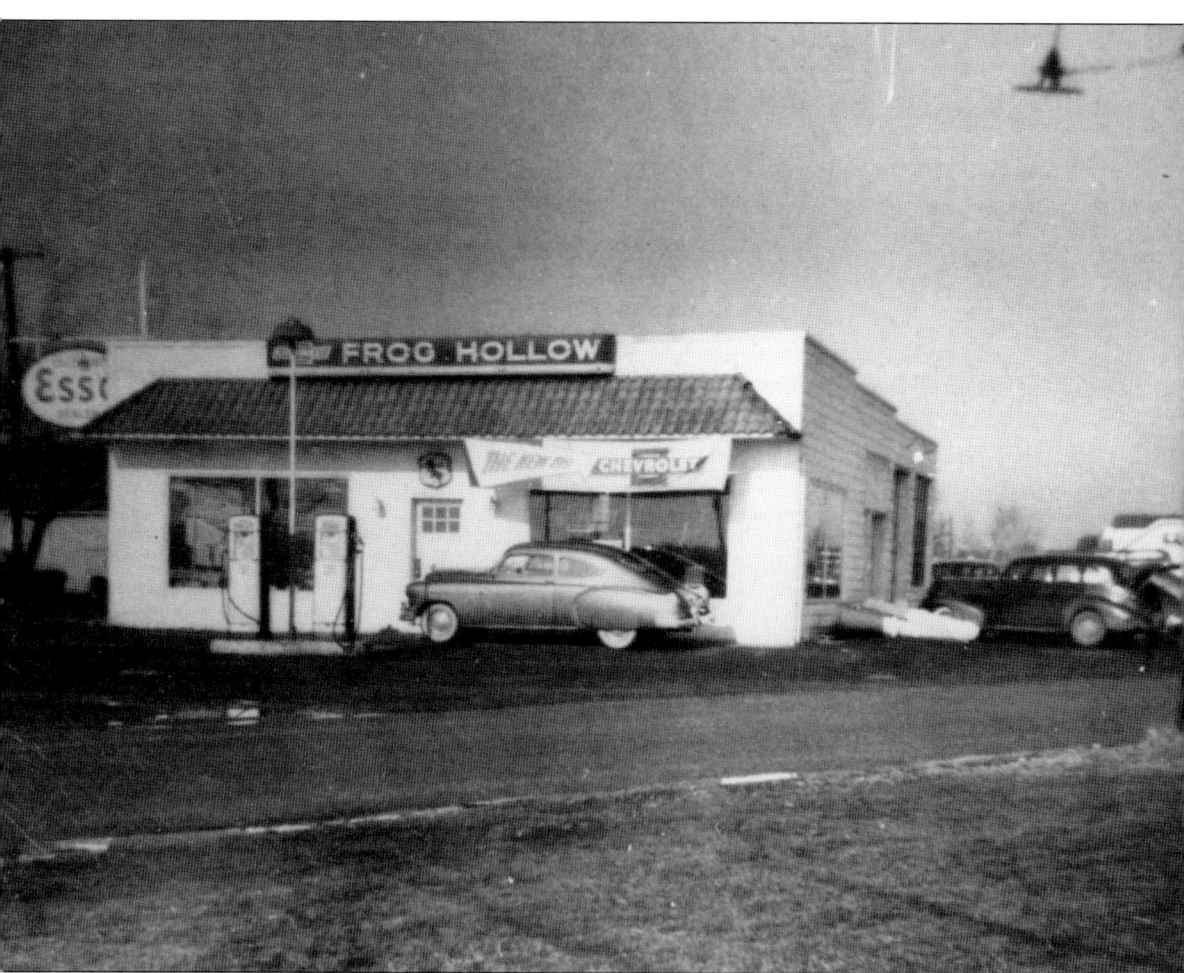

In 1927, they built a house and garage showroom on the site. That same year, an agreement was signed with Chevrolet Motor Division, and Ben Reinke was now a Chevrolet dealer. Only 11 units were sold the first year, and sales were progressing, increasing slowly, until the end of World War II, when developers bought up farm after farm and built thousands of homes in the surrounding area. Sales jumped, and old Frog Hollow ran out of room, so in 1957 a new facility was built on the property to the north. There it continued to grow, and sales climbed into the 600 range. Ben passed away in 1972, and the business was carried on by his son Duke, who had been a partner since 1950. Emily passed away two years later. In 1977, Frog Hollow closed its doors. Today, Frog Hollow Collision and Carl's Fence are located here. (Courtesy of Plainedge Public Library.)

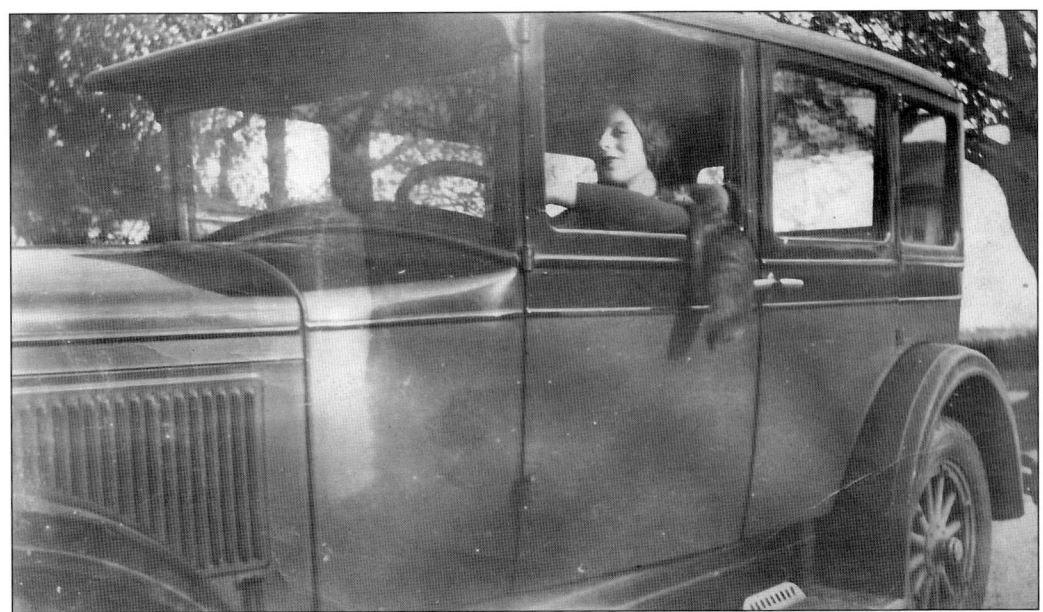

Alice Lane (Kranz) is behind the wheel of a "Hup-Mobile" in 1929 on Central Avenue in Central Park.

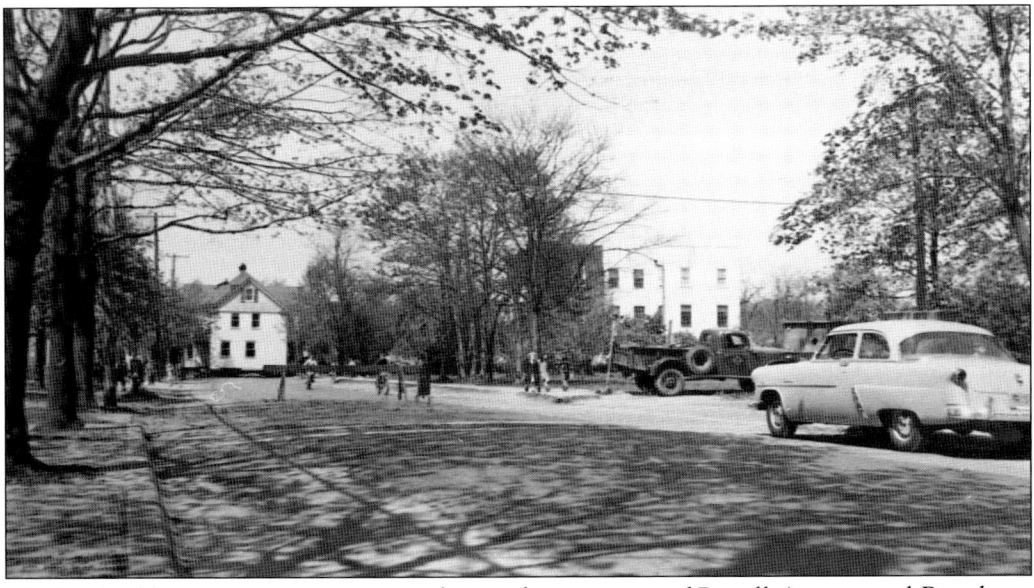

The Rathcabbin Apartments were on the northeast corner of Powell Avenue and Broadway. Originally built by Charles Powell in 1854, the wooden structure was one story. A two-story wooden addition and a three-story clapboard addition were added in 1906, but a fire in 1912 destroyed half of the attic. In 1937, J.W. Kelly purchased the house and enlarged it into a three-story brick building. Kelly turned it into apartments primarily for upstate schoolteachers, who boarded there while teaching at the Powell Avenue School. It was torn down in 1995, and Central Park Estates condominiums replaced the structure. The Rathcabbin Apartments are pictured here, behind the truck to the right. On the left, the Jarvis House is being moved from Broadway to its new location on Broadway and Barbara Street in 1956. (Courtesy of Nassau County Parks, Recreation & Museums.)

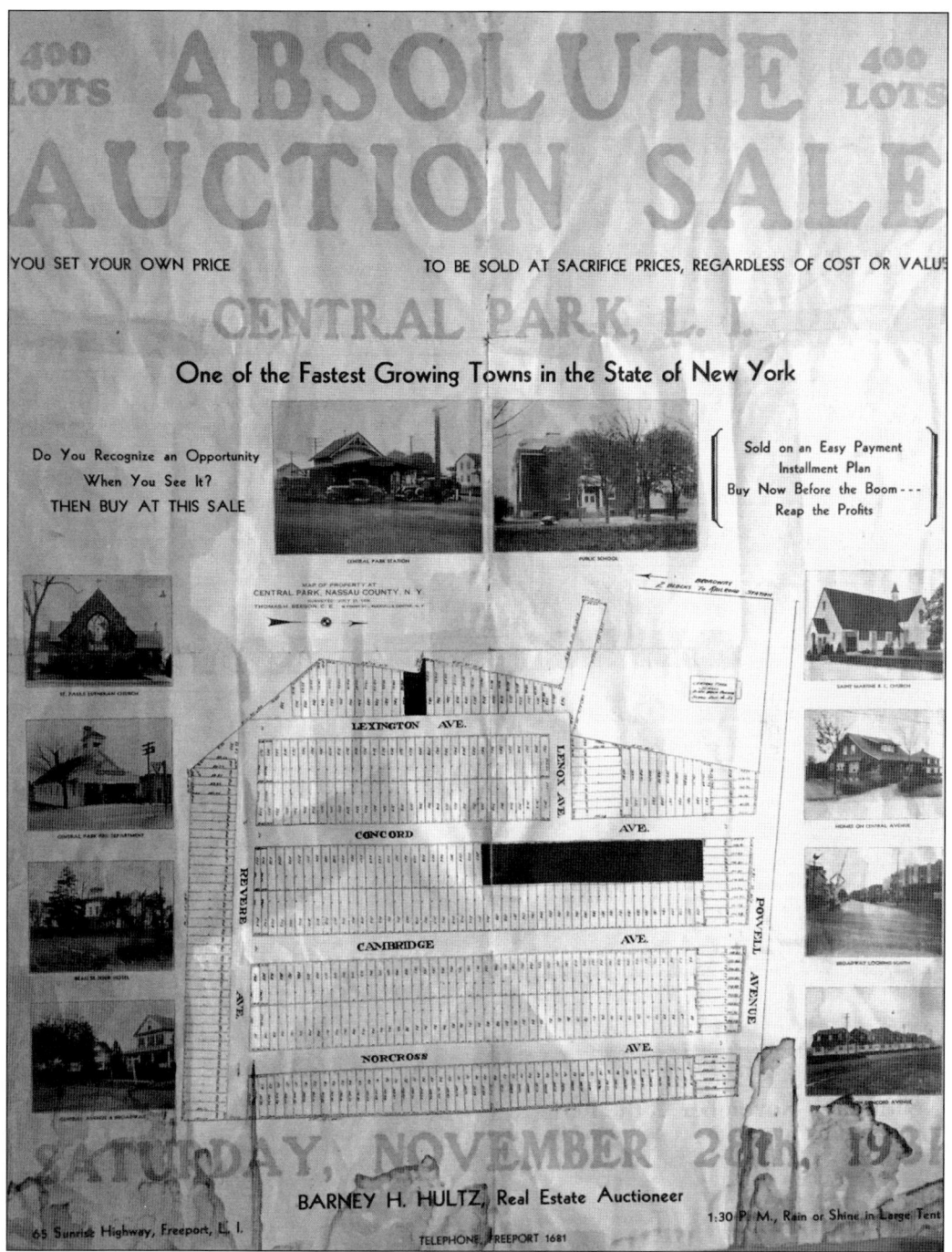

This is a poster for a land auction in Central Park from 1931. This available land was a new subdivision of 400 lots to be built behind where the current Bethpage Public Library is located. It is being advertised as "One of the fastest growing towns in the State of New York." The poster depicts a very developed town with a public school, the Powell Avenue School, St. Martin Roman Catholic Church, St. Paul's Lutheran Church, the Central Park Train Station, a strip of stores and merchants on Broadway, the Central Park Fire Department, and the Beau Sejour Hotel.

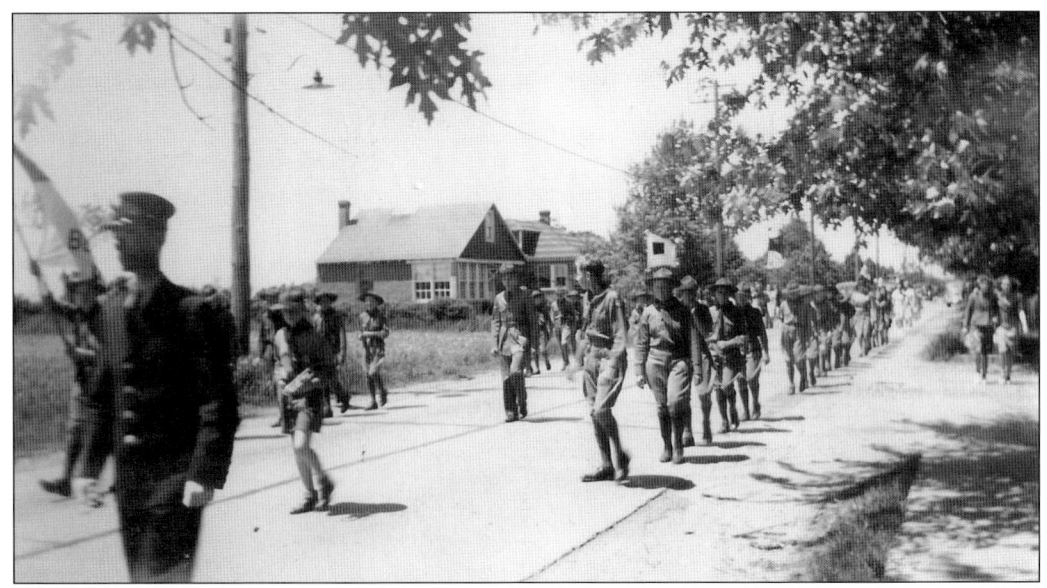

This Memorial Day parade in Central Park is flowing down Central Avenue in 1930. Charles Schwartz, who operated a florist shop on Central Avenue, arranged the Memorial Day parade for over 50 years.

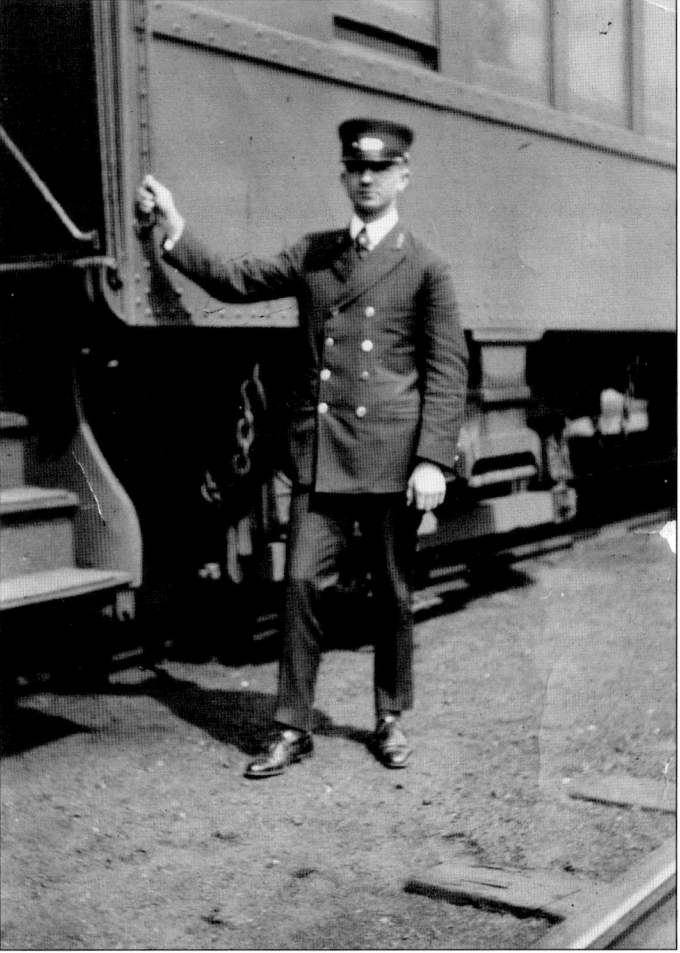

Pictured here in 1933 is Al Kranz, Long Island Rail Road conductor for 50 years.

Six

Central Park to Bethpage

In 1912, railroad executive Benjamin Yoakum purchased 1,368 acres of land and hired Devereux Emmet to design and build an 18-hole golf course, which opened in 1923 and was leased to the private Lenox Hills Country Club. Upon Yoakum's death in 1929, the Long Island Park Commission took over the lease operating the Lenox Hills Country Club as a public facility. In 1931, the park commission purchased the Yoakum Estate and other area farms to create Bethpage State Park. In 1932, Jessie Merritt, the Nassau County historian and a direct descendent of Thomas Powell, proposed naming the properties Bethpage State Park. Members of the Central Park Improvement Association formed and suggested that a name change for the town would be desirable. William Ahern wrote to Robert Moses, president of the Long Island Park Commission, and pointed out that the name Central Park had caused difficulties for the postal service and asked if they would object to the town changing their name to Bethpage. Farmingdale considered the name change for their town and argued that Central Park was not incorporated, had no village board, and was nonexistent politically. Farmingdale continued their argument while Central Park organized a committee and circulated a petition to change the name. The disagreements continued throughout the communities regarding the name and location of the railroad, all done in an effort to gain leverage.

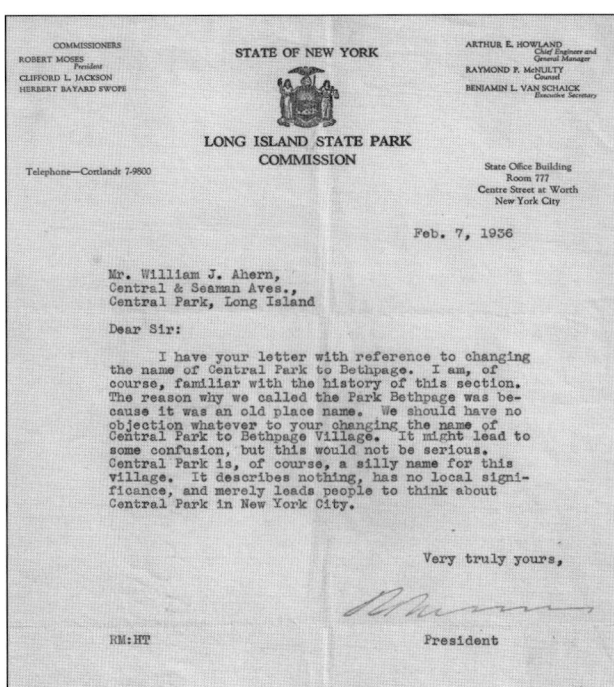

One reason for changing the name was that the mail was always being sent to nearby towns such as Central Islip, Center Port, Center Moriches, and even the actual Central Park in New York City. Some people felt that the name Central Park had no historical background, and they preferred the name given by Thomas Powell. However, the name Bethpage was in use by an adjacent community, which resisted suggestions of a merger. That community insisted they were the original Bethpage and instead renamed itself Old Bethpage. This letter from Robert Moses of the Long Island State Parks Commission to William Ahern in February 1936 made note of some minor confusion that could come from renaming Central Park to Bethpage Village.

Ahern also wrote to George LeBoutillier, vice president of the Long Island Railroad, for support. This March 1936 reply from LeBoutillier to Ahern expresses approval for changing the name of the station to Bethpage.

DIVISION OF POSTMASTERS

IN REPLYING
REFER TO INITIALS AND DATE
AP

Post Office Department
FIRST ASSISTANT POSTMASTER GENERAL
Washington

February 18, 1936

Mr. William J. Ahern,
   Central Park, Nassau County,
     Long Island, New York.

My dear Mr. Ahern:

    Receipt is acknowledged of your letter of February 10, 1936, relative to changing the name of a post office at Central Park to Bethpage or some name including the word Bethpage.

    If a majority of the patrons desire the name of the post office changed, they should submit a petition to the Department to that effect, giving their reasons for desiring the change. It should also be stated whether the railroad company would be agreeable to changing the name of its station to agree with the proposed name of the post office.

    Inasmuch as there is only one post office in the United States by the name of Bethpage at the present time, it being a small third class office, the Department would not object to changing the name of the local post office to Bethpage. However, the Department prefers to have the names of post offices contain only one word if possible. In this connection, you are advised that a complete alphabetical list of post offices in the United States is contained in the United States Official Postal Guide of July, 1935, beginning on page 995. A copy of this publication can be consulted in any post office upon request.

                               Sincerely yours,

                                 W. W. HOWES
                  First Assistant Postmaster General

B1-18

This February 1936 letter from W.W. Howes, first assistant postmaster general in Washington, advised Ahern to organize a petition and to provide a one-word name for the post office. A petition signed by 435 residents of Central Park, over half the number of patrons of the post office, was prepared and sent to Howes. Finally, in August 1936, the US Post Office approved the name change to Bethpage. The change from Central Park to Bethpage was one of the last complete name changes of Nassau County's post offices.

In 1931, the Long Island State Park Commission prevented the subdivision of the Yoakum estate and preserved it as a great future reservation for public recreation by special legislative authorization, which took an option on the entire property. This option was extended from year to year until 1934, when the Bethpage Park Authority was created. The Long Island State Park Commissioners, acting as the Bethpage Park Authority, issued bonds to pay for the property, of which $100,000 was taken by the state comptroller and the remainder by the Yoakum estate. The title was vested in the authority on May 18, 1934. Pictured here is the Bethpage Golf Course Clubhouse. (Courtesy of Nassau County Parks, Recreation & Museums.)

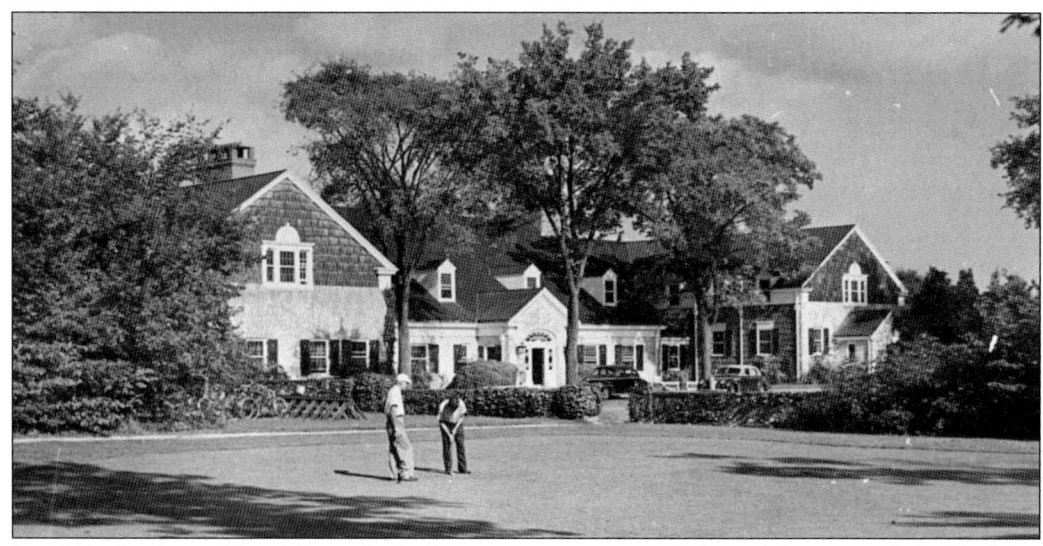

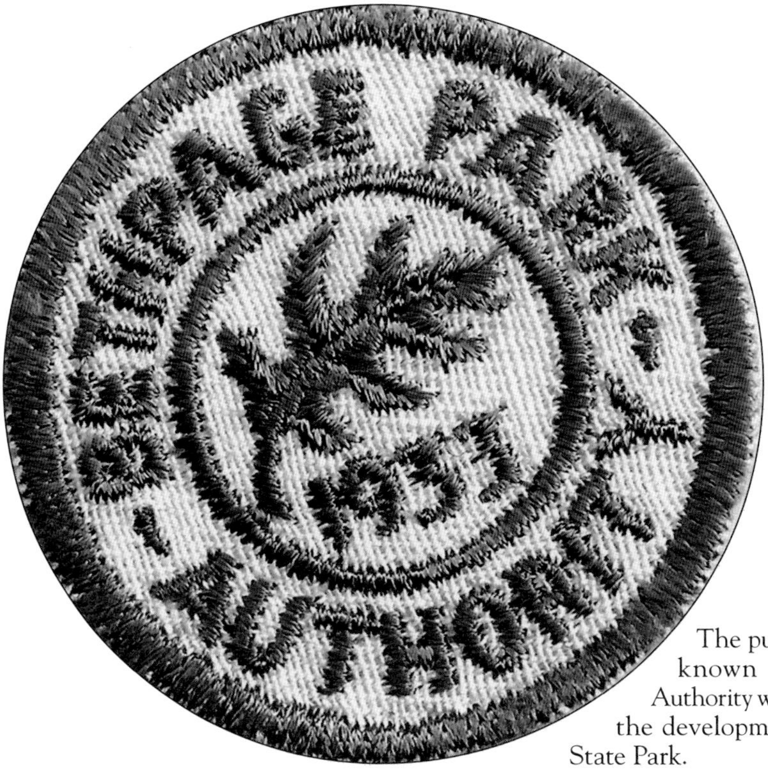

The public benefit corporation known as the Bethpage Park Authority was formed, which oversaw the development plans for Bethpage State Park.

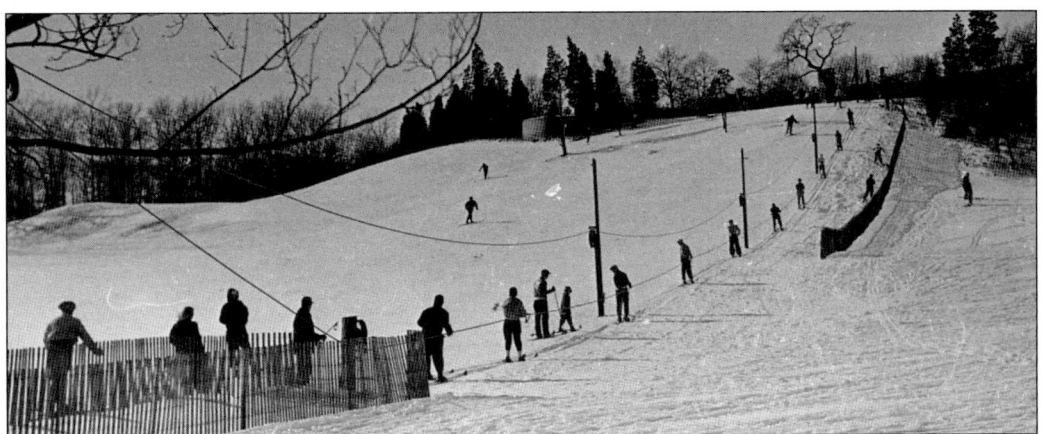

In 1933, Gov. Herbert Lehman called a legislative session to help relieve unemployment. Robert Moses proposed legislation that formed the public benefit corporation known as the Bethpage Park Authority. Consisting of members of the Long Island State Park Commission, the park authority was empowered to issue bonds for the acquisition, improvement, and operation of Bethpage State Park. Pictured here are residents skiing down a hill in front of the Bethpage Golf Course Clubhouse in winter. (Courtesy of Nassau County Parks, Recreation & Museums.)

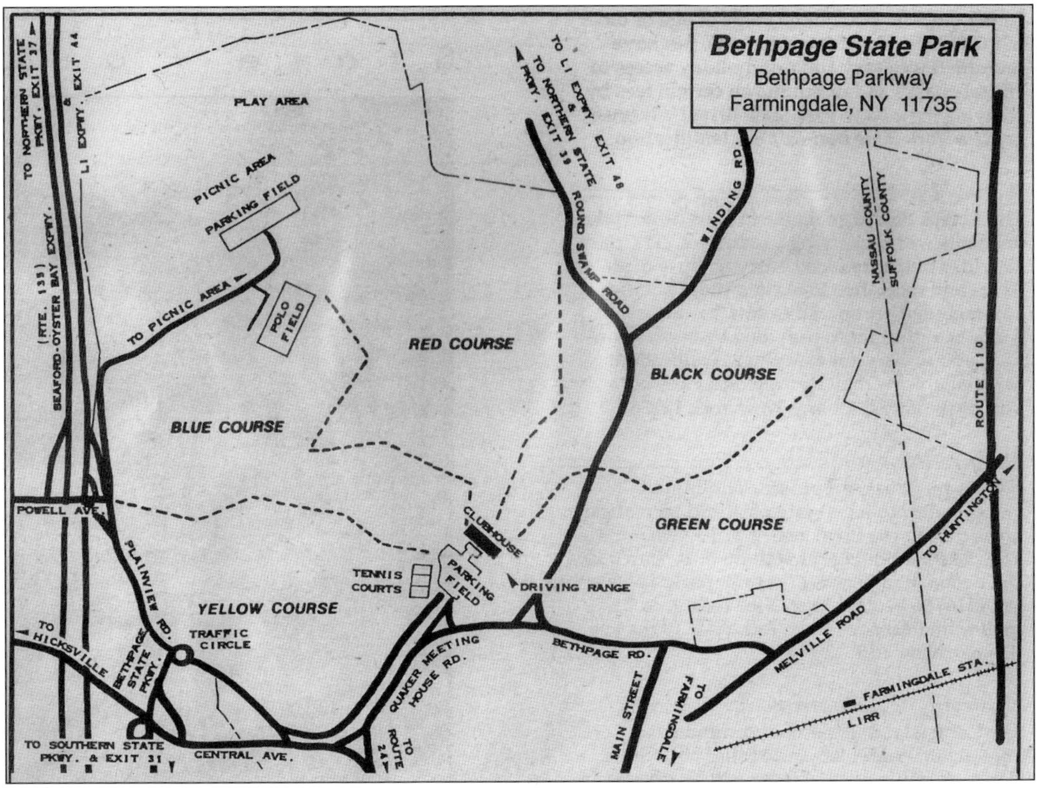

The development plans for Bethpage State Park provided for remodeling the existing 18-hole golf course, constructing three new courses, a large modern clubhouse, a polo field, bridle paths, trails, picnic areas, recreational fields, and playgrounds, all of which still exist on the grounds of the park. These improvements began under the auspices of the Bethpage Park Authority in 1934 as a work-relief project.

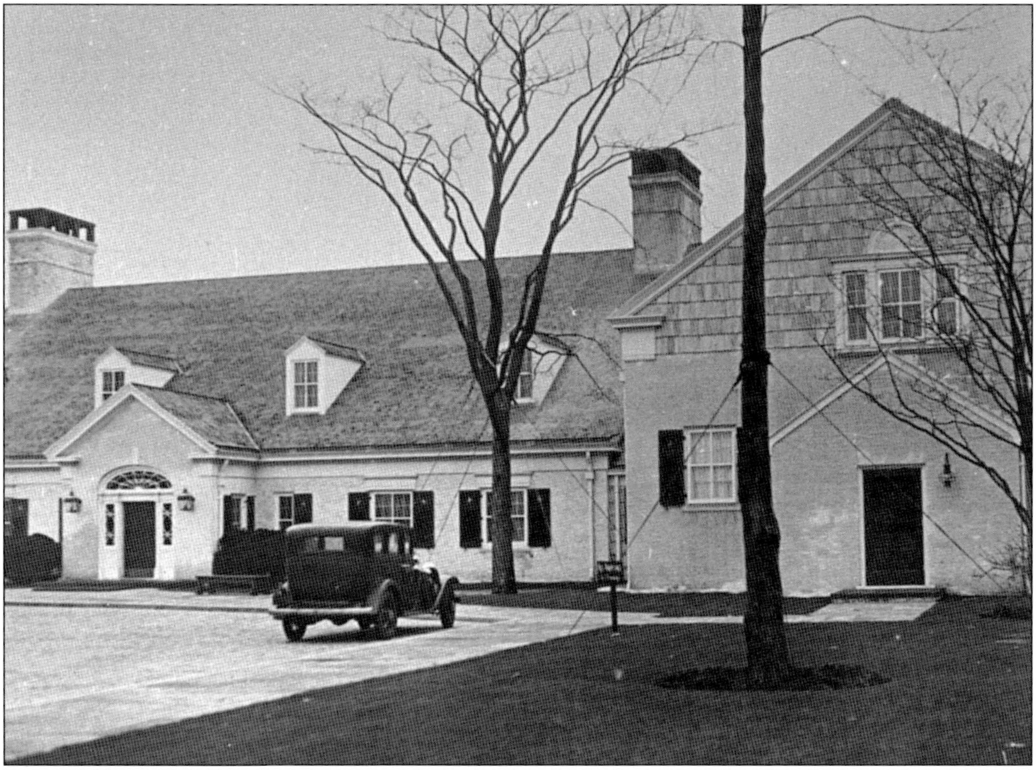

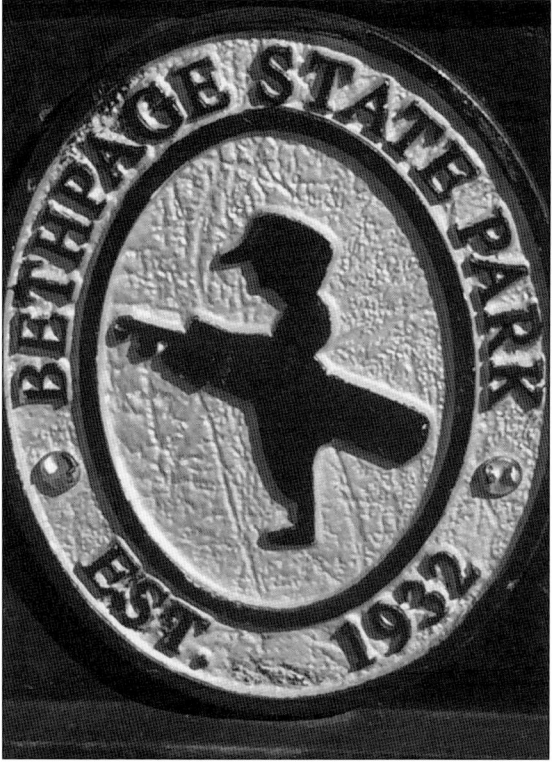

The Green and Red Courses opened in 1932, and the Blue Course opened in 1935. The clubhouse and the three golf courses opened to the public on August 10, 1935. The Black Course opened in 1936 and the Yellow Course in 1958. The Bethpage State Parkway was opened in 1936 to serve as a connection from the Southern State Parkway to Bethpage State Park. With the parkway's opening, the park immediately became a popular destination. The Bethpage Black Course hosted the 2002 and 2009 US Open Golf Championships. (Courtesy of Nassau County Parks, Recreation & Museums.)

Moses oversaw every detail of the construction, inspiring designers and architects to excel and produce beautiful work. Among his trademark innovations were the wrought-iron directional signs that still stand today at Bethpage State Park. Moses also recommended that the caddy boy profile be cut in every shutter adorning the new brick clubhouse. (Photograph by the author.)

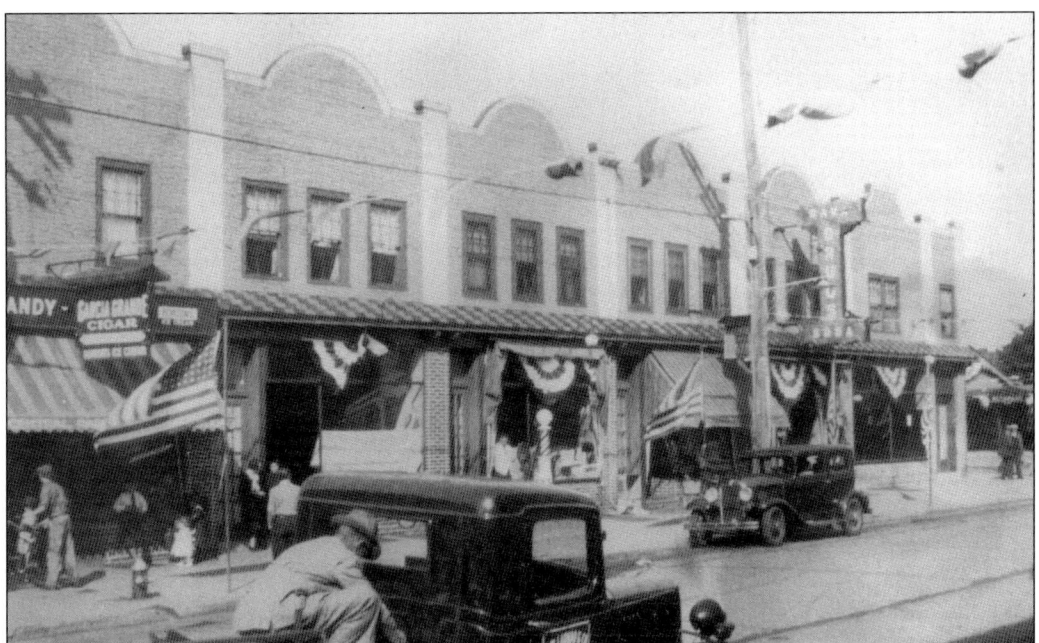

The name Bethpage was declared officially by both the post office and the LIRR on October 1, 1936. The Bethpage Progress Celebration Committee was organized, and plans were made for a week of celebration. They made the week of October 7–12 a noteworthy event, with a parade, ceremonies at the railroad station, including the installation of a new Bethpage sign, a beauty contest, a pageant, and a block party on Broadway.

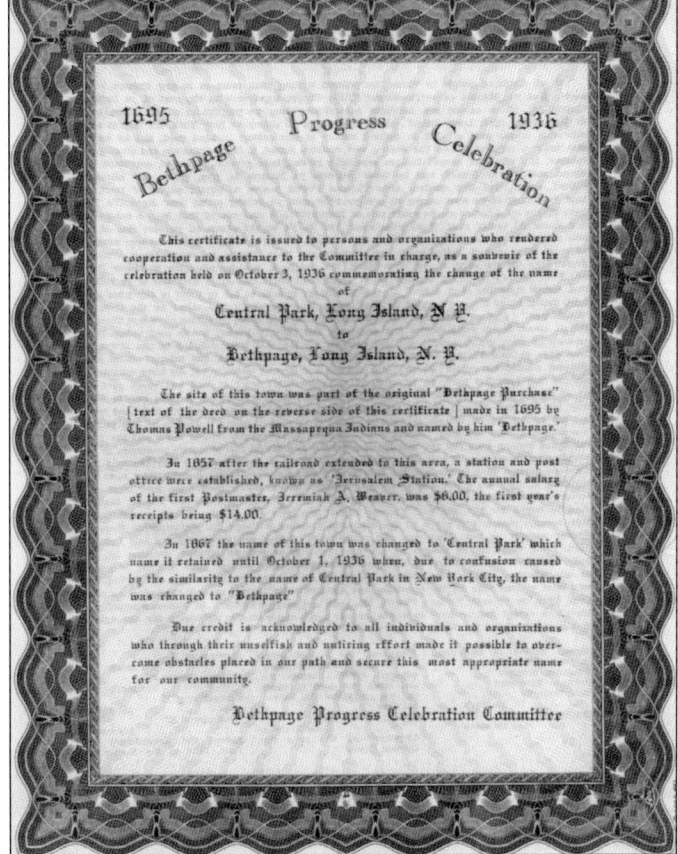

This certificate declares the name officially changed to Bethpage in October 1936.

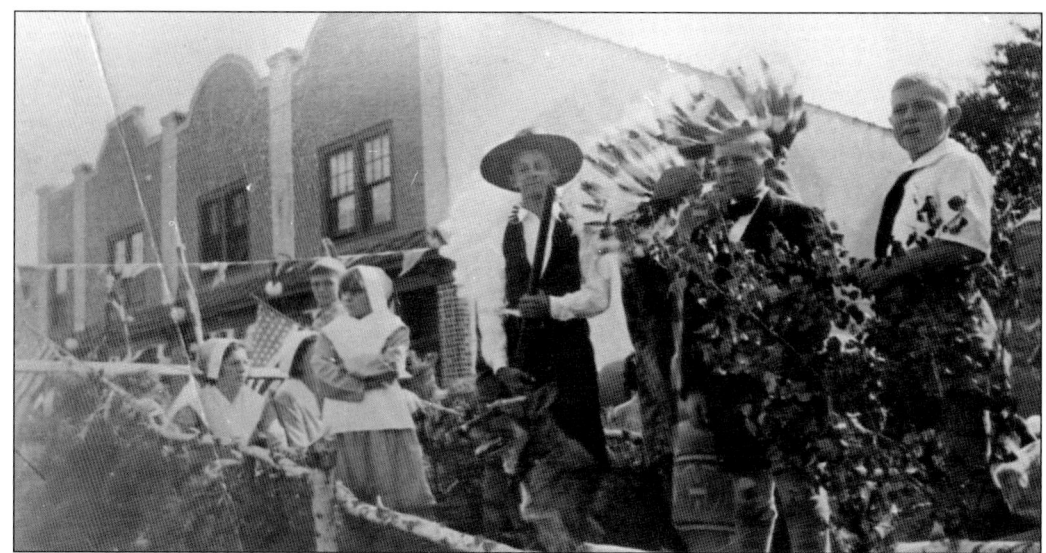

Bethpage residents and children dressed in costumes along the parade route celebrate the name change to Bethpage in 1936. On September 20, 1989, a proclamation was presented to the Central Park Historical Society and president Daniel M. Schiavetta, designating the first Saturday in October as Bethpage Day. The first Bethpage Day was on October 6, 1990, in the Bethpage Community Park. It is a day to celebrate Bethpage and recognize all the organizations, houses of worship, schools, merchants, and residents of the town.

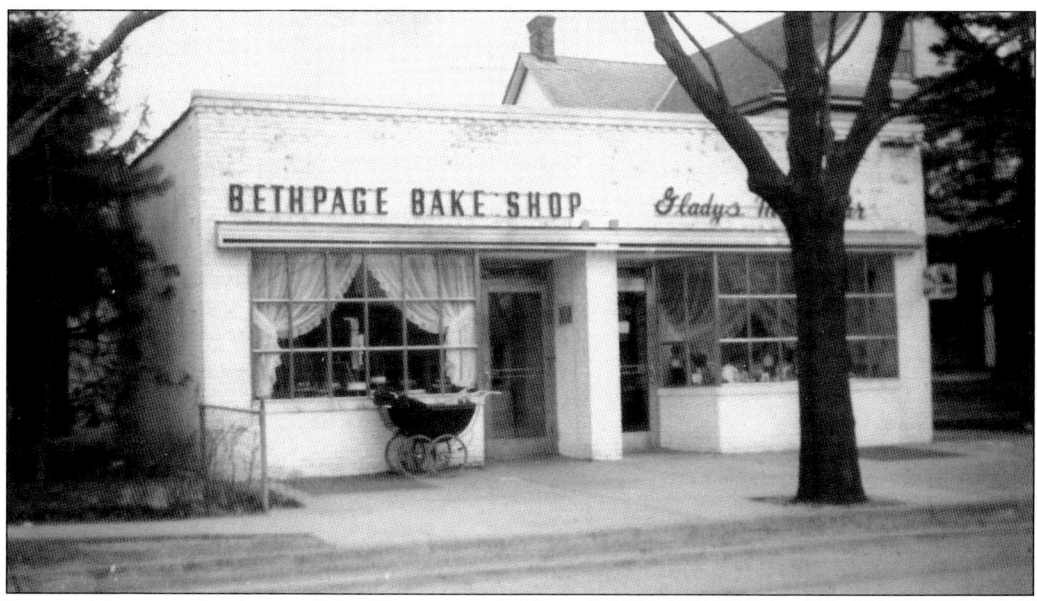

Pictured here are Bethpage Bake Shop, originally owned by Edward Sengstacken, and Gladys Gift Shop, a few of the local businesses on Broadway.

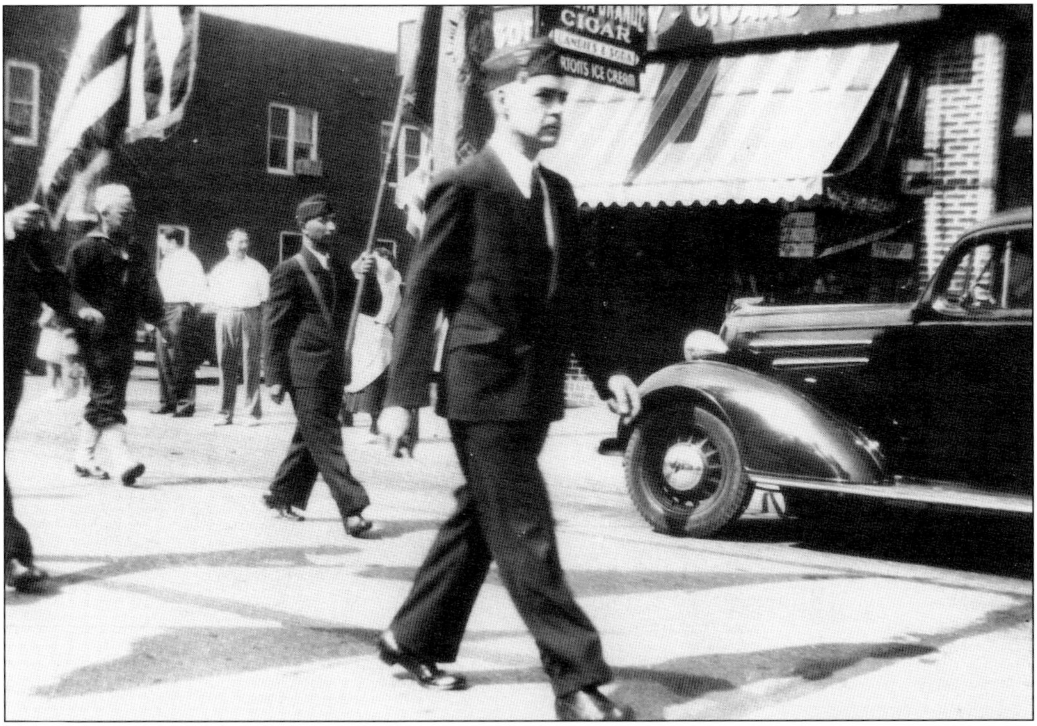

Pictured here is the town's first Memorial Day parade after the name change to Bethpage in 1937. American Legion member Antonio Finamore, holding the flag, marches on Broadway and Baldwin Place. Antonio Finamore and Stella Ruggiero were the first bride and groom to be married in the new congregation of the newly established St. Martin of Tours R.C. Church on November 18, 1923.

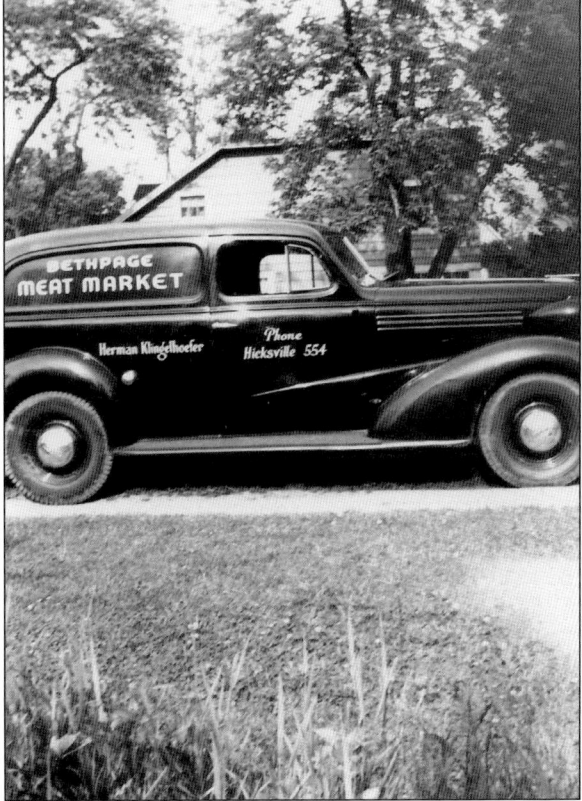

Herman Klingelhoefer's business changed from Central Park Meat Market to Bethpage Meat Market in 1936.

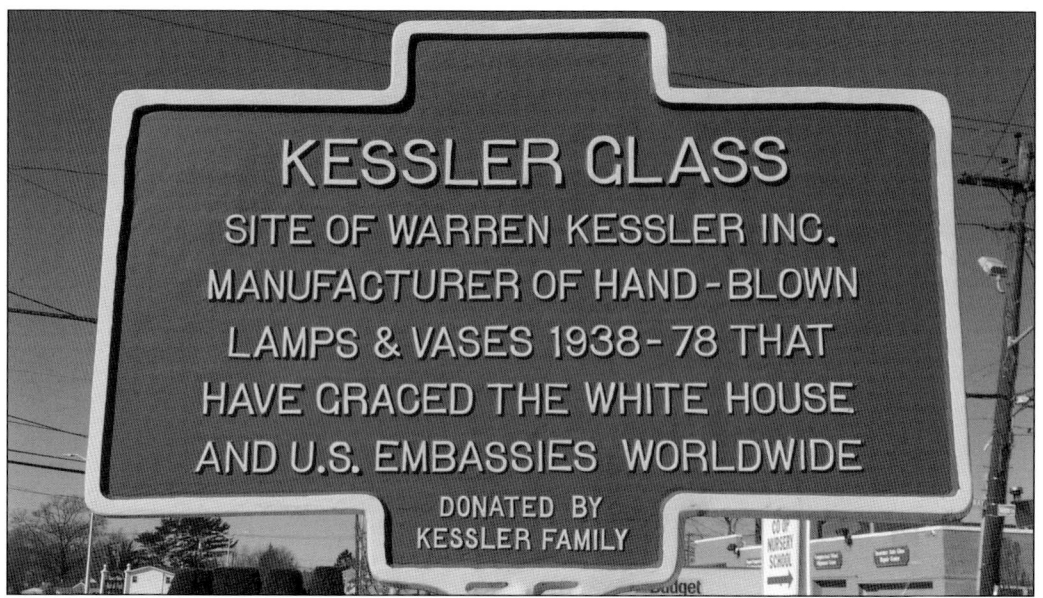

In 1939, Warren Kessler built a factory on the site of the Feuchsel Pickle Works, north of the railroad tracks. Kessler glass was one of the finest American glass companies, and its craftsmen began shaping exquisite products. Creating handmade glassware was traditionally a European art. Kessler Glass manufactured lamps and decorative glassware, which included lamps and lighting units for the remodeling of the White House during the Truman administration and lighting fixtures for all of the American embassies. There is a historic marker at the original location on Broadway. (Photograph by the author.)

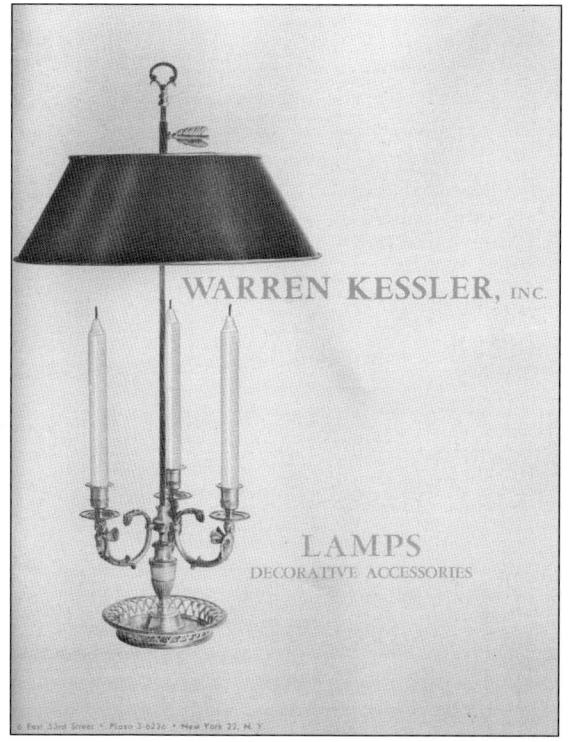

This is a catalogue listing for Warren Kessler lamps and decorative accessories. Kessler lamps were included in the remodeling of the Truman White House, were sold in major department stores, and graced hotels and theaters. (Photograph by the author.)

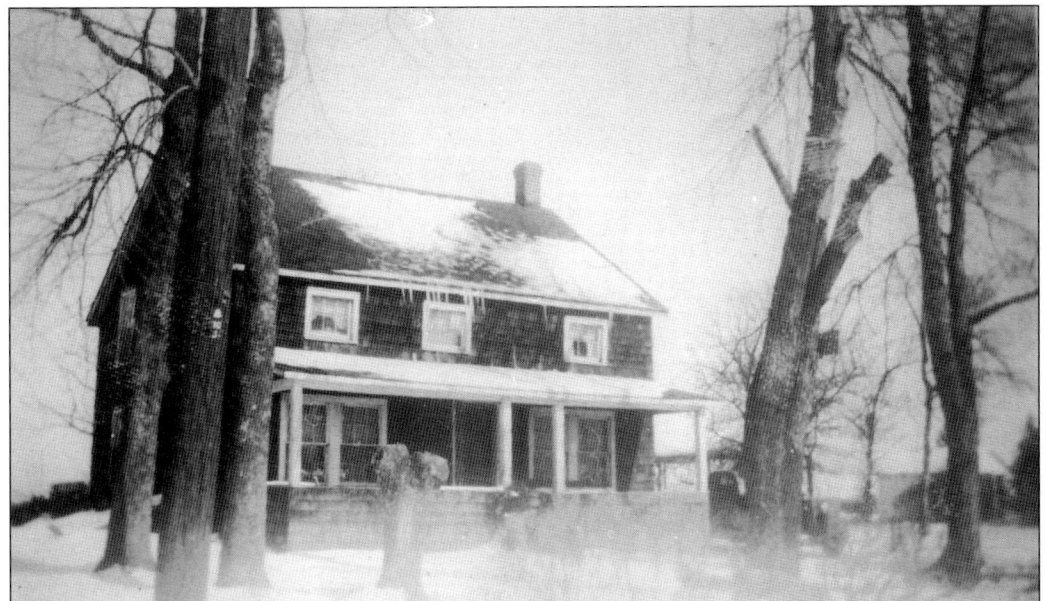

This early residence was located on Harrison Avenue in an area known as McCordville. A builder named Robert McCord built several houses in this area, and it is one of the early developments bounded by Harrison Avenue to the north, Central Avenue to the south, North Robert Damm Street to the east, and Hicksville Road to the west. The iron fire ring was on the corner of Peach Street and had to be rung until the volunteers arrived. (Courtesy of Joyce Calo.)

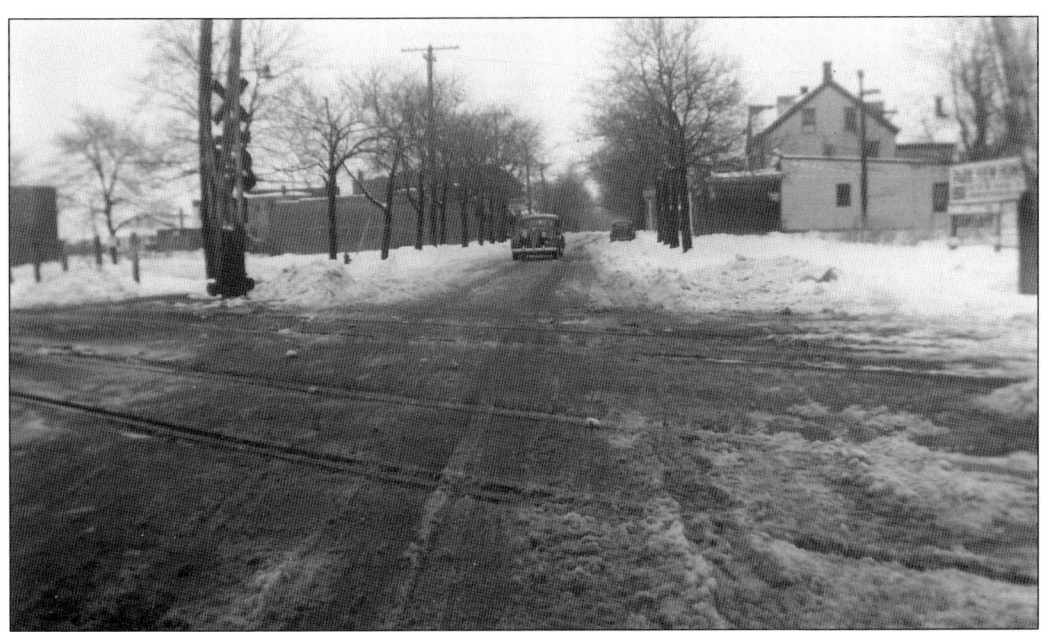

Pictured here is Broadway, looking north from railroad tracks in 1940. On the right is Maurer's Hotel, formerly the Central Park Hotel built by Dreyfuch. Today, on the west side is Bob and Fred's Collision, and on the east side is CVS.

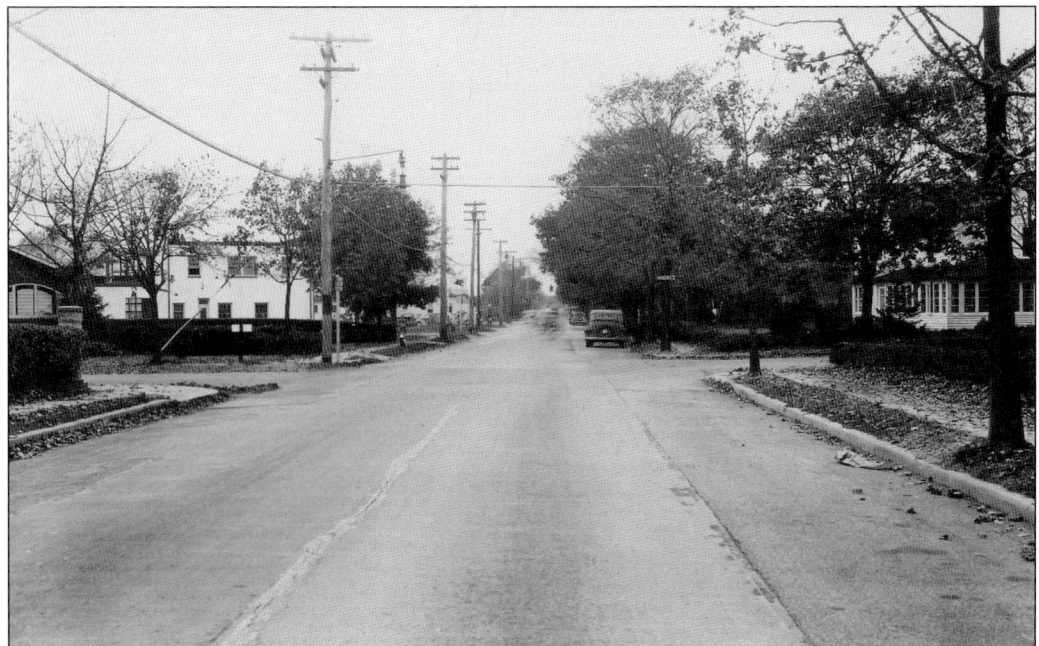

Pictured here is Central Avenue, looking west. The sign for Anselmi's Restaurant points the way north up Broadway in 1940. In the early 1900s, Enrico Anselmi opened Anselmi's Italian Restaurant, just north of the current middle school on Broadway, and featured Herman Stenzler's Orchestra Friday and Saturday evenings. The restaurant closed in 1969.

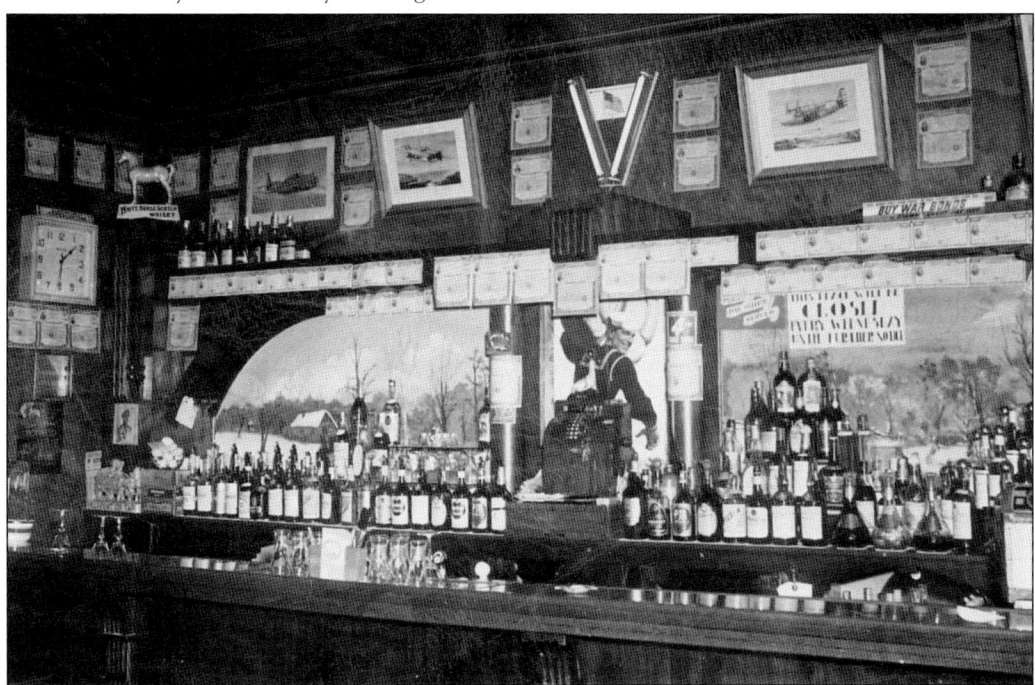

Lou Maggi owned the Pine Lodge Bar and Grill located on Broadway and Washington Street. Pictured here is Maggi's bar during World War II in 1944. It later became Annie's Place and is now Who-ville Bar and Grill. (Courtesy of Nassau County Parks, Recreation & Museums.)

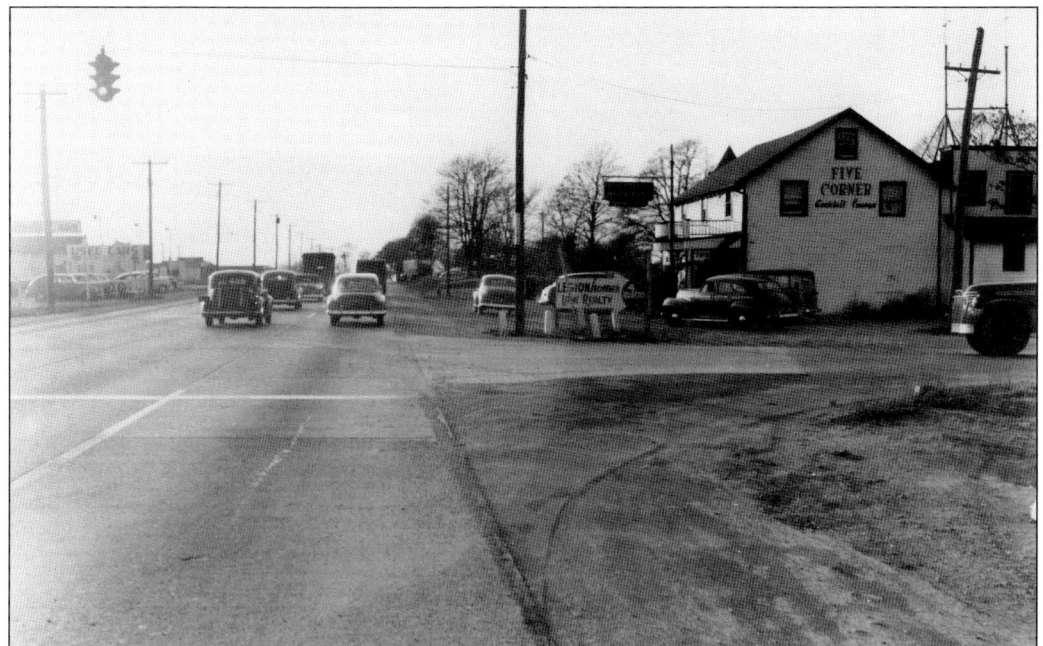

Five Corners Restaurant was built around 1858 by Emma Stebner. In the late 1920s, she gave the restaurant to her youngest daughter, Bertha Kunzig, who operated it until it was destroyed by a fire in 1958. The Five Corners Restaurant was located on the northwest corner of Hempstead Turnpike and Stewart Avenue, and it catered weddings, parties, clubs, and social functions.

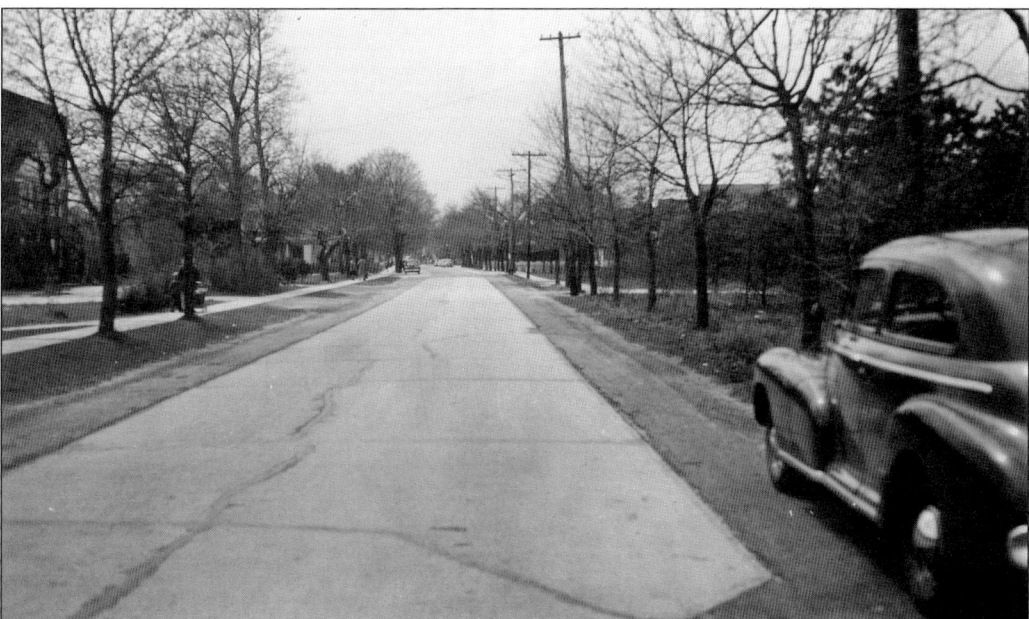

In 1948, the school district was forced to make plans for a new school due to the ever-increasing population. The Broadway School, now the JFK Middle School, was constructed on land that in earlier years was used for farming. In the spring of 1951, all grades from kindergarten to eighth grade—650 children—occupied the building. Pictured here is Broadway, looking south. The Broadway School is on the left.

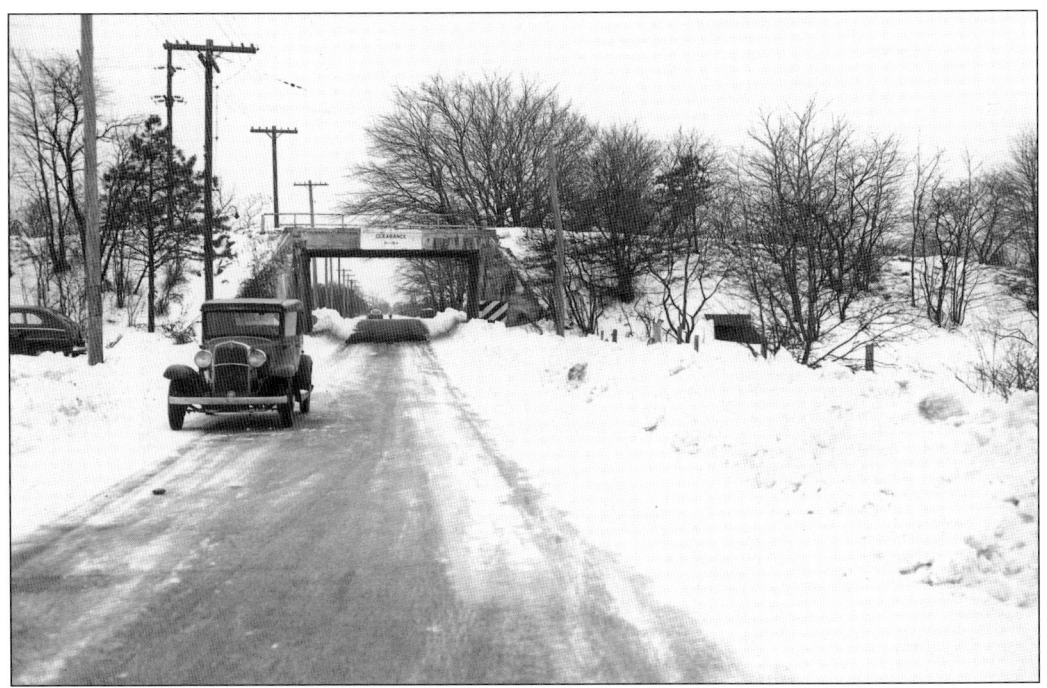

One of the motor parkway bridges, pictured looking south, was still standing 10 years after the motor parkway closed. This photograph is Stewart Avenue, looking south, and Arthur Avenue in 1948.

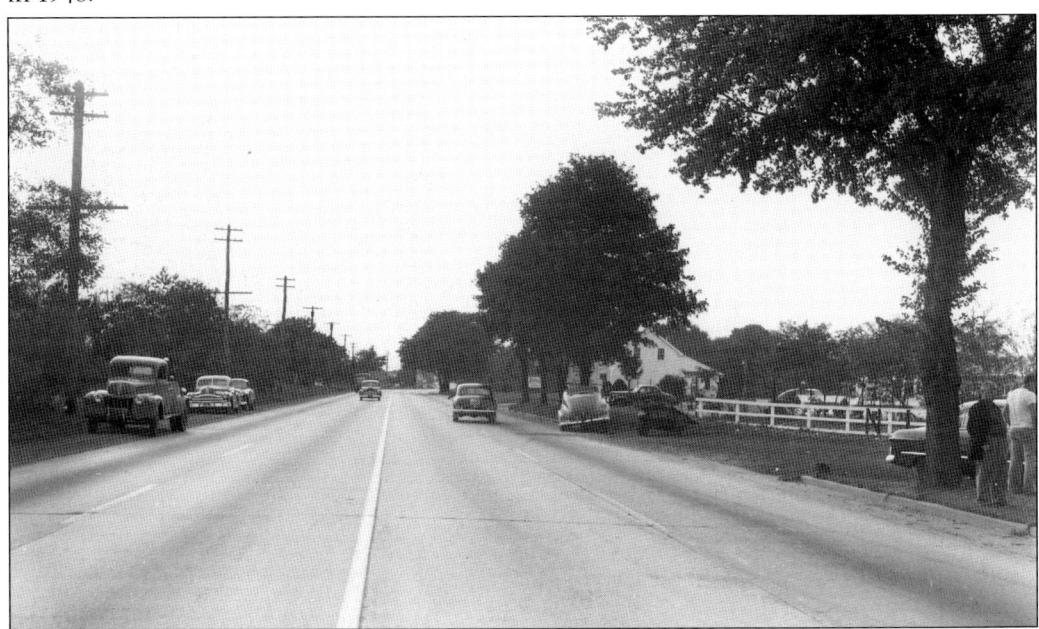

This is Hempstead Turnpike, looking west, in 1948. There were only two lanes in each direction, compared with the six lanes today. Zorn's Poultry Farm is on the right, and the photograph was taken where the Seaford–Oyster Bay Expressway exits westbound for Hempstead Turnpike. There appears to be no development on the south side of the street, where the Embassy Diner is today.

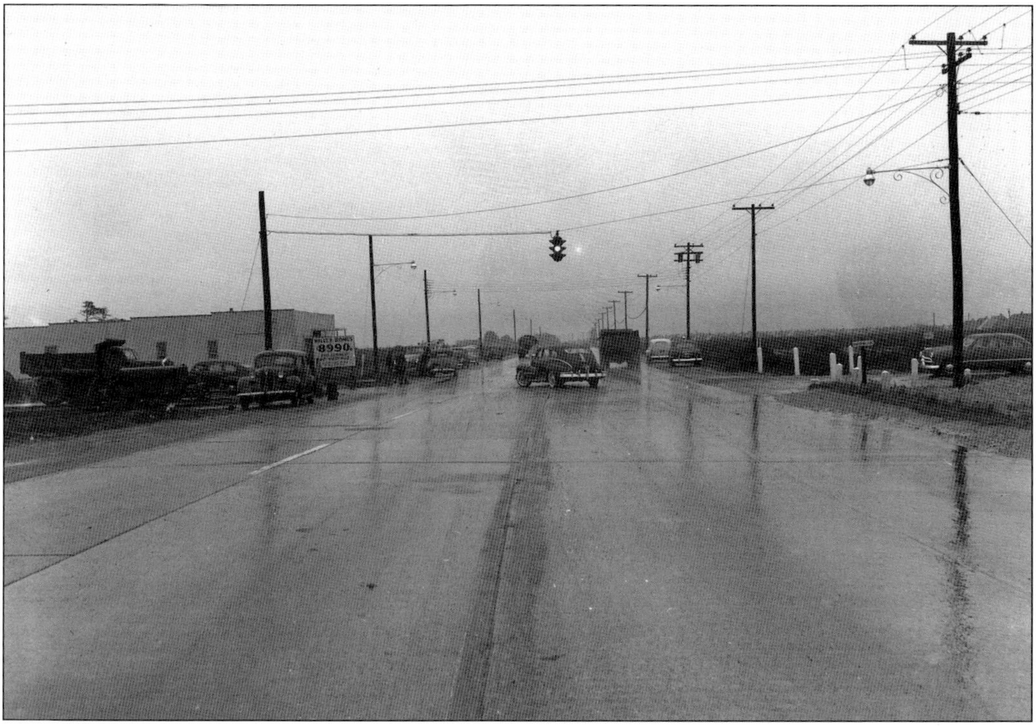

Pictured here is an accident at the intersection of Hempstead Turnpike and Gardners Avenue, looking eastbound in 1949. The sign on the left advertises Miller Homes being sold with a full basement and hot-water heater for $8,990. Today there are six lanes going east and west and four lanes for north and south. Friendly's is on the northeast corner, with large shopping centers occupying the other three corners.

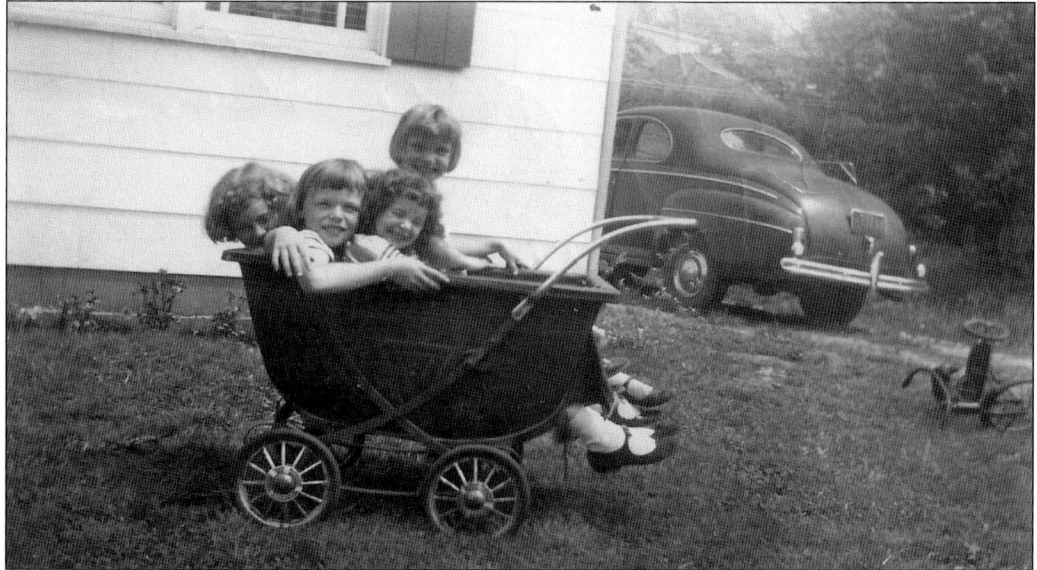

Pictured from left to right are Ruth Lane, Beverly Carolan, Joyce Lane, and Adrienne Carolan playing in a carriage on Carriere Street in 1954. Carriere Street is named after Raymond Carriere, the first young man from Bethpage killed in World War II. (Courtesy of Joyce Calo.)

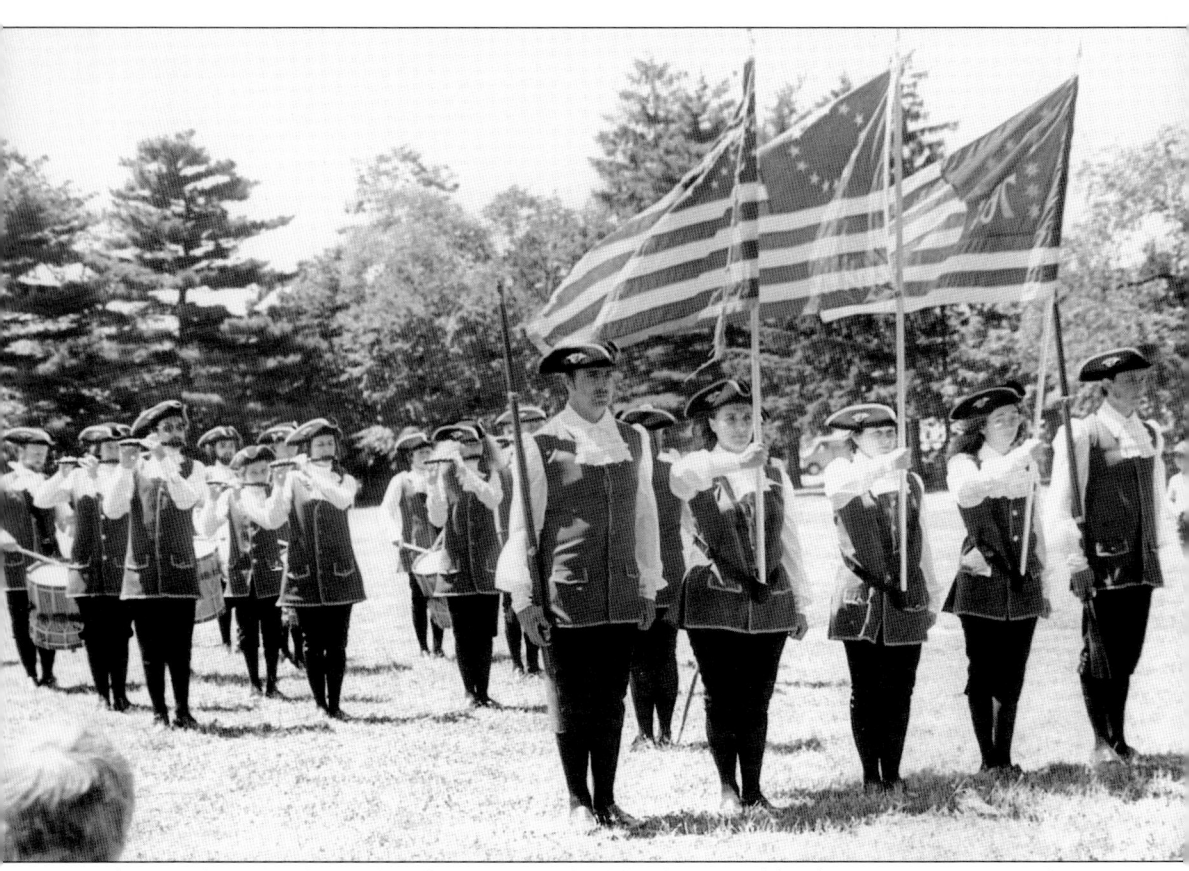

The Butehorn brothers of Bethpage formed a fife, drum, and bugle corps consisting of young children playing marching music. At some time, they went out of existence. Eventually, they became the Bethpage Colonials in 1958. Achievements and Appearances made a recording for the Valley Forge Freedom Foundation with Buddy Ebsen narrating the story about the freedom fighters. The Colonials provided the background music and played the "Star-Spangled Banner." They appeared four times in Macy's Thanksgiving Day parades and played at Macy's, which was on national television. They were featured at the New York World's Fair from 1964 to 1965. They led the famous Gasparilla Pirate Parade in Tampa, Florida, in 1966. They played for the Daughters of the American Revolution at the Plaza Hotel in New York twice. They played political rallies for President Ford and President Nixon and played the "Star-Spangled Banner" at the opening football game for the New England Patriots and Giants game. There were nearly 100 members, all taught to be patriotic, respectful, and great Americans.

Seven
LOOKING TOWARD THE SKY

Leroy Grumman and others worked for the Loening Aircraft Engineering Corporation in the 1920s, but when it was bought by Keystone Aircraft Corporation, the operations moved from New York City to Bristol, Pennsylvania. Grumman and his partners started their own company in an old factory in Baldwin, New York. All of the early Grumman employees were former Loening employees. The company was named for Grumman, its largest investor, and opened its doors on January 2, 1930. Keeping busy by welding aluminum tubing for truck frames, the company eagerly pursued contracts with the US Navy. Grumman designed the first practical floats that allowed US Navy land planes to function as seaplanes with a retractable landing gear, and this launched Grumman into the aviation market. In 1932, the first Grumman aircraft was for the Navy; the Grumman FF-1 was a biplane with retractable landing gear. In 1936, a local townsman successfully persuaded his friend Leroy Grumman to relocate his expanding aircraft business from Farmingdale to Bethpage. It was at this time that the founders Leroy Randle Grumman, Leon "Jake" Swirbul, William "Bill" Schwendler, Clint Towl, Ed Poor, and Joe Stamm purchased farmland from the Looney family, Mary Moesch, the Neders, and the Kutsurs. They expanded their operations and opened their first plant in Bethpage in 1936.

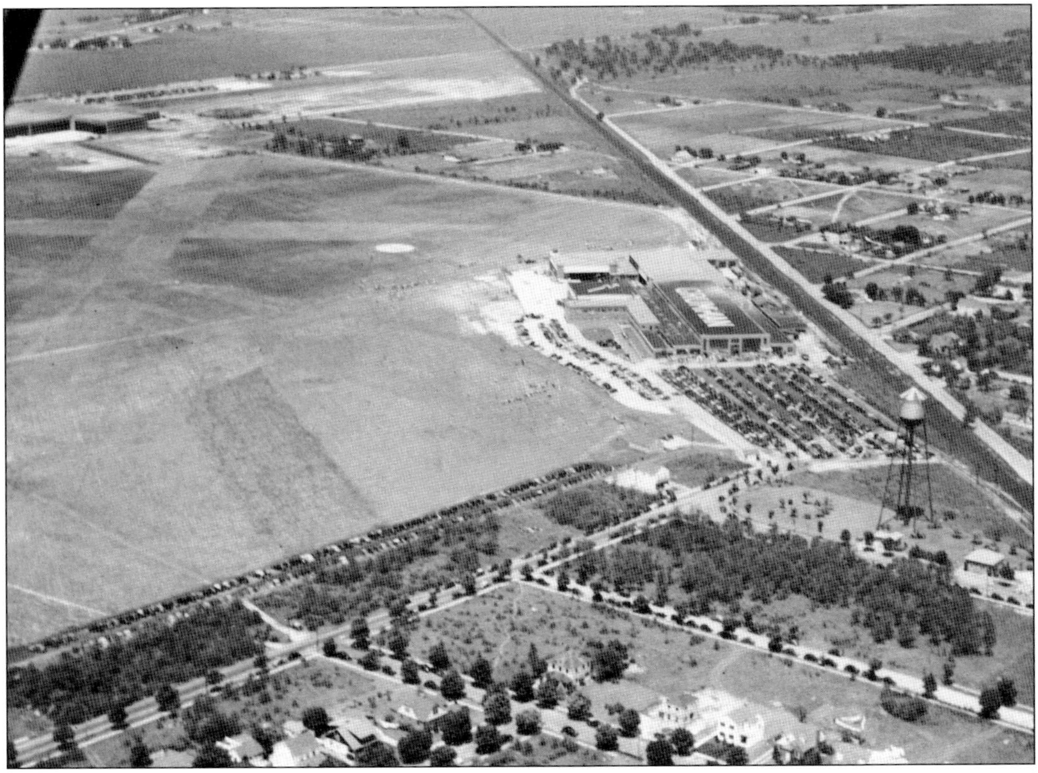

They opened their first plant in 1936, soon becoming the largest employer for Bethpage and Long Island. Grumman had a close relationship with the Navy, but by the mid-1930s, company officials were worried about the sole reliance on military business and decided to design planes for the commercial market. The first ventures into the civilian realm occurred in 1936 when it developed the G-21 Goose and the G-22 Gulfhawk. (Courtesy of the Northrop Grumman History Center.)

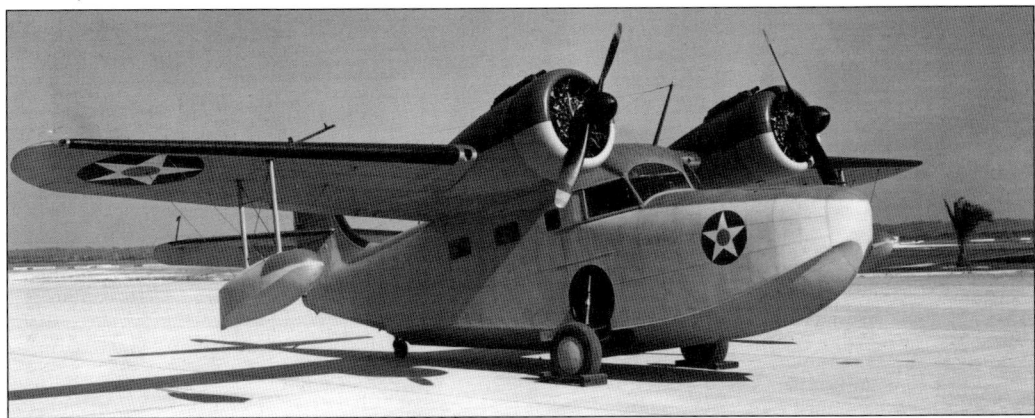

The Goose filled the needs of businessmen who wanted a water taxi service for commuting between their Wall Street waterfront offices and their remote Long Island estates. It was a two-engine, mono-wing seaplane that held eight passengers and two crew members. By World War II, the Goose had proved itself versatile enough that both the Navy and Army Air Corps were using modified versions. Pictured here is a Grumman G-21 Goose in 1941. (Courtesy of the Northrop Grumman History Center.)

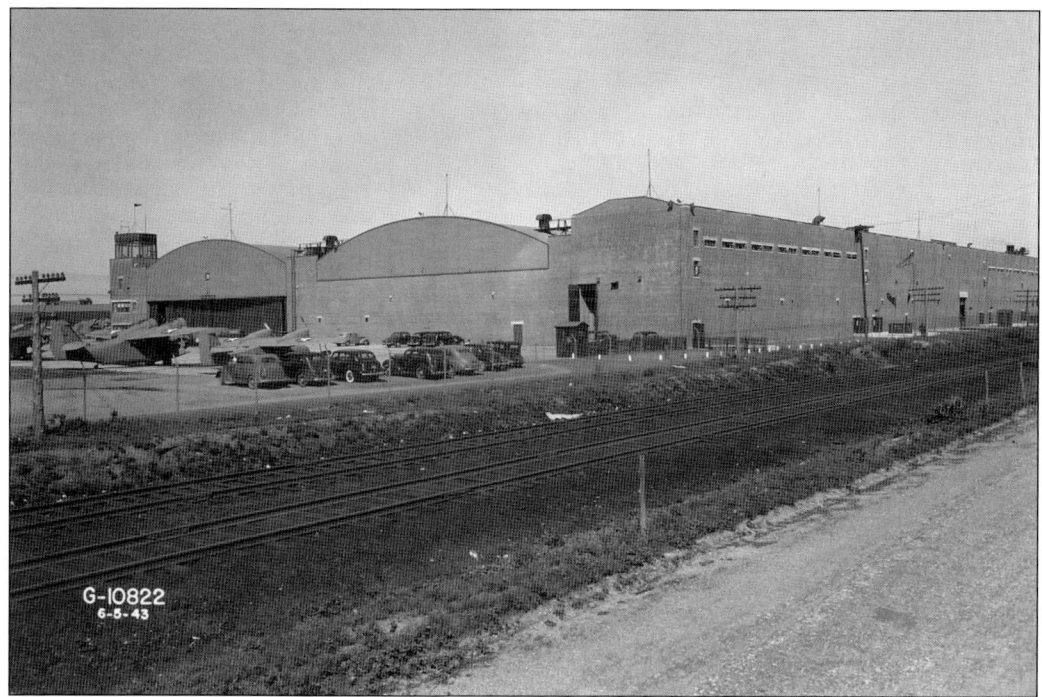

Their business boomed during the 1930s and 1940s in answer to the Navy's demands for quality aircraft, and by 1944 Grumman had won the Navy E Award for production efficiency five years in a row. It was also awarded for its high morale, as it turned out 500 airplanes per month. Pictured here is Grumman in 1943. (Courtesy of the Northrop Grumman History Center.)

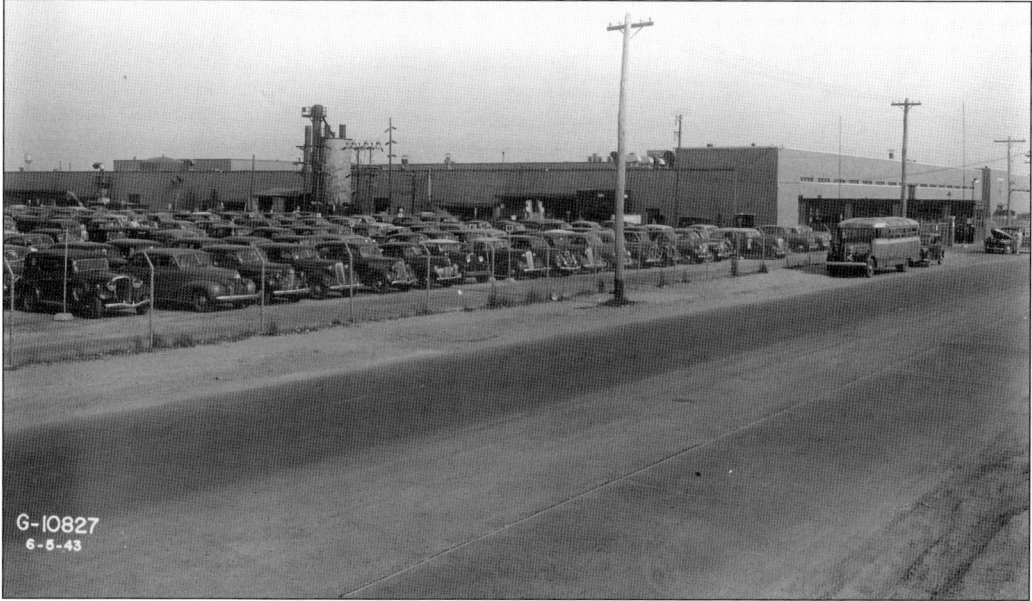

By the fall of 1941, Grumman had grown to approximately 6,500 workers. But to produce all of the planes the Navy needed during World War II, Grumman's workforce grew at a rate of 1,000 workers a month until it peaked in September 1943 at about 25,500 employees. (Courtesy of the Northrop Grumman History Center.)

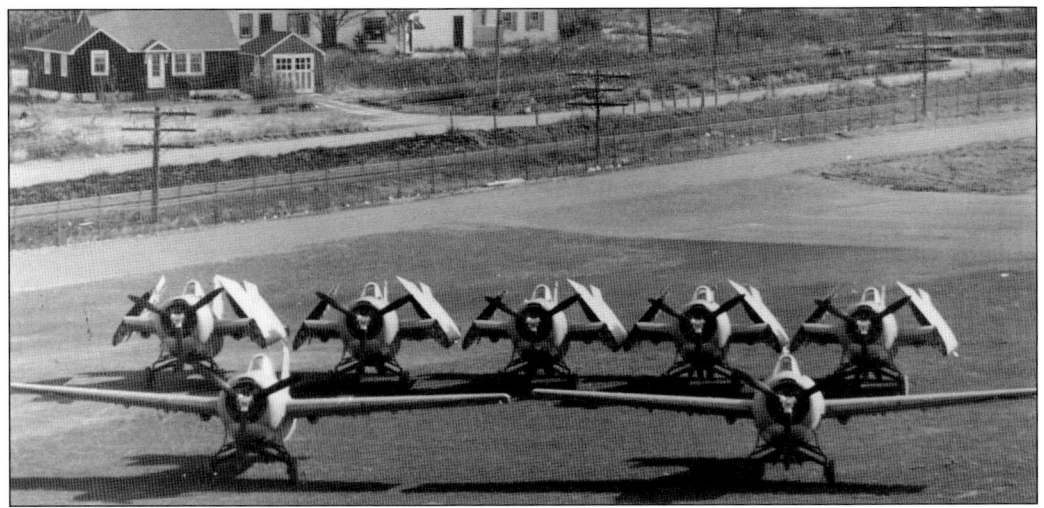

Grumman Navy fighter aircraft became known for its cat names. Grumman's first major warplane was the F4F Wildcat, a single-seat, single-engine, carrier-based strike fighter equipped with a Grumman invention called sto-wings, which allowed the wings to fold in half for storage on cramped aircraft carriers. It had six machine guns and two 100-pound bombs. Pictured Grumman F4F-4 Wildcats show that five with Grumman's sto-wings could occupy the space of two without sto-wings, thereby increasing the striking force of carriers by about 150 percent. (Courtesy of the Northrop Grumman History Center.)

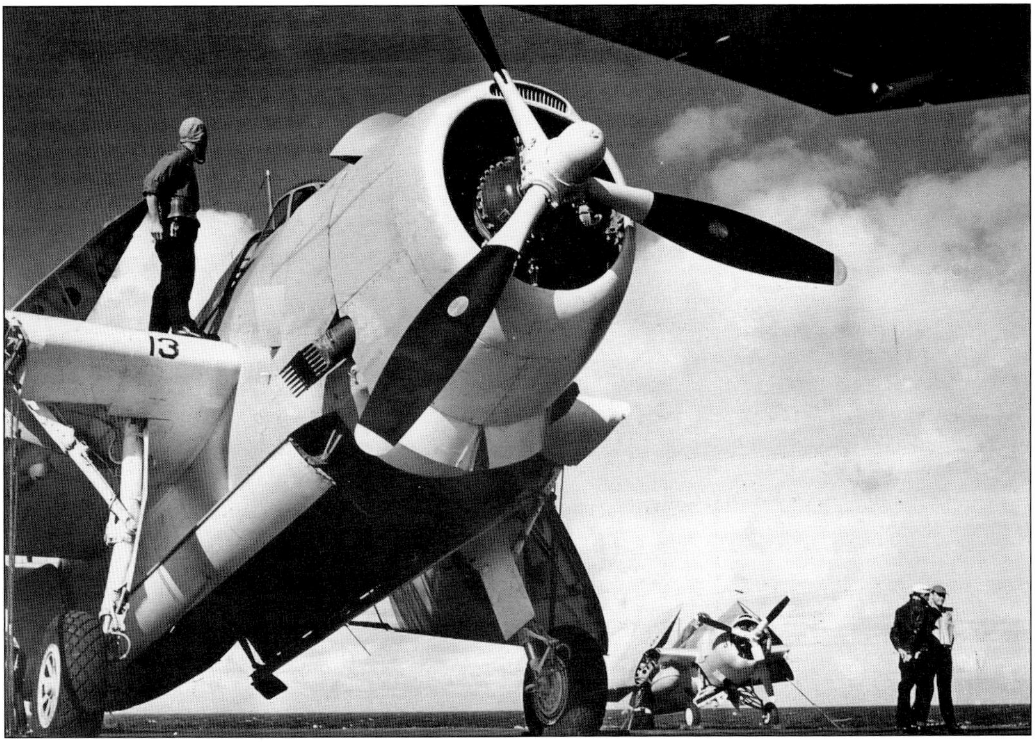

The Navy used the Avenger effectively against enemy submarines, particularly in tandem with Wildcats. Grumman delivered the first TBFs to the Navy in January 1942. (Courtesy of the Northrop Grumman History Center.)

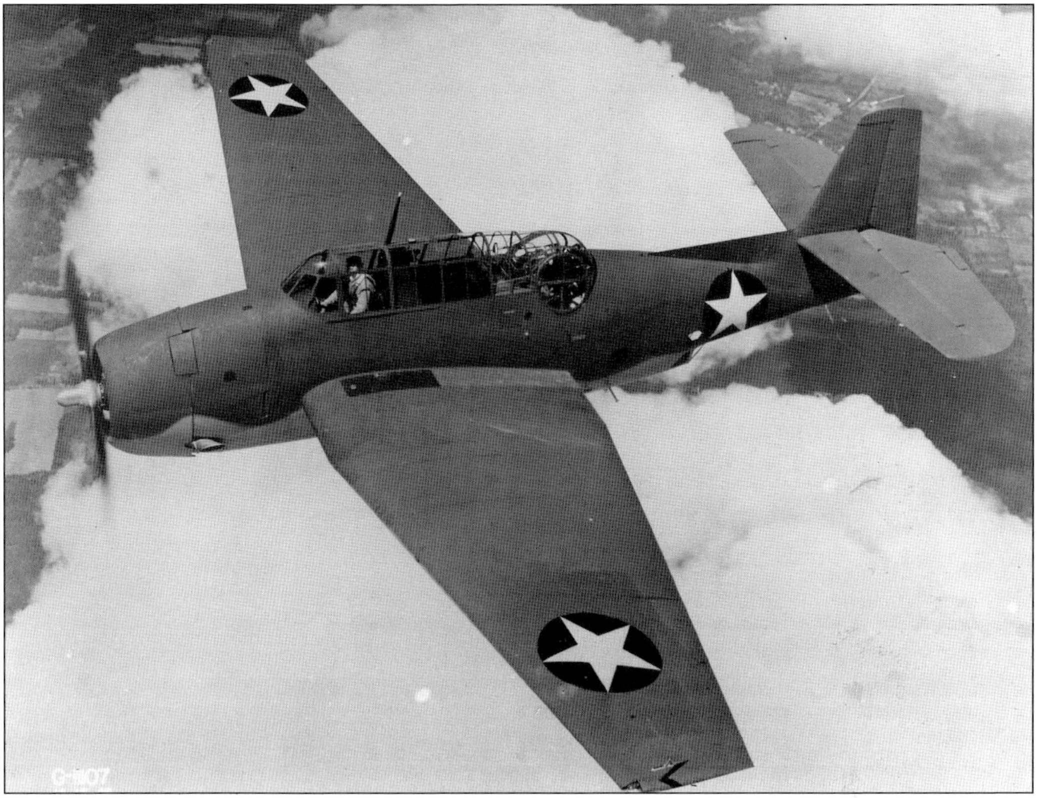

Grumman's TBF Avenger also contributed significantly to the Allied victory. The Avenger was a single-engine, mono-wing, torpedo bomber that held a pilot, turret gunner, and bombardier. When fully loaded with bombs and torpedoes, the TBF was twice the weight of the Wildcat. With a machine-gun turret mounted behind the pilot, the Avenger was a formidable combat plane and performed well on low-altitude attacks and dive-bombing runs. (Courtesy of the Northrop Grumman History Center.)

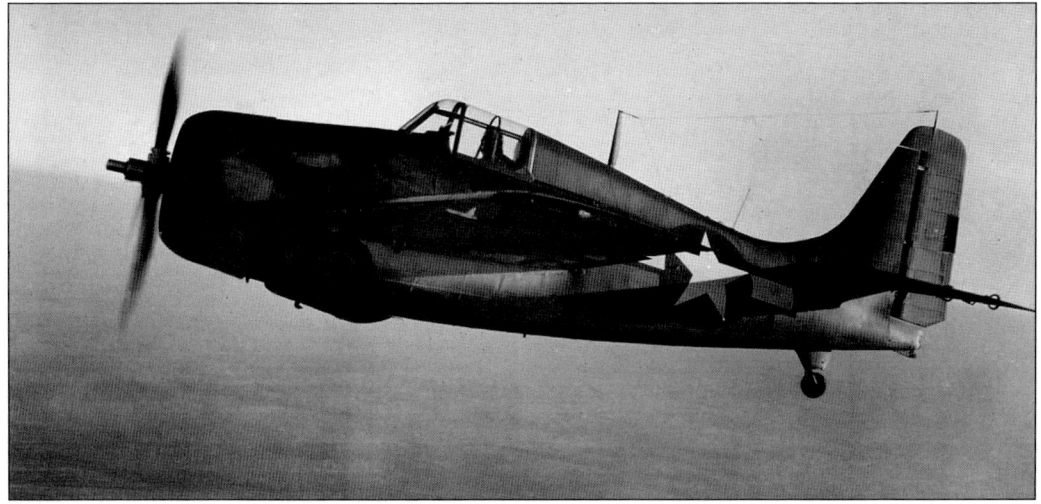

Grumman's first major warplane, the F4F Wildcat, takes to the skies in 1942. (Courtesy of the Northrop Grumman History Center.)

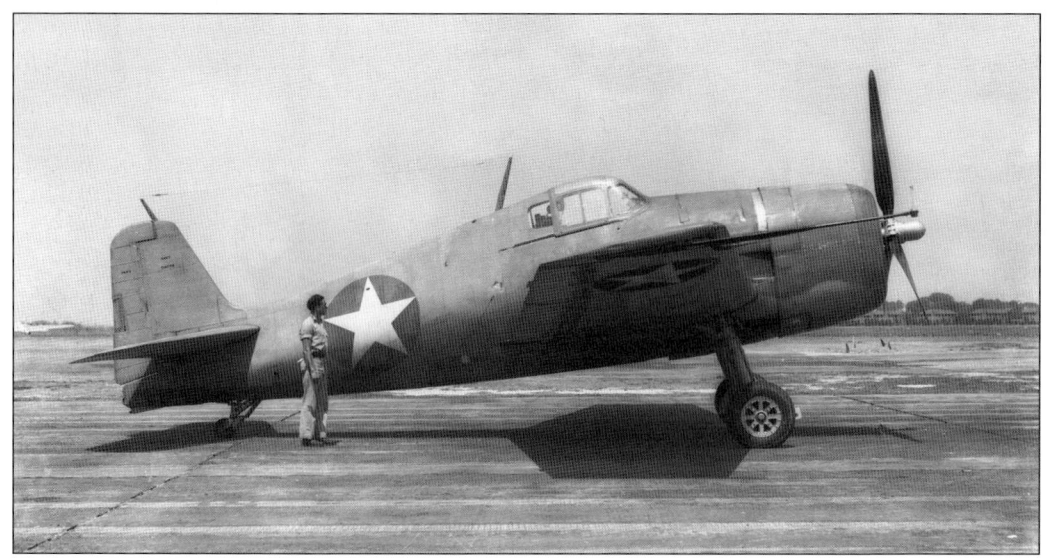

Grumman built one of the classic combat planes of World War II, the F6F Hellcat. Essentially a more sophisticated version of the F4F Wildcat, Grumman engineers specifically designed it to defeat the Japanese Zero. It could fly about 60 miles per hour faster than the Wildcat, about 300 miles farther without refueling, and carry more armament. Like the F4F, the Hellcat was a single-seat, single-engine strike fighter with sto-wings. (Courtesy of the Northrop Grumman History Center.)

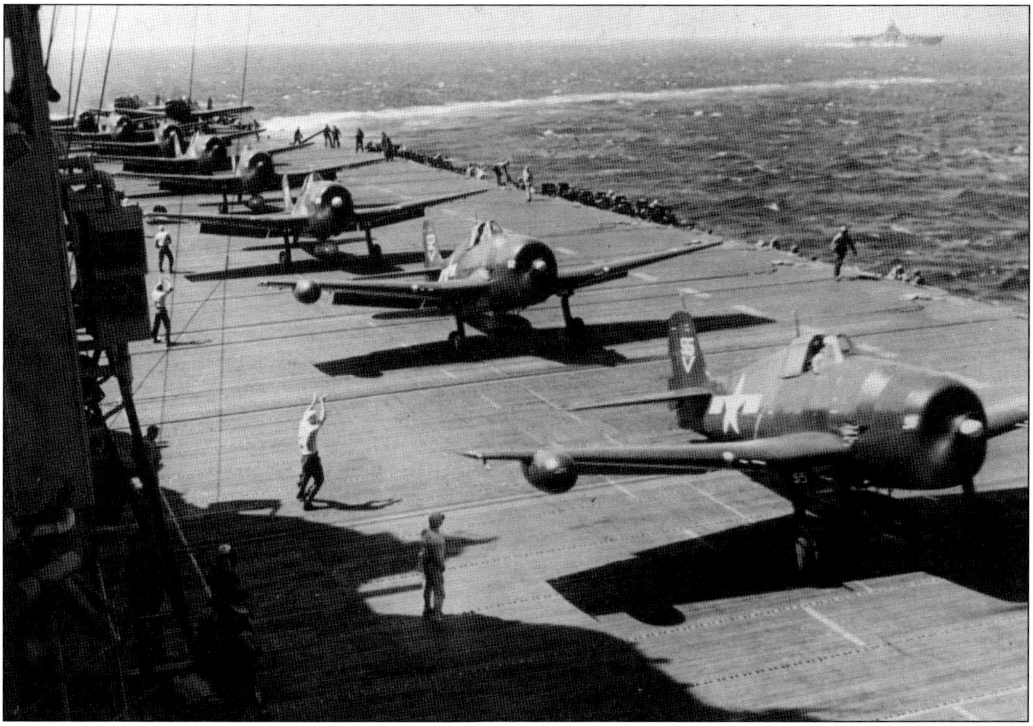

The first Hellcats saw action in the Pacific in September 1943 and quickly gained a reputation for outstanding performance and craftsmanship. Many sustained extensive combat damage and still returned their pilots safely home. (Courtesy of the Northrop Grumman History Center.)

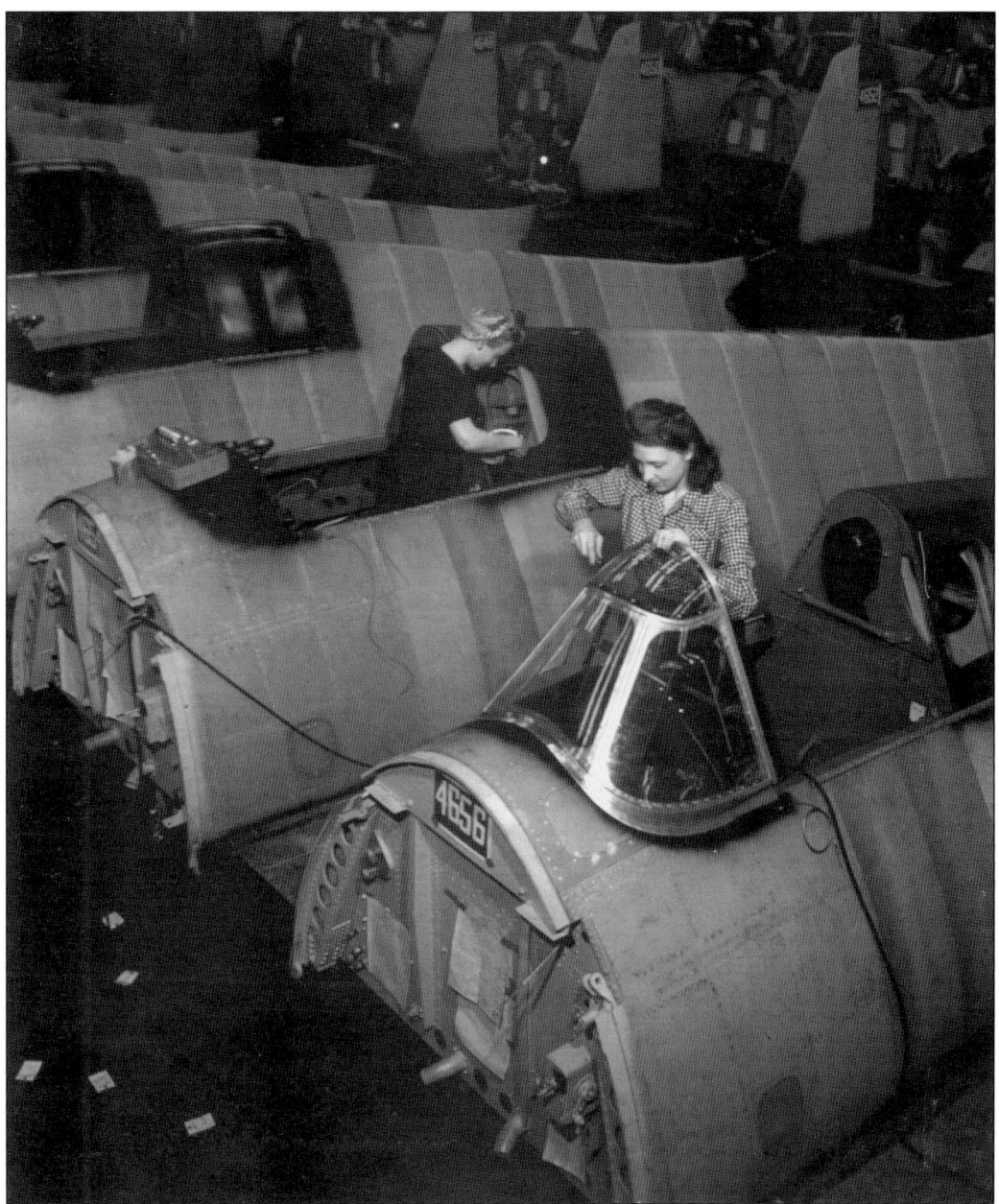

Grumman produced 12,272 Hellcats from June 1942 to November 1945, the largest number of fighters ever made in a single aircraft factory. Naval aviators racked up an impressive record with the Hellcats. Of the 6,477 aerial victories they claimed during the war, 4,947 went to F6F Hellcat pilots. In March 1942, three months after the United States entered World War II, six women walked on to the factory floor at Grumman's Plant No. 1. They were the first female aircraft workers on Long Island. By the end of 1943, there were 8,000 more women in the Grumman War Productions Corp. Eventually, women comprised approximately 30 percent of Grumman's wartime workforce of 25,400 workers. These "Janes Who Made the Planes" built Wildcats, Hellcats, and Avengers for the Navy. Pictured here are women workers on an FGF Hellcat assembly line installing windshields in 1942. (Courtesy of the Northrop Grumman History Center.)

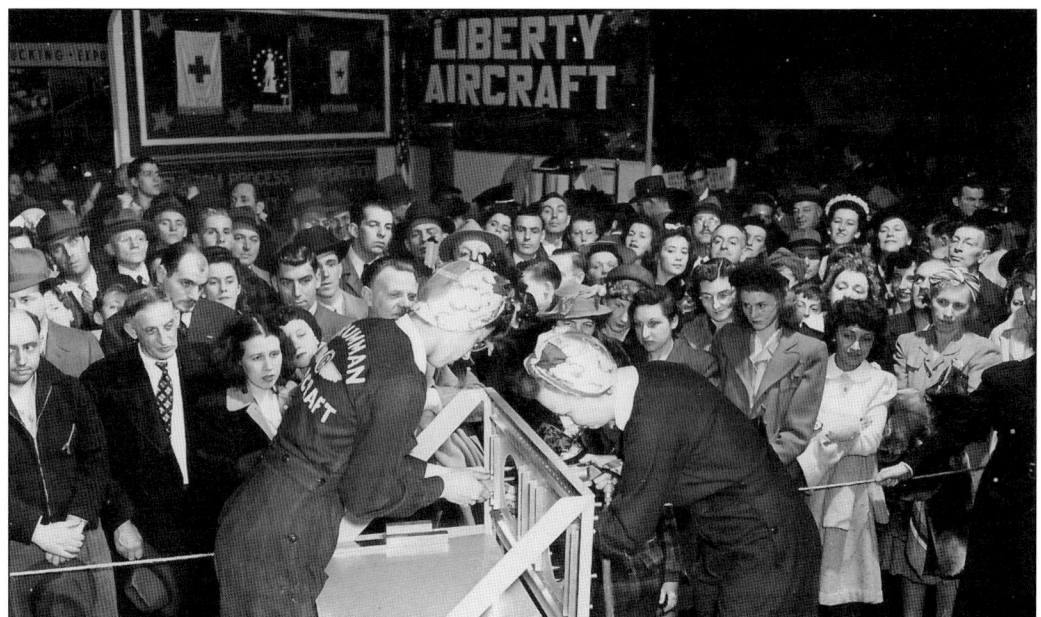

Many men were called to active duty in the military, and Grumman hired more women for its workforce. By 1943, women made up approximately a third of the wartime production force. Martha Muskowske (right) and Betty Relli, members of Port Washington's championship riveting team, work their way to a new record of 19.2 rivets per minute. This contest was held at the Nassau at War Exposition at Adelphi College in April 1943. (Courtesy of the Northrop Grumman History Center.)

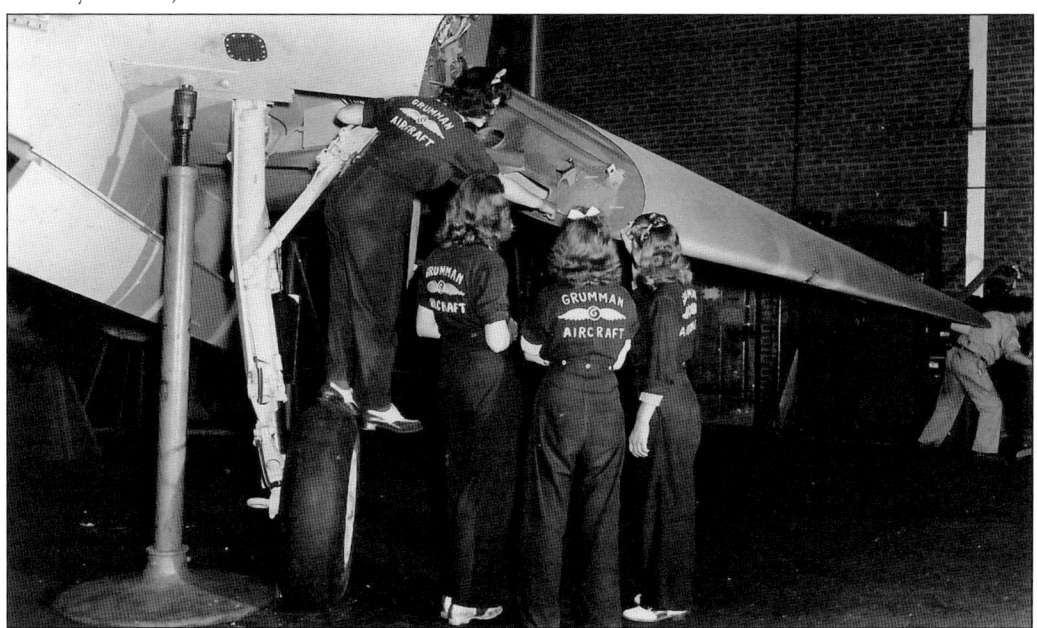

Women played just as important a role as men. With the help and support of the women, demands were met for warplanes and other equipment that was needed. Pictured here are women working on a wing in their Grumman coveralls in 1943. (Courtesy of the Northrop Grumman History Center.)

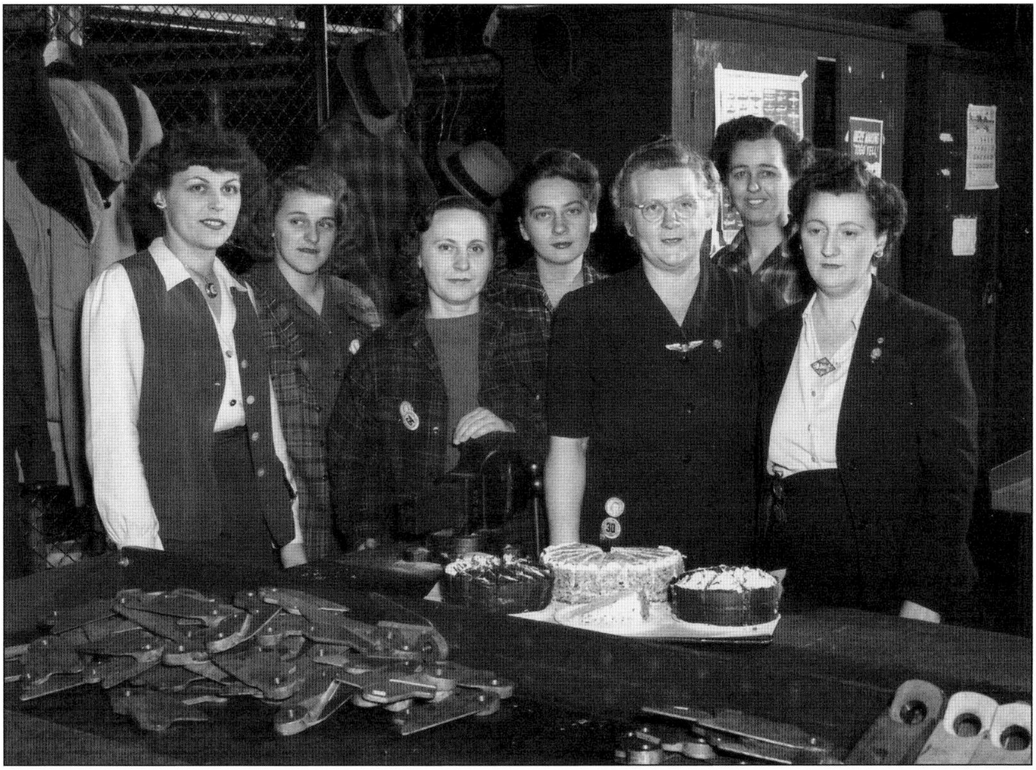

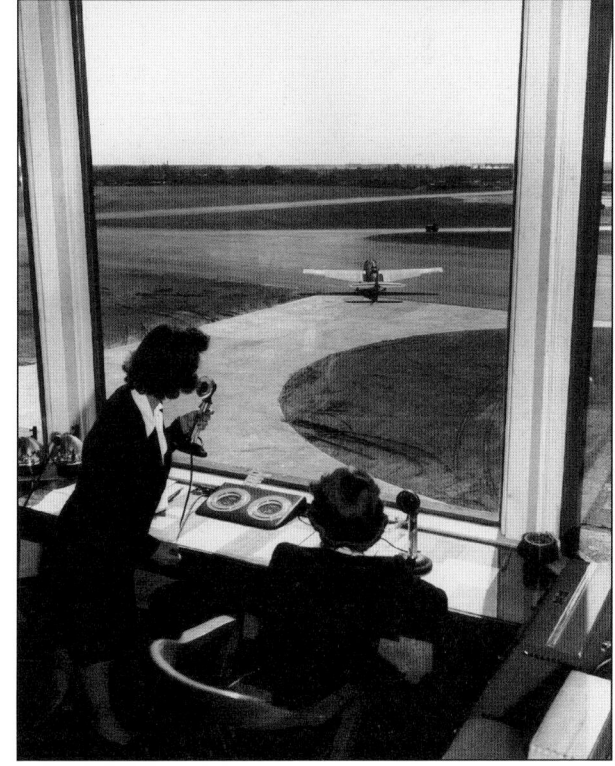

Women served in the Grumman factories as builders, inspectors, assemblers, and other positions that helped contribute to the company's success. The first group of women to work in the shop are pictured celebrating the anniversary of their first year in the main inspection crib. From left to right are Vivla Clark, Victoria Wozniak, Nellie Natterer, Harriet Kosick, Josefa Seffert, Charlotte Denton, and Ruth Lane. (Courtesy of the Northrop Grumman History Center.)

Some women even had the opportunity to become test pilots. These women flew test flights for years and served their nation admirably. Pictured here are women working in the control tower in Bethpage in 1942. (Courtesy of the Northrop Grumman History Center.)

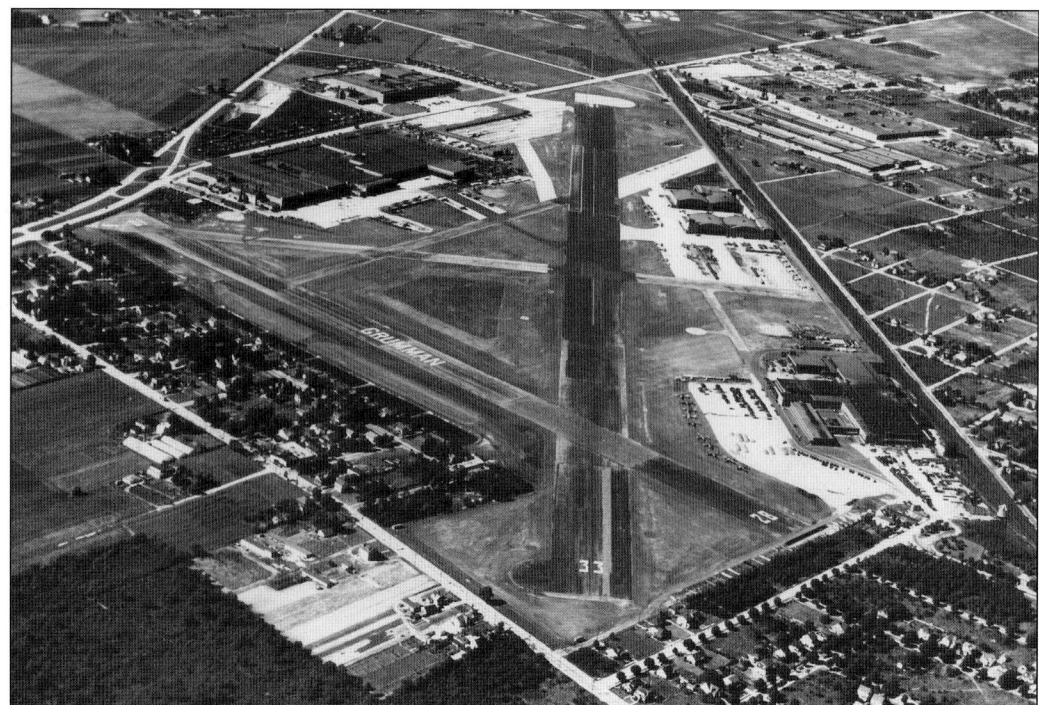

As World War II was ending, the aviation industry began developing the jet engine, and Grumman worked on perfecting the new technology. By 1949, they created the F9F Panther, the company's first combat jet and the Navy's primary fighter plane of the Korean War. It was a carrier-based aircraft that used several weapons systems and handled a variety of missions. During the war, F9Fs would fly more than 78,000 combat missions. This is an aerial view of Grumman and runway and the tremendous development of the property in Bethpage in 1945. (Courtesy of the Northrop Grumman History Center.)

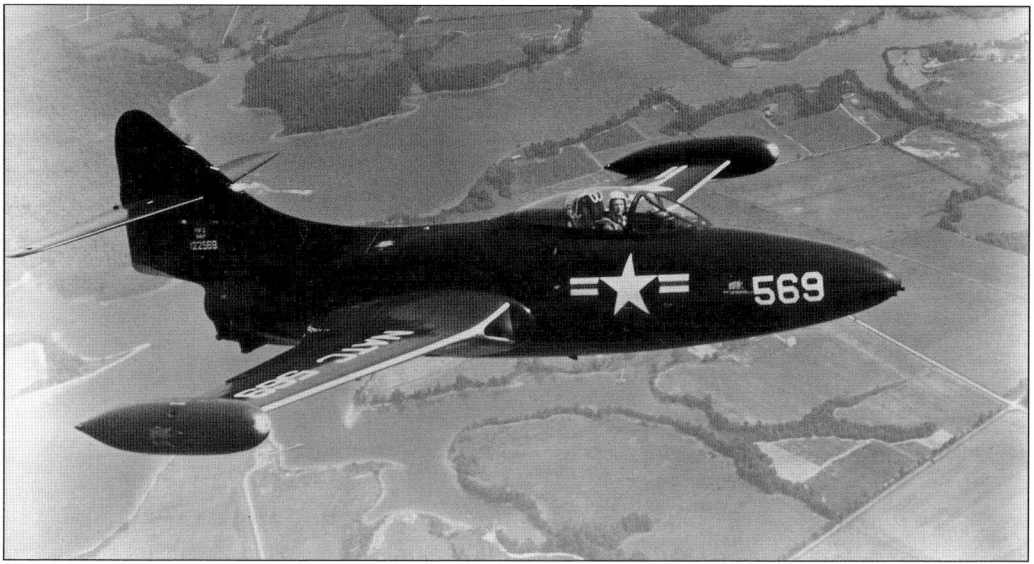

Pictured in the late 1940s, this Grumman F9F-2 is being tested by the US Naval Air Test Center in Maryland. (Courtesy of the Northrop Grumman History Center.)

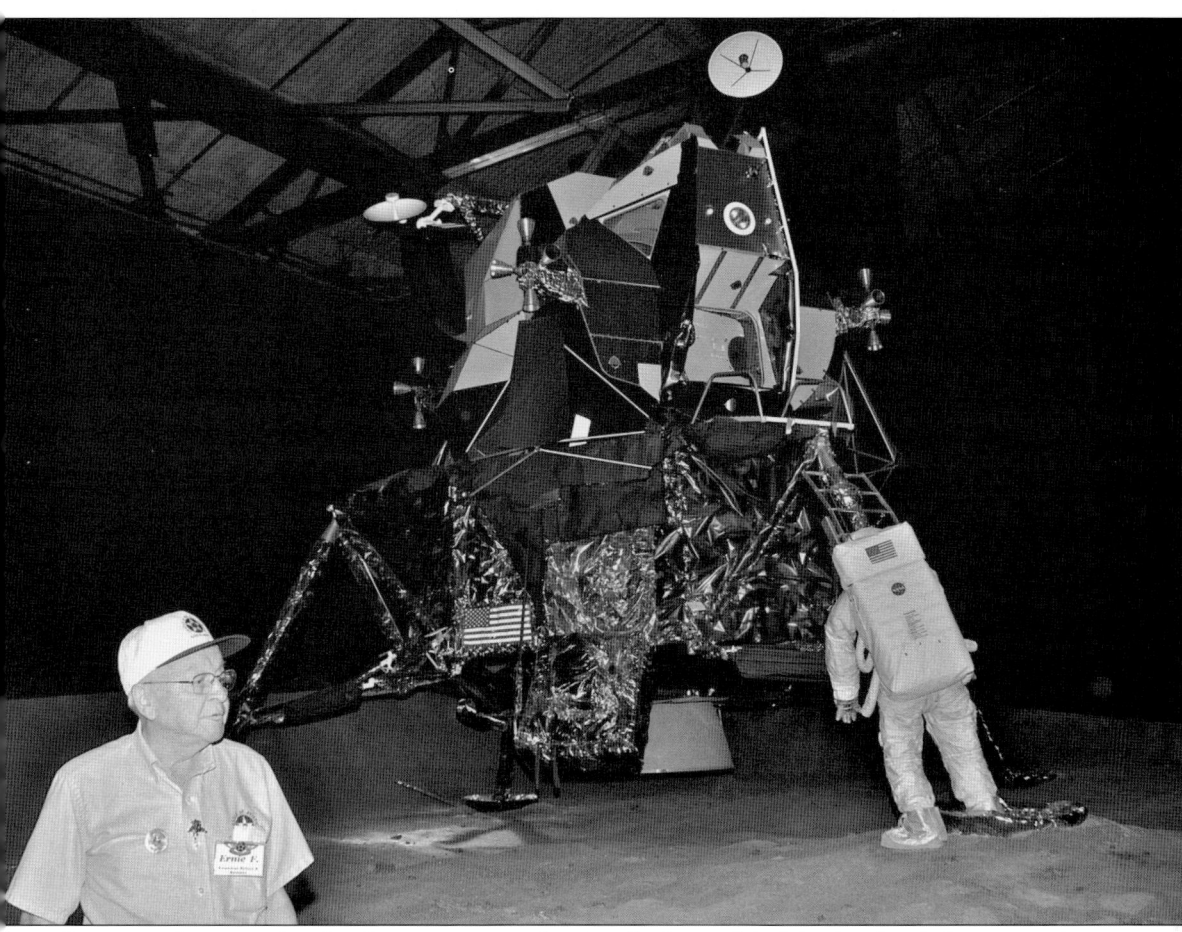

Grumman became the chief contractor on the Apollo Lunar Module that landed men on the moon. They received the contract on November 7, 1962, and built 13 lunar modules. The descent stage held the engine that allowed it to descend to the lunar surface. On top of the descent unit rested the ascent stage with the ship's control room and the engine that lifted it off the moon. The first one landed on the moon during the July 1969 Apollo 11 mission. In 1969, the company changed its name to Grumman Aerospace Corporation. As the Apollo program neared its end, Grumman was one of the main competitors for the contract to design and build the space shuttle, but lost to Rockwell International. The company ended up involved in the shuttle program nonetheless, as a subcontractor to Rockwell, providing the wings and vertical stabilizer sections in the early 1970s. Pictured here is Ernie Finamore, former Grumman employee and volunteer at Nassau County's Cradle of Aviation Museum, standing in front of the lunar module on exhibit at the museum. (Courtesy of Rita Rusch.)

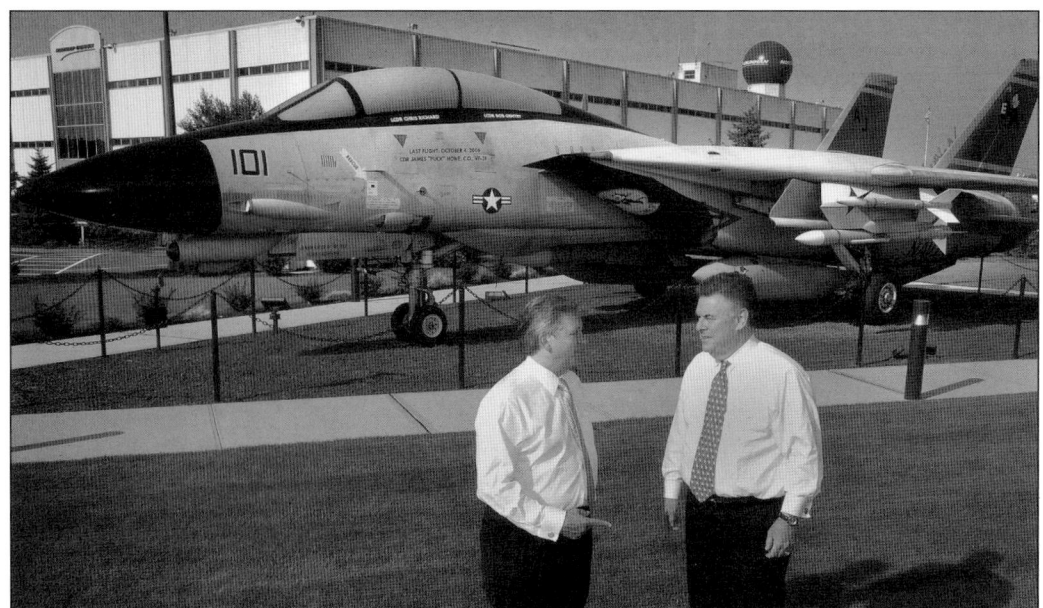

In September 1972, the Tomcat began replacing the Phantom as the Navy's frontline jet fighter. Due to its flexibility, superior weapons system, and speed (it could travel at Mach 2.5), the F-14 remained the Navy's best fighter for over 20 years. At its peak in 1986, it employed 23,000 people on Long Island. With the end of the Cold War, Grumman began to run into serious financial difficulties in the 1980s. The company built the Grumman Long Life Vehicle (LLV), a light transport mail truck designed for and used by the US Postal Service. The LLV entered service in 1986. By 1994, the company was facing financial problems and could no longer stand on it own. Northrop, a competing company, purchased Grumman, forming the Northrop Grumman Corporation. Pictured here are County Executive Ed Mangano (left) and Congressman Peter King (right) standing in front of the Grumman F14 display outside the Northrop Grumman plant. (Courtesy of Mike Tamborrino.)

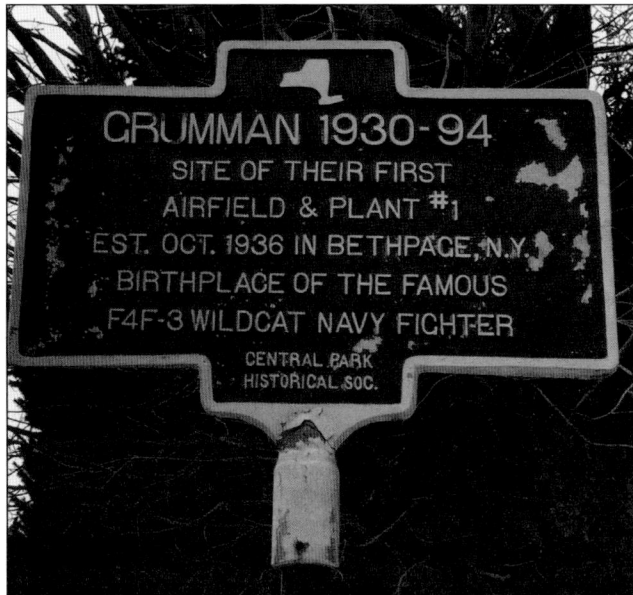

This is the historic marker at the site of the first Grumman airfield, located north of Central Avenue. (Courtesy of Amanda Laikin.)

Eight
Zorn's: A Taste of History

In 1924 and 1925, the Zorn family—parents Josef and Julianna, son Peter, Josef's brother August, and sisters Tessie and Julia—immigrated to Ridgewood, New York, from their native Germany. When Peter Zorn was 18 years old, he worked on a farm in Montgomery, New York. He then had a chance to go to Poughkeepsie, New York, to follow his passion in the butcher trade, which he had learned in Germany. After a year, he went to New York City, where he continued his trade for eight years. Peter Zorn took advantage of the superior opportunities provided by the soil, climate, and proximity to large markets, and he became one of the largest growers of eggs, chickens, and turkeys on Long Island. He was thoroughly familiar with the marketing of meats and poultry when he moved out to Flushing, Long Island, and began the production of poultry and eggs, operating under his own name. In 1935, the Zorn family opened and operated nine poultry farms, eight farms on Long Island, and one in Mullica Hill, New Jersey.

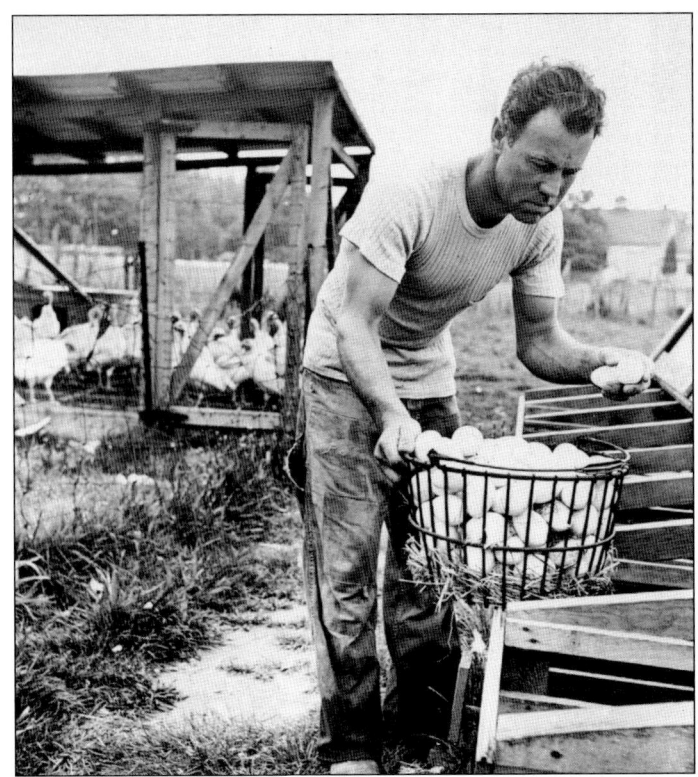

In 1935, first-generation Josef and Juliana Zorn operated the Central Islip farm located on Suffolk Avenue. They raised live chickens on 16 acres until 1955. Josef operated another farm in Bohemia in 1935, again raising only live chickens on five acres. This farm was operated until it was sold to his sister Tessie and her husband, Henry. They ran the farm until 1958. Pictured here are chicken coops at the Bethpage farm and eggs being collected to pack for retail. (Courtesy of Merrill Zorn.)

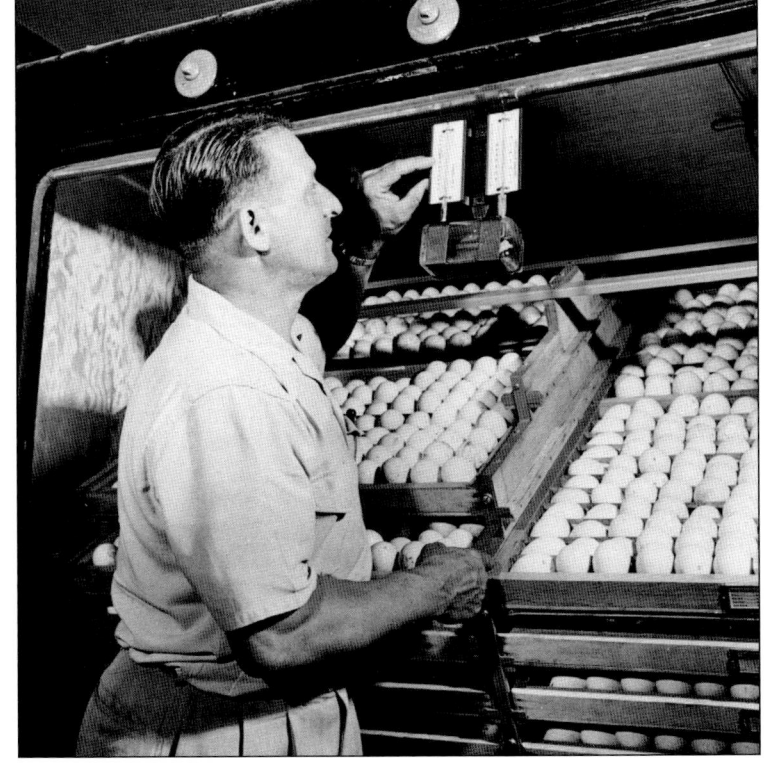

From 1936 to 1940, Pete Zorn rented five acres in Glenwood Landing, which was part of the poultry estate. It was a dairy farm, a florist, and poultry farm. In 1940, August Zorn bought the five-acre farm on Columbus Avenue in Brentwood and raised live chickens. Pictured here is Pete Zorn in his turkey-egg hatchery, where St. Joseph Hospital is located today. (Courtesy of Merrill Zorn.)

Peter Zorn became president of the Long Island Broiler Growers Cooperation Inc., and was a committee member of the Nassau County Farm Bureau. In addition, he was the president of the Long Island Poultry Association. Pictured here is second-generation Pete Zorn with poults, one day old turkeys. (Courtesy of Merrill Zorn.)

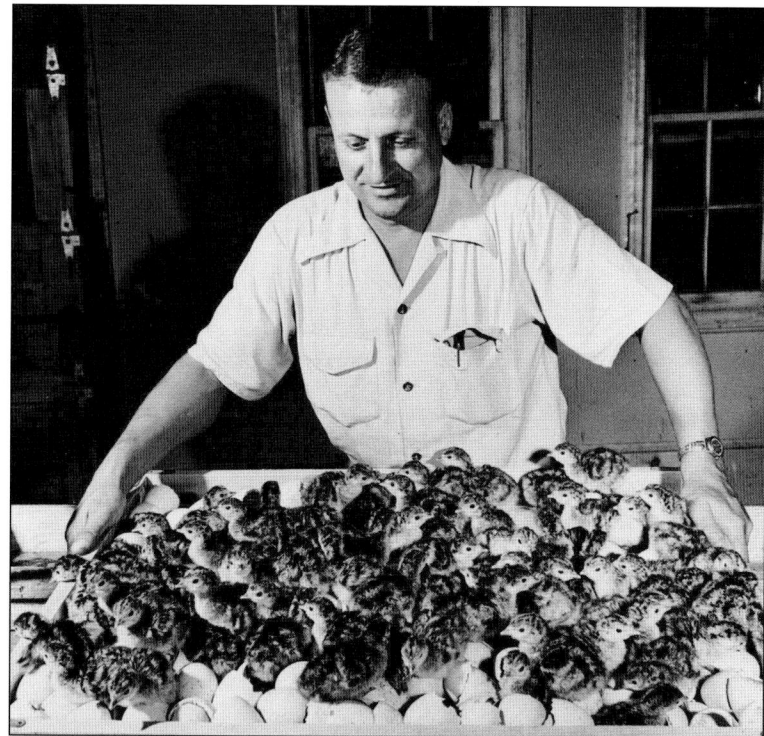

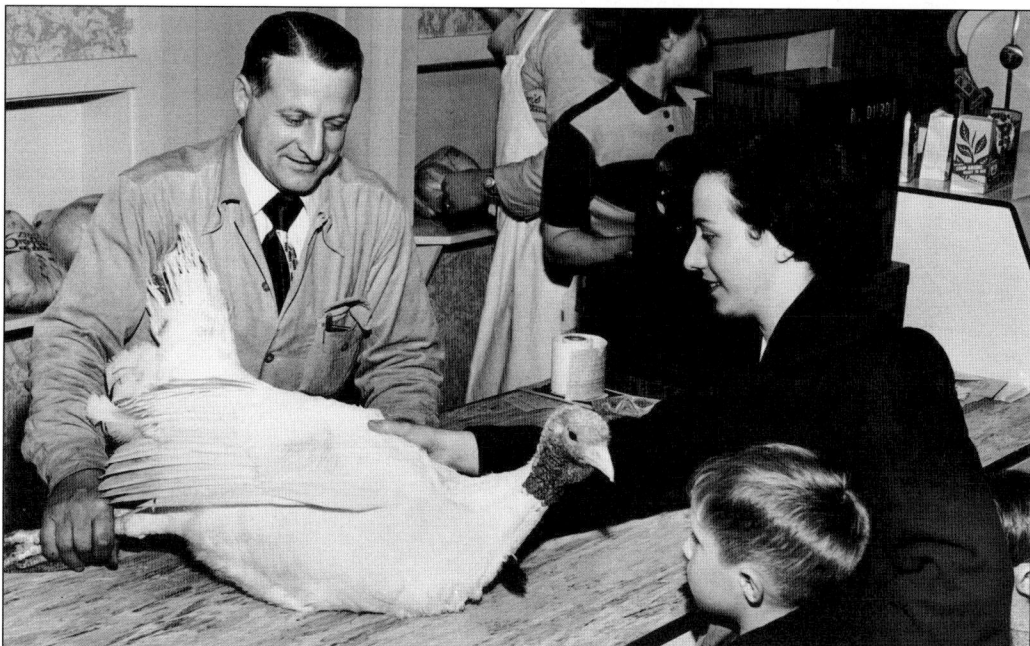

In 1941, Peter Zorn wanted to raise and sell turkeys year-round. He was told one cannot raise turkeys on Long Island, but Zorn would not be deterred and bought 2,000 poults. The only problem was that the buyers offered less money than it took to grow them. Being the entrepreneur that he was, he took a piece of plywood and put "Buy your turkeys here" on it. Pictured here is Pete Zorn at the counter in their Bethpage store. Behind Peter is his wife, Sine. (Courtesy of Merrill Zorn.)

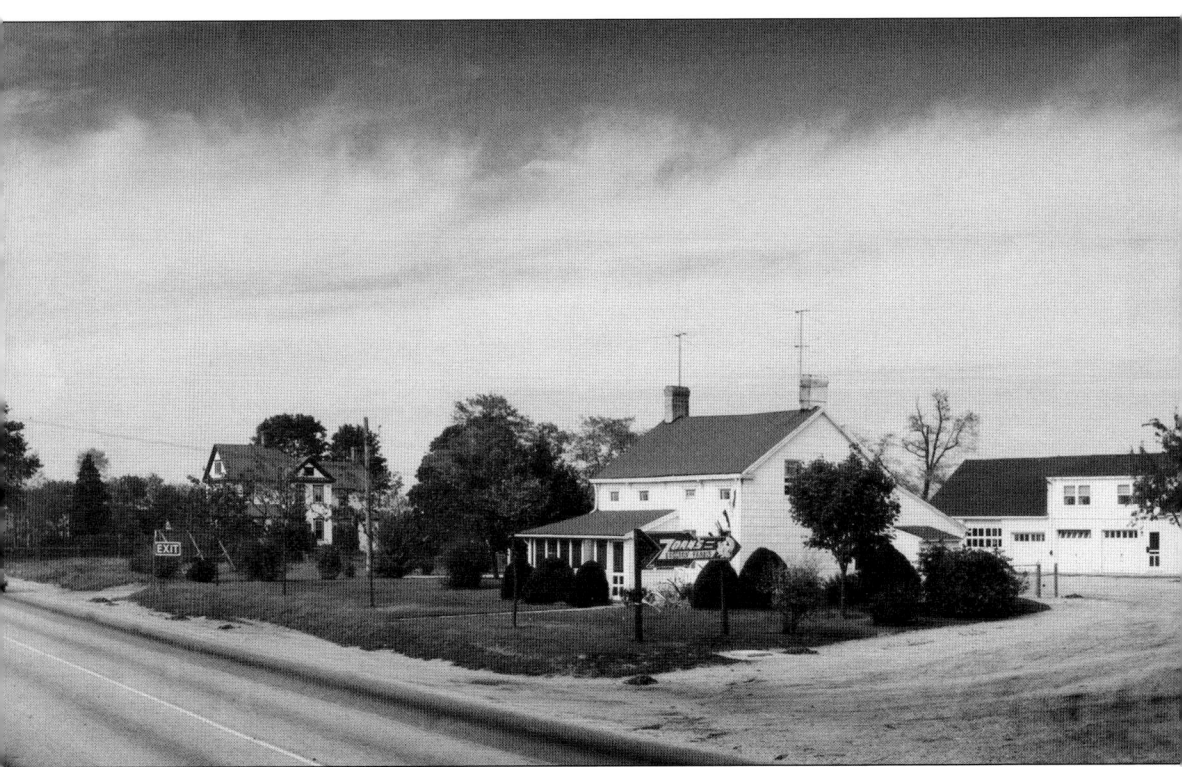

In 1940, the Zorn Bethpage farm was born. Next door to Peter Zorn's 10 acres was the Krusher property, where St. Joseph Hospital is now, and they had a barn in which they kept their three horses on one side and a hatchery on the other. Across the street (Hempstead Turnpike), he rented 10 acres on which he built the first unit of his present plant and has carried on a steady growing business in poultry, eggs, and chickens. Parts of his operations were a 23,000-egg-capacity turkey incubator together with all the necessary modern equipment. His first store was a windowless,

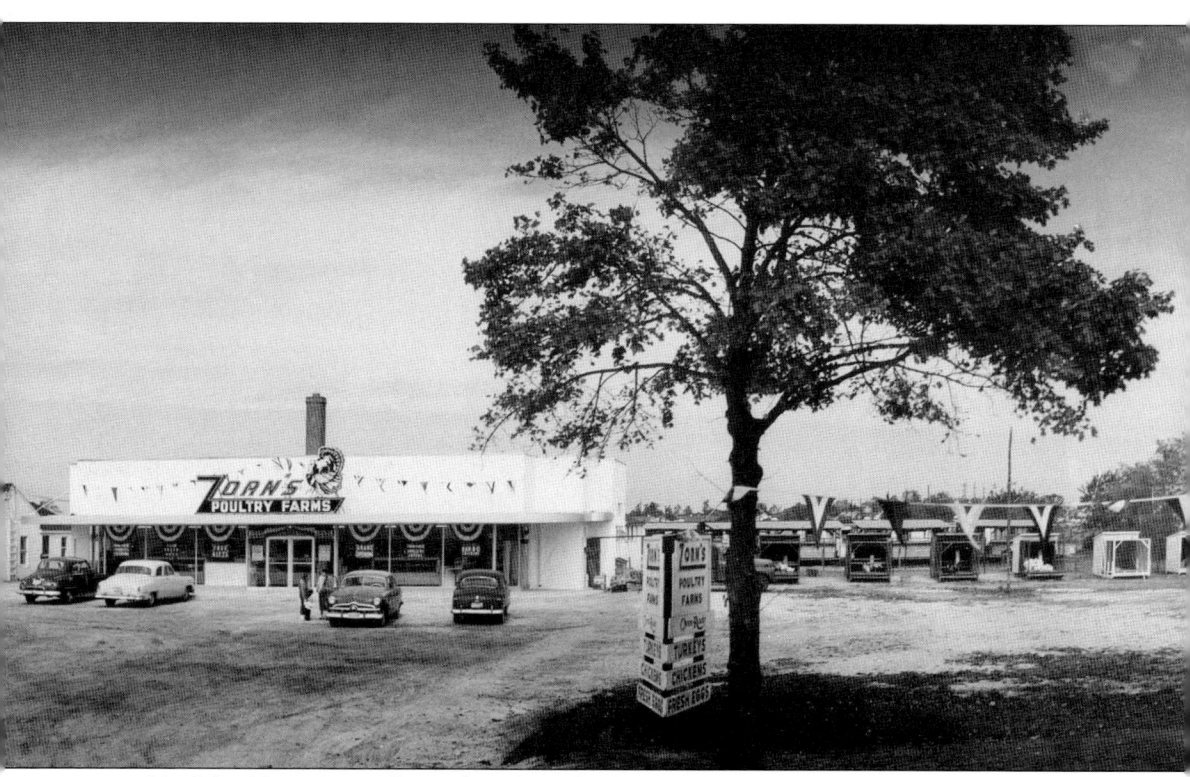

cement-block building that still stands today. This became his first and only retail store and the beginning of his retail empire. They raised live chickens and sold them wholesale to various vendors from Queens and Brooklyn, among other places. They came with empty trucks and crates to pick up the chickens. He sold turkeys only at Christmas and Thanksgiving. All of the family farms were chickens farms, and they were sold live only. Pictured above is the grand opening of the Bethpage retail store in September 1940. (Both images courtesy of Merrill Zorn.)

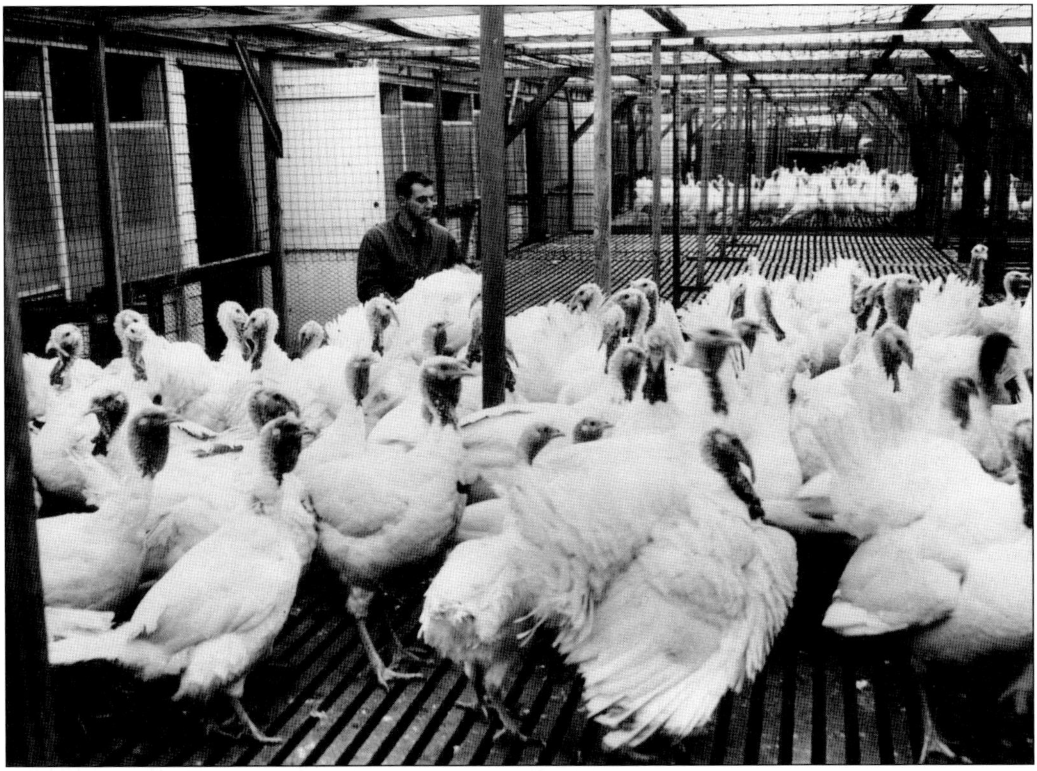

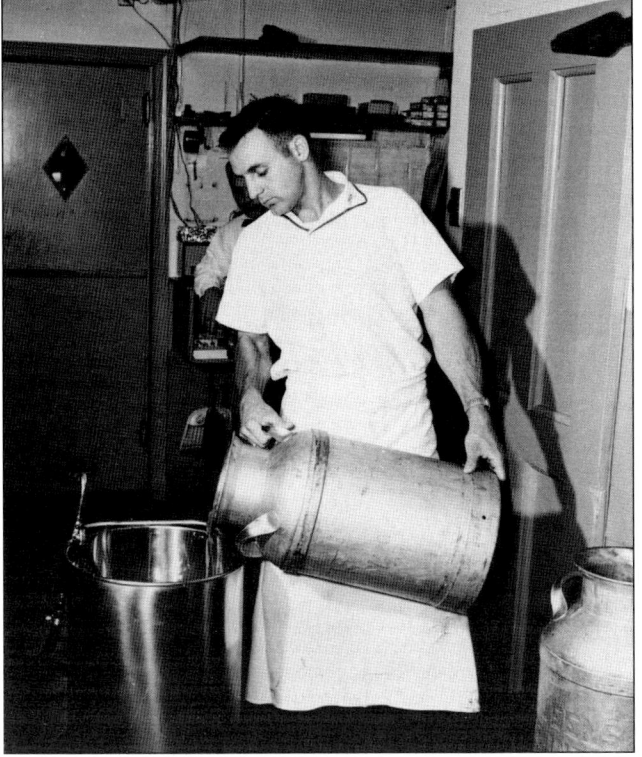

In 1943, Zorn's farm was the first to eviscerate a turkey; they called it oven ready. Everyone else sold their turkeys dressed (plucked only, head and feet attached). Pictured here is Joe Zorn in the turkey pens at the Bethpage farm. (Courtesy of Merrill Zorn.)

The following year they phased out live chickens and only sold fresh chickens and turkeys. Pictured here is third-generation Joe Zorn pouring gravy to pack out for retail. (Courtesy of Merrill Zorn.)

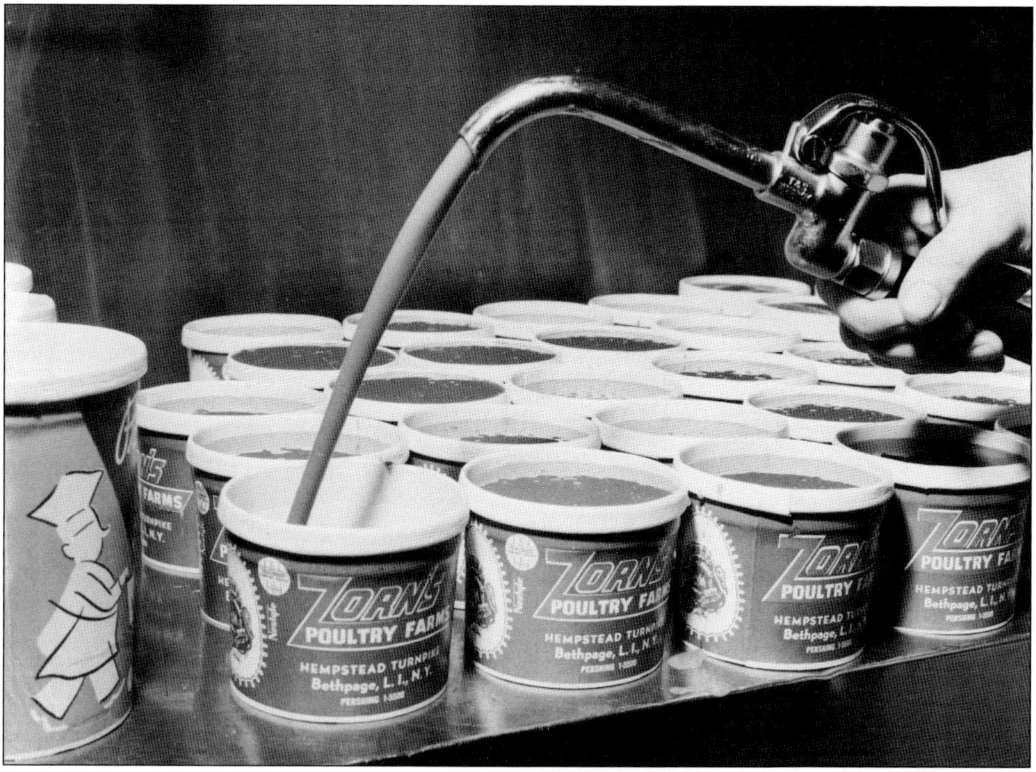

In 1945, Peter Zorn went to an Army base camp in Upton, New York, bought five Army barracks, and towed them to Bethpage for part of the building that stands now and some garages. That same year, they started selling fresh, uncooked chickens and turkeys year-round. Pictured here is Zorn's gravy being packed out in containers for the retail store. At the time, this was a state-of-the-art gravy dispenser. (Courtesy of Merrill Zorn.)

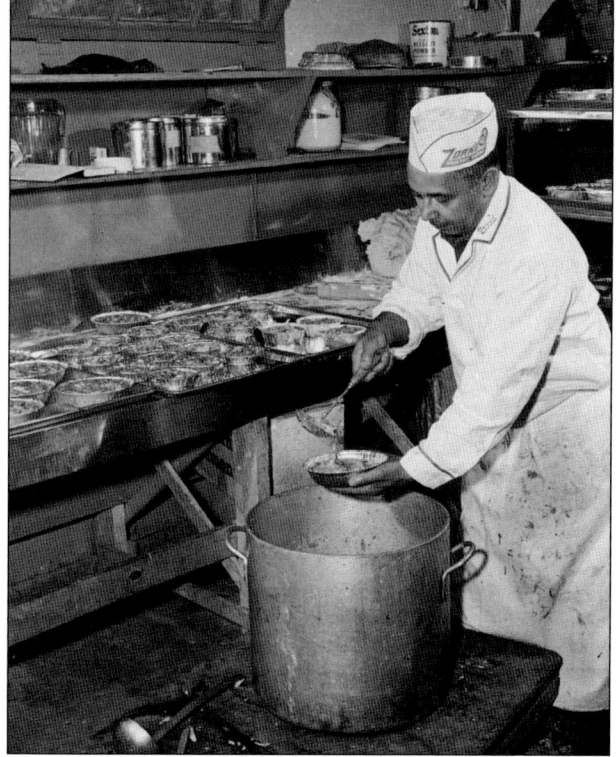

In 1946, they got a plucking machine; it looked like a barrel or an oil drum with finger-like projections that were attached to the outside of the barrel that spun at high speeds. The turkeys were dipped in hot water and would be held on the outside, and a spinning drum would take the feathers off. Pictured here are chicken pot pies being prepared in the retail store. (Courtesy of Merrill Zorn.)

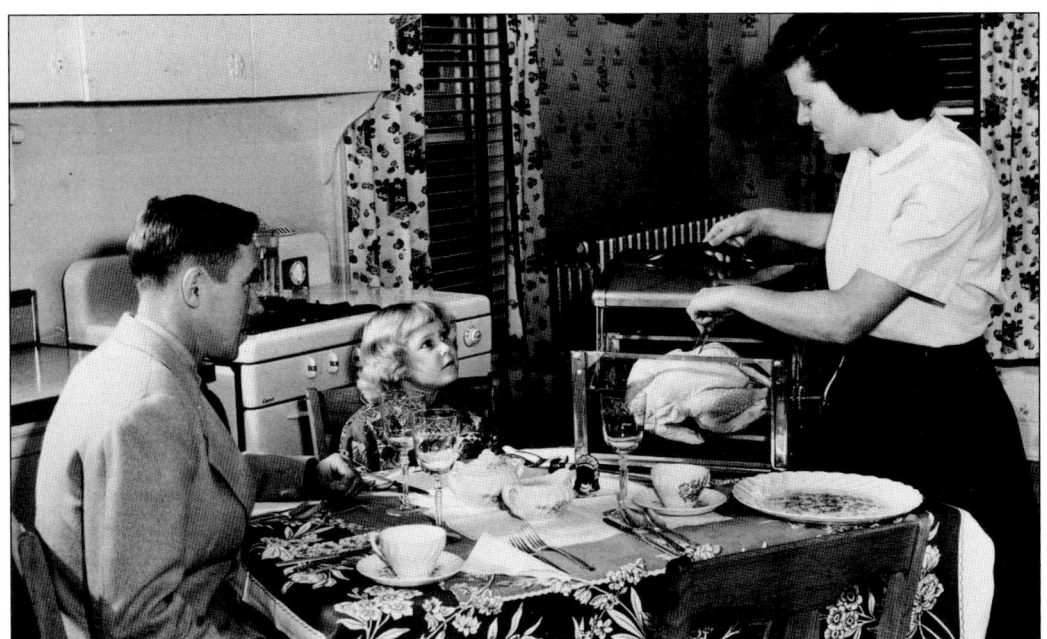

In 1949, Zorn's was the first on Long Island to have a rotisserie machine. He also sold gravy, coleslaw, potato salad, macaroni salad, and french fries. In the late 1940s, Grumman executives came to Zorn's for turkeys for their employees. They started making gift-boxed turkeys, which are turkeys in a decorated gift boxes, a practice still carried out today. Pictured here are Pete Zorn's first manager, Darwin Bruce, and his wife, Pat, using a rotisserie. This photograph was taken in the house in front of the Bethpage store for an advertisement. (Courtesy of Merrill Zorn.)

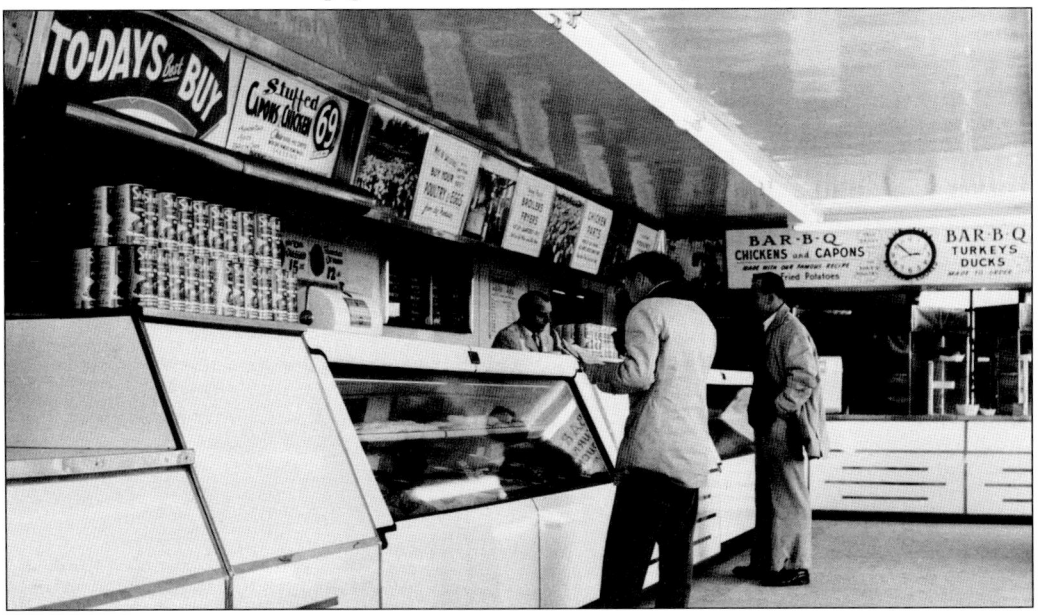

In 1952, the white store in Bethpage was built as you see it today. Peter Zorn wanted a different way to cook the chickens, so he got a big pot of boiling water and a fish net to dunk the chickens in the water he then breaded and fried them. The same breading recipe is used today for their southern fried chicken. (Courtesy of Merrill Zorn.)

Nine
BUILDING A COMMUNITY

In 1917, a group of Catholic men petitioned Bishop McDonnell to establish a parish here in Bethpage, as they had to travel to St. Kilian's in Farmingdale or to St. Ignatius in Hicksville to attend ,ass. Among these men were Joseph Walsh Sr., Frank A. Nolan, Harry A. Stolz, and William J. Ahern. The bishop, however, turned down the petition because he felt that such a small farm community could not support a third parish in the area. Nonetheless, the bishop was so impressed with the fervor of these earlier Bethpage Catholics that he did purchase the land that is the site of St. Martin of Tours Church and school today. Undaunted in their efforts, this small group of men, some three years later, conducted a pledge campaign with great success. They produced pledges of $10,000, an amazing sum for such a sparsely populated community. More amazingly, one of the largest single donations was made by a local storekeeper who was not of the faith. Armed with these pledges, another petition was presented to the new bishop, the Right Reverend Thomas E. Molloy. The time was now ripe for a new parish.

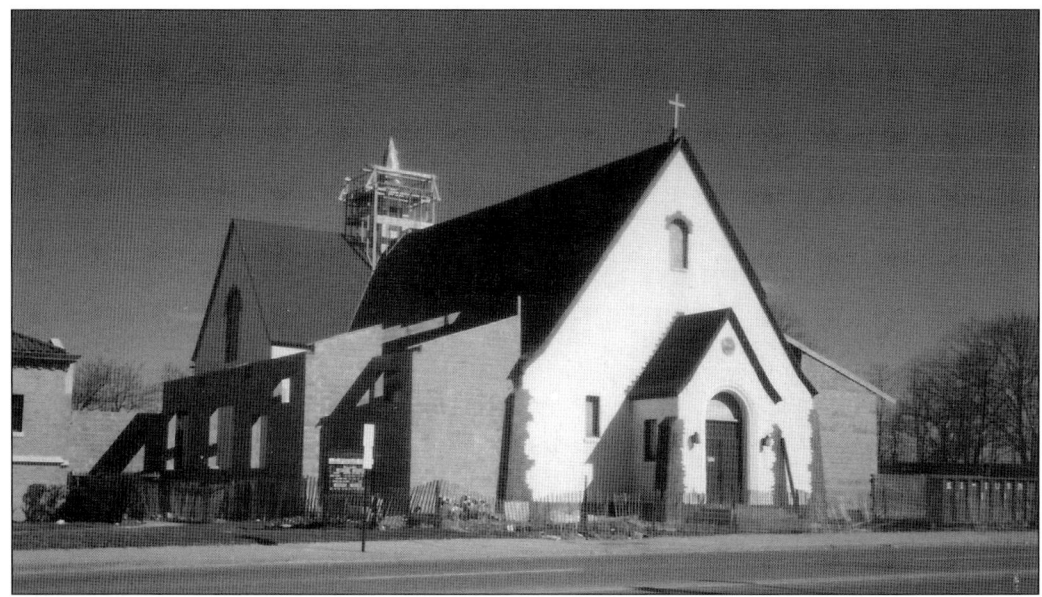

Bishop Molloy appointed the Reverend Daniel A. Dwyer as the founding pastor. Father Dwyer arrived on October 12, 1923, and on Sunday, October 14, 1923, he offered the first mass in the Roosevelt Republican clubhouse on Broadway. A small group of Catholics attended this successful beginning. Father Dwyer set up residence in a house at 188 Herman Avenue while the Republican club continued to serve as the first church. Pictured here is St. Martin of Tours Church during its expansion in 1996.

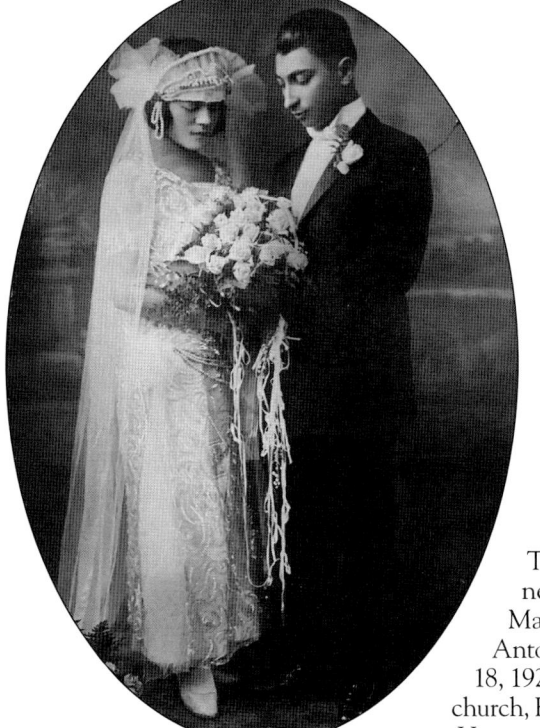

The first bride and groom to be married in the new congregation of the newly established St. Martin of Tours R.C. Church in Central Park was Antonio Finamore and Stella Ruggiero on November 18, 1923. As the flooring was not finished in the new church, Father Dwyer officiated the wedding in his house on Herman Avenue. (Courtesy of Nora Logerfo.)

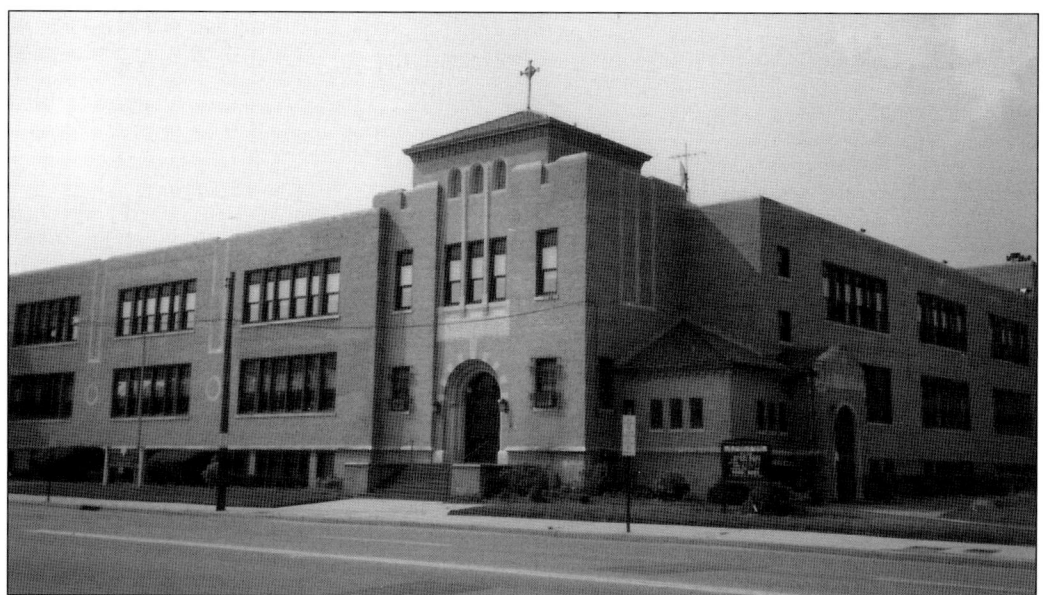

Father Dwyer was able to rent the house that once was the St. Vincent de Paul building on Broadway. Several months later, the building was bought by the parish and served as church and parsonage. On March 21, 1924, ground was broken for the church building, much of the labor being completed by the parishioners. The new church building was dedicated on November 9, 1924. In later years, it became evident that a school was needed to educate the children of the parish. The ground-breaking ceremony took place in May 1954 and opened in September 1955.

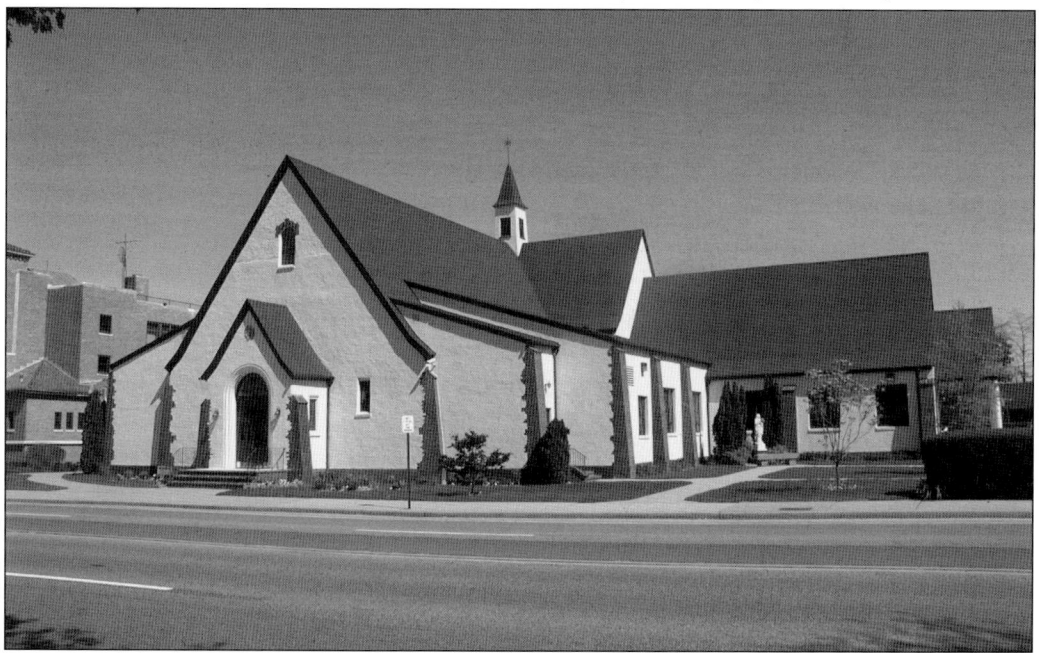

Almost 40 years later, there was a need to enlarge the beautiful, but very old, church building. On July 2, 1995, the parish ceremoniously closed the doors of its church so the new construction could begin. The newly enlarged church was dedicated on September 15, 1996. Pictured above is the St. Martin of Tours school and St. Martin of Tours Church as it appears today.

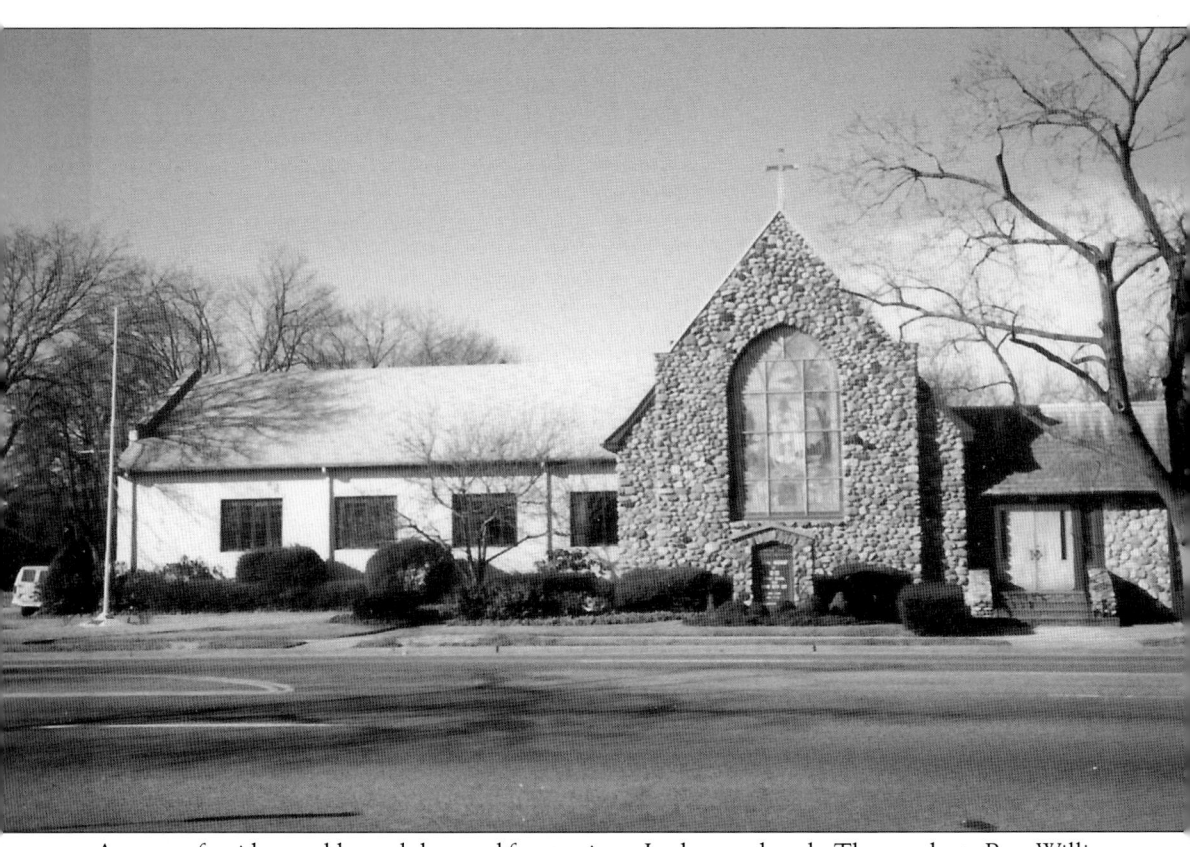

A group of residents addressed the need for starting a Lutheran church. They spoke to Rev. William Rush of Trinity Lutheran Church in Hicksville, and an organizational meeting was held on March 5, 1923, at the Roosevelt Republican Hall. It was attended by 35 people, and $8 was collected. Pastor William Rush of Hicksville offered to conduct services on Sunday afternoons in the Central Park Firehouse on Stewart Avenue. The first worship service was held on March 11, 1923. On November 1923, the current property was purchased, and the cornerstone for the church was laid. Construction was started, and the church was called St. Paul's Evangelical Lutheran Church. The stone for the exterior were gathered by parishioners from nearby farmlands surrounding the church. The Scherer family moved to a home in Central Park on the corner of Central Avenue and Scherer Street, which is still standing today. Scherer had a masonry business for years, and he did the stonework on St. Paul's Lutheran Church in 1924. The church continued to prosper, and the parish house was added in 1955.

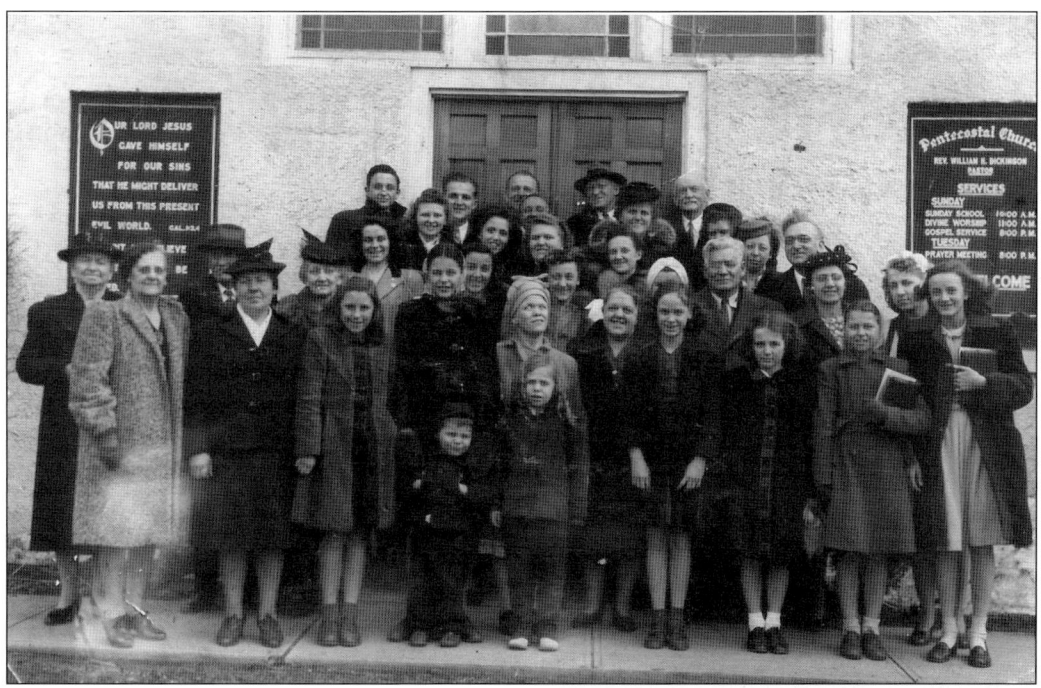

The Central Park Pentecostal Church met for eight years in a room above Deubel's Restaurant on the corner of Stewart and Central Avenues. In 1922, the people built a small chapel on the east side of Stewart Avenue, south of Central Avenue. They met here until 1952, when they merged with the Assembly of God Church. In 1953, the congregation began to construct the present church and educational building. The labor was done by members of the congregation. The Bethpage Assembly of God church was finished in 1957. Pictured are members of the Bethpage Assembly of God congregation in 1942. (Courtesy of Joyce Calo.)

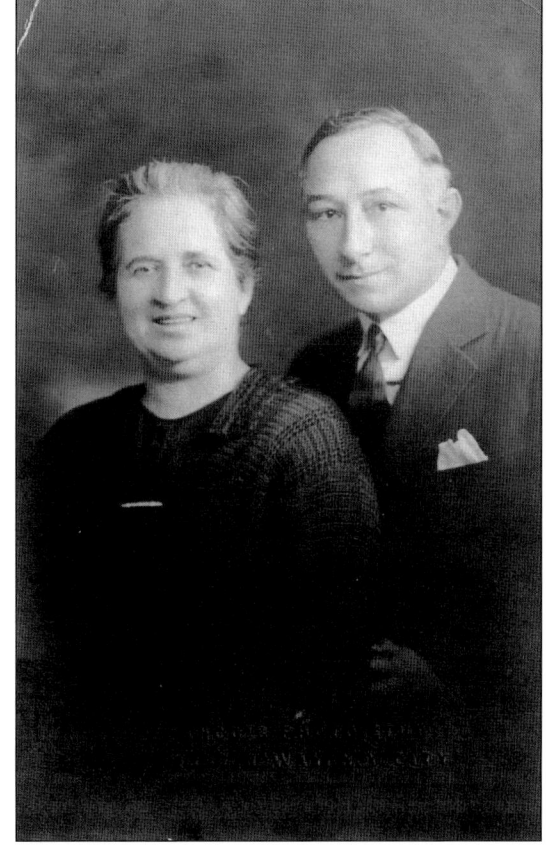

Pictured here around 1920 is the first pastor of Bethpage Assembly of God, the Reverend Robert Shumann, and his wife. (Courtesy of Joyce Calo.).

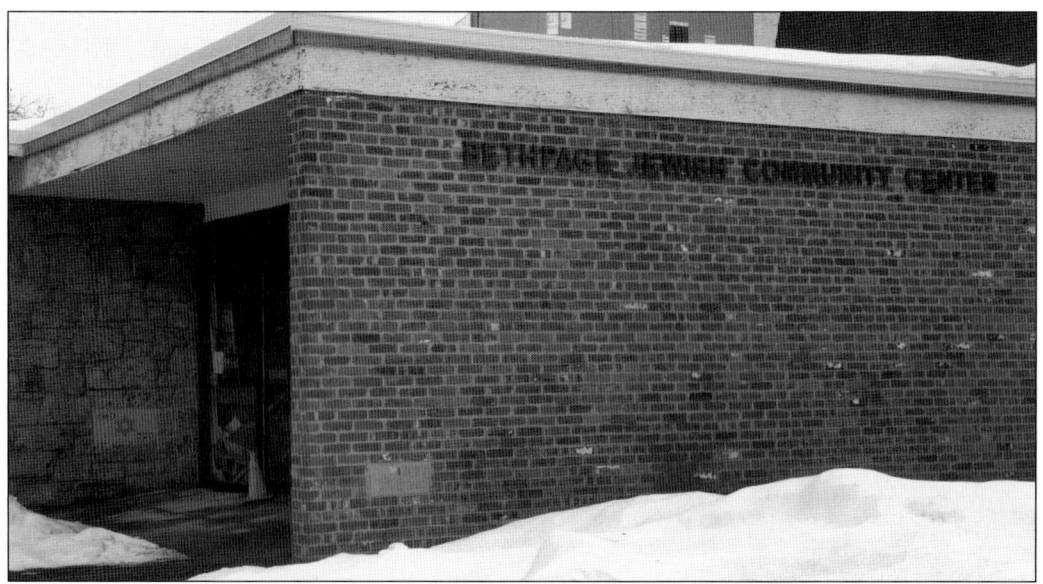

In 1955, the Jewish community in Bethpage joined together and held their first meeting in a member's home. Then, the Assembly of God Church on Stewart Avenue was made available to the community. As membership grew, the need for additional space was evident. Land was purchased on Broadway in 1957, and the Jewish temple was dedicated on April 24, 1960. In 2007, the temple closed, and members are attending other temples in surrounding communities. (Courtesy of Mike Tamborrino.)

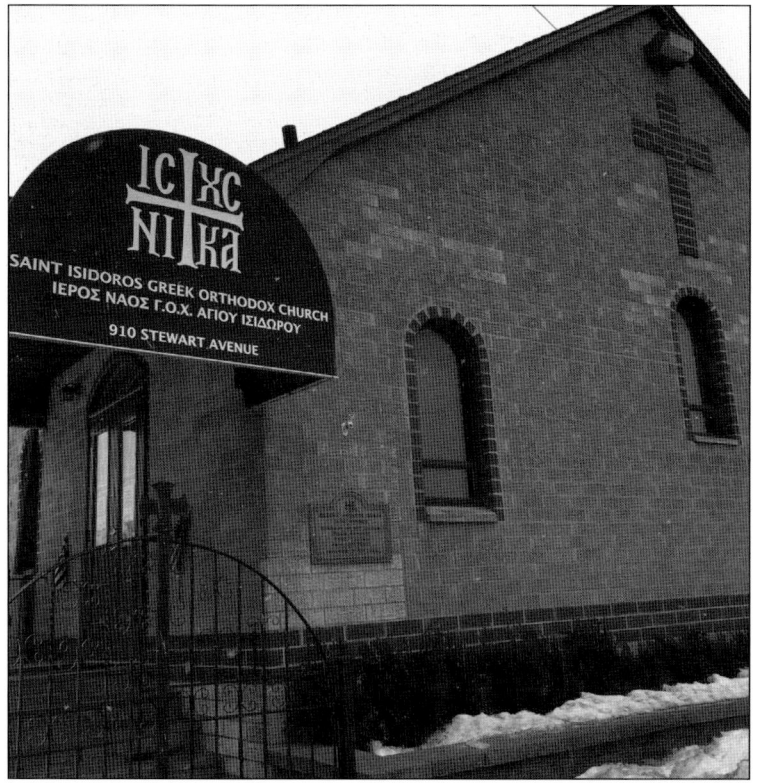

St. Isidoros Greek Orthodox Church was founded in 1974 by Rev. Petros Astyfides, Bishop of Astoria, from Chios, Greece. Built on Stewart Avenue, just north of Cherry Avenue, it serves a traditional Orthodox parish following the Patristic (Julian) Calendar. Their liturgy is mostly in the Greek language, but Orthodox of non-Greek ancestry. The Orthodox church is the original Christian church, and their liturgy and services can be traced back to the apostles. (Courtesy of Amanda Laikin.)

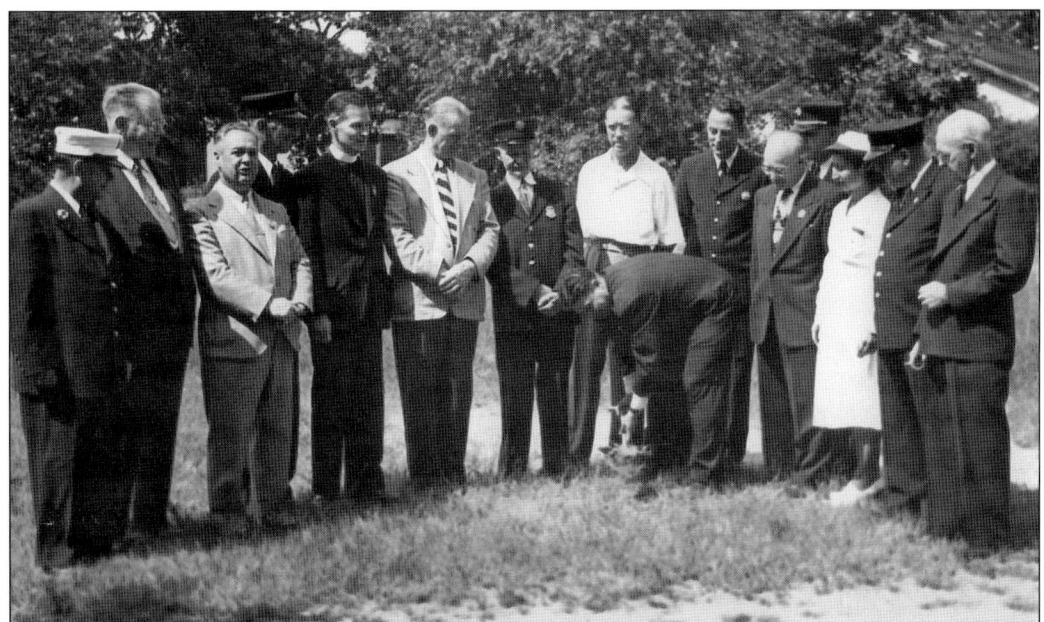

As the population of the town grew, so did the needs of the fire department. In 1949, the Bethpage Fire Department headquarters was built on Broadway. The building included a meeting hall, a wing for the library, an office for the water district, as well as a garage to house the trucks and equipment. Pictured here is the ground-breaking ceremony for the new fire headquarters on Broadway. (Courtesy of Frank Debobes.)

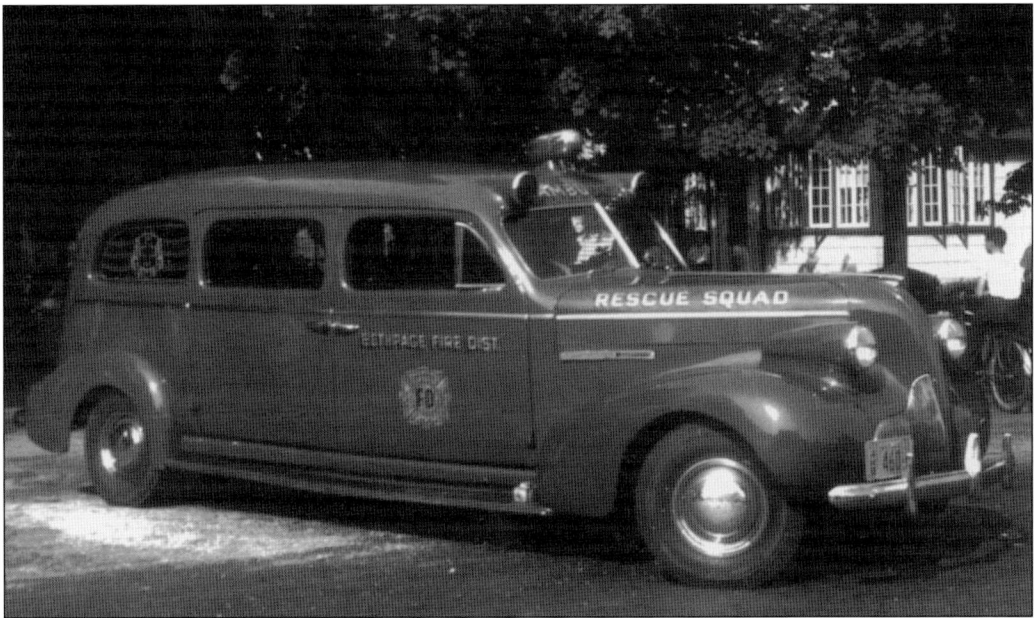

Around 1945, many firemen were called to active duty in the military and left the department short-handed. The fire commissioners made the decision to lower the age of eligibility to be a firemen from 18 years of age to 16, a great opportunity for the young men to become active firefighters. Pictured here is an early ambulance of the Bethpage Fire Department. (Courtesy of Frank Debobes.)

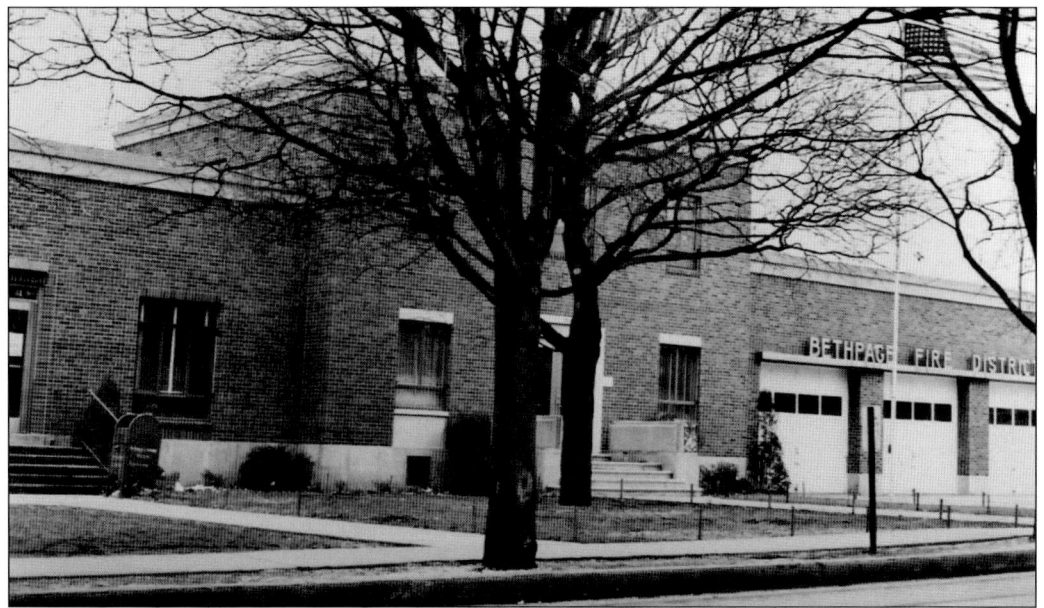

In 1955, the Bethpage Fire District Board of Fire Commissioners began planning for a growing community. Homes were quickly being built, and Grumman Aerospace was expanding on a 600-acre facility. There was a need for more fire protection on the north and south sides of the fire district since response times were too long from the Broadway headquarters. In 1958, the Bethpage Fire District consisted of 6,700 homes and had received 600 calls. In 1964, the firehouse on Broadway was expanded for more men, trucks, and equipment. (Courtesy of Plainedge Public Library.)

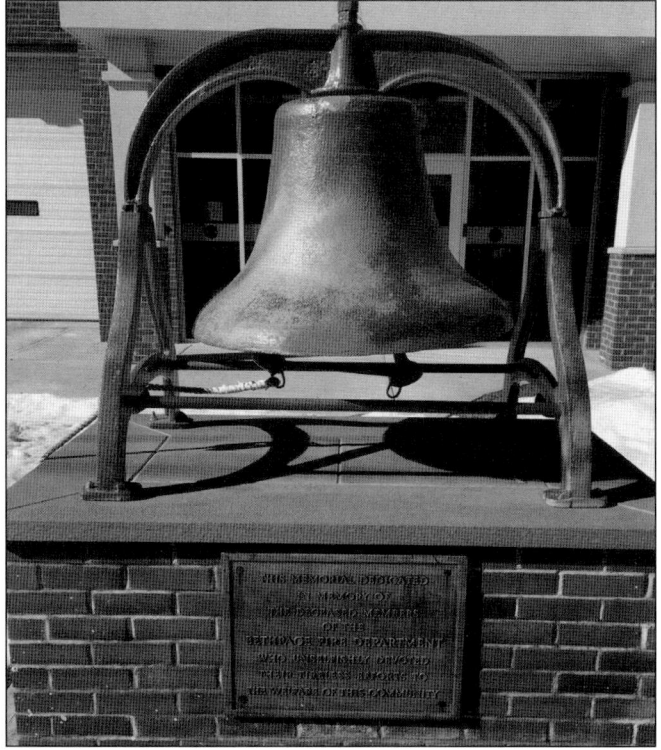

This brass bell was first located inside the cupola of the original firehouse on Stewart Avenue. It is now located in front of the Bethpage Fire Department Headquarters building on Broadway. (Photograph by the author.)

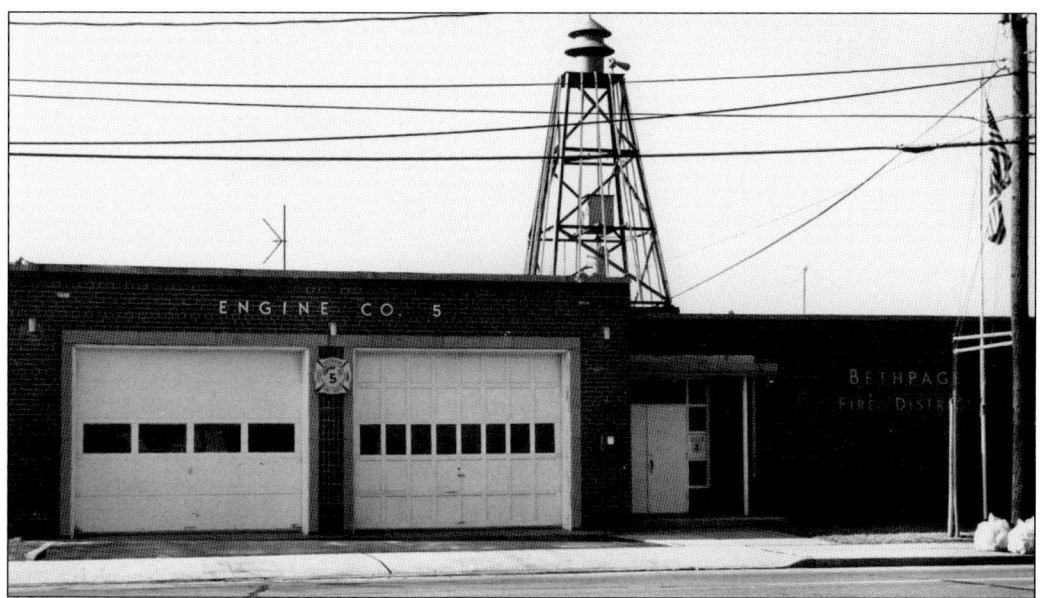

Two new companies were to be formed from the headquarters' membership who resided in these areas. Engine Company 5 was on the south side of the district on Union Avenue. Engine Company 4 was formed on the north side of the district on Stewart Avenue across from Farmers Avenue. Engine Company 4 was established with a charter membership of 15 men, and a new firehouse consisting of two bays was built on land donated by the Grumman Corporation. (Courtesy of Plainedge Public Library.)

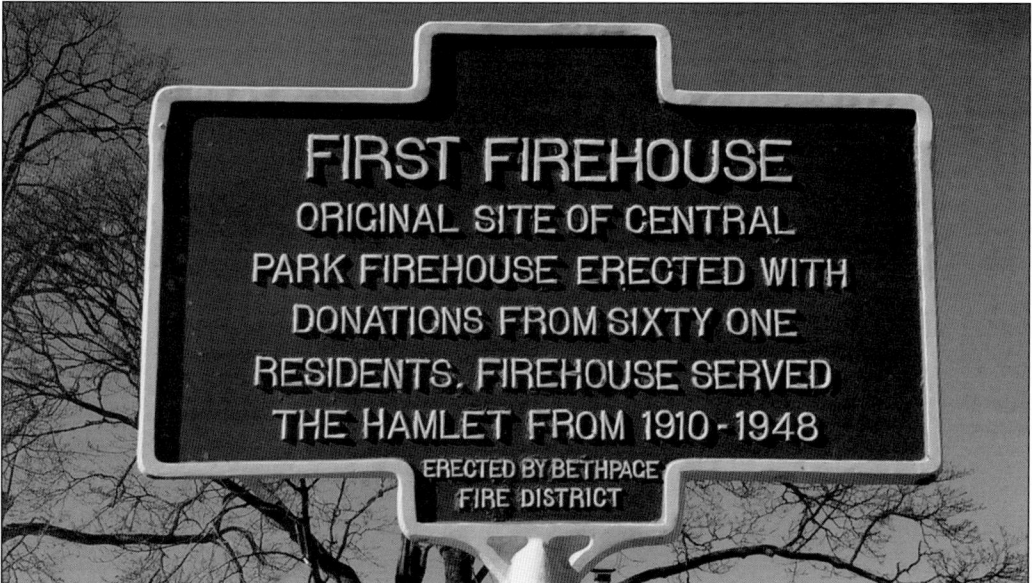

In 1970, a new addition was added to accommodate a ladder truck and a new mechanics shop. Time, age, larger fire apparatus, and growing membership forced the board of fire commissioners to make plans for a new building for Engine Company 4. The plans for the new building started in 1996. After much planning, construction began in March 2003 and was completed in April 2004. Pictured here is the historic marker at the site of the first firehouse on Stewart Avenue. (Photograph by the author.)

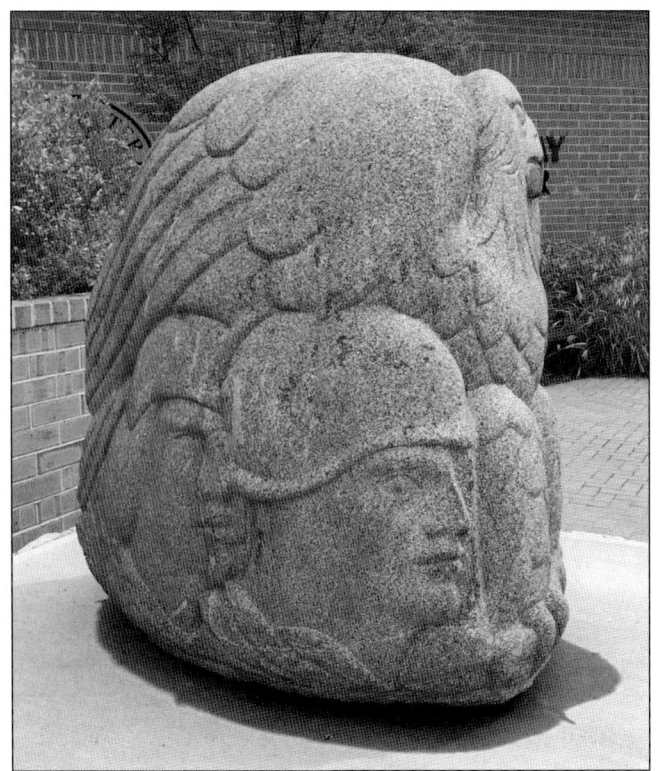

In 1933, Polygnostis Vagis purchased a house on Evergreen Avenue in Central Park, where he would work for the next 32 years. In 1952, he completed his monument—a memorial to the armed forces. The monument is about four feet tall and carved in black granite that came from Locust Valley. A neighbor and friend hauled the slab to Bethpage. Pictured here is the left side of the war memorial, *US Armed Force*. (Photograph by the author.)

After rendering the stone into a square block, Vagis carved four faces in profile. Vagis chose four local young people from Bethpage who were serving in each of the four chosen divisions of the military. Ruth Nicholson Haugen modeled as a member of the Women's Army Auxiliary Corps (WAAC), Carl Nicholson for the Navy, Robert Nicholson for the Army, and Judy Lang for the Navy Women's Reserve (WAVES). Pictured here is the centered view of the war memorial. (Photograph by the author.)

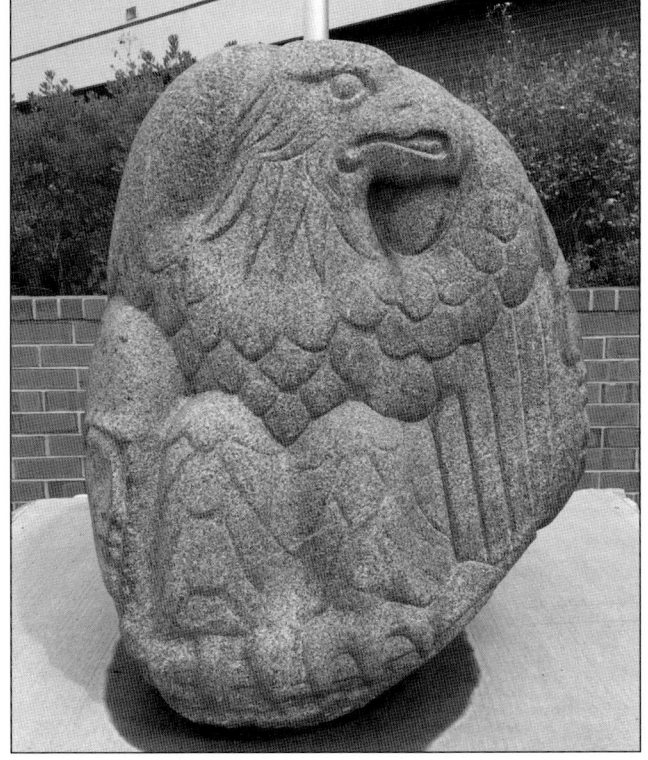

In the 1950s, Vagis exhibited his work at the Whitney Museum of Art, New York Museum of Modern Art, the Metropolitan Museum of Art, and the International Exposition at the Carnegie Institute in Philadelphia. Polygnostis Vagis was one of 101 sculptors whose work has been admitted to the nationwide competitive exhibition, American Sculpture 1951, in the Great Hall of the Metropolitan Museum of Art. Vagis's entry was the *Moon* in cast stone. Vagis died on April 14, 1965. Pictured is the right side of the war memorial. (Photograph by the author.)

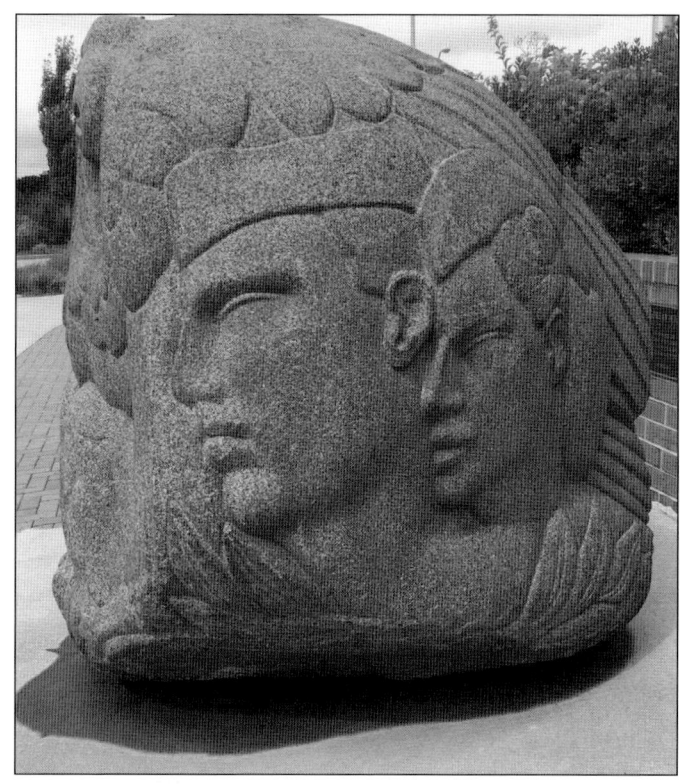

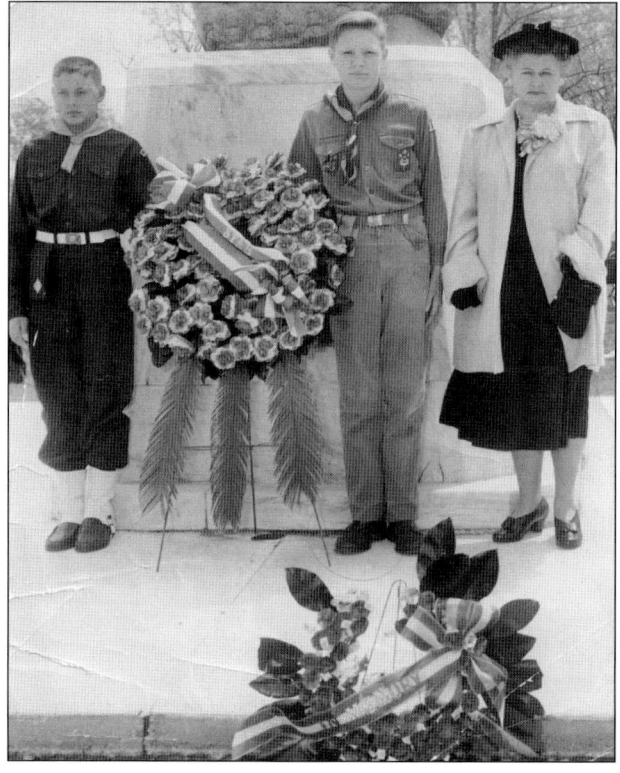

Cousins John and James Wilson hold a wreath at a memorial service in Bethpage. Mary Moesch (wife of Charles Moesch), representing the Gold Star Mothers, looks on. Her son Richard Moesch was killed in the Korean War. The bottom part of Polygnostis Vagis's monument *US Armed Force* can been seen behind them. The memorial is now at the Bethpage Community Park.

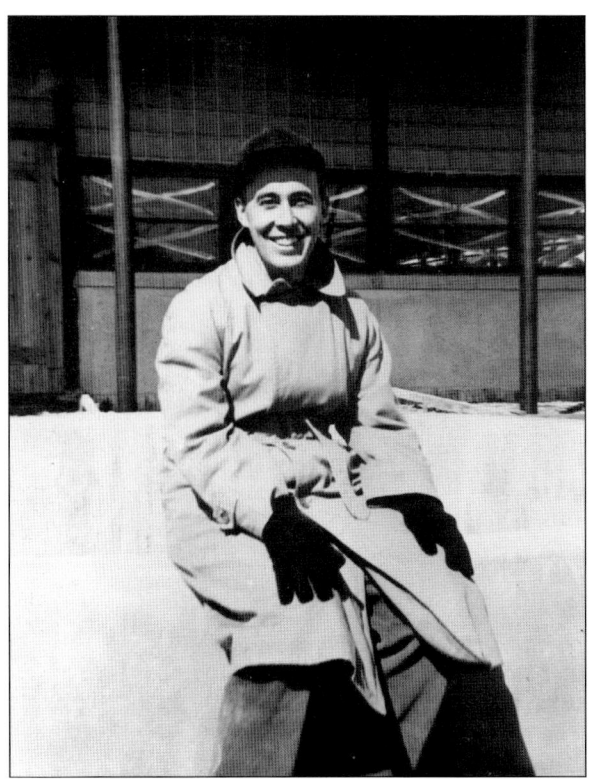

Alonzo Gibbs, pictured here in 1951, moved with his family to Valley Stream. In 1933, he moved with his family to a farm in Plainedge and attended Farmingdale High School. In 1941, he received a certificate from Columbia University on aircraft structural design. He was employed by Grumman Aircraft Corporation and started in the engineering department when Grumman was located in Farmingdale. He had the opportunity to work on the lunar excursion module. He pursued his love of writing and wrote many young-adult novels, poetry, and essays. Alonzo married Iris Ebish on June 17, 1939, and they shared a love of nature, art, books, and history. (Courtesy of Plainedge Public Library.)

Alonzo and Iris wrote for the *Long Island Forum* for 40 years. These writings were later compiled into books, *Harking Back* and *Bethpage Bygones*. These document the history of the community from the time of the Bethpage Purchase by Thomas Powell on through the early 1900s. Alonzo died in 1992. (Photograph by the author.)

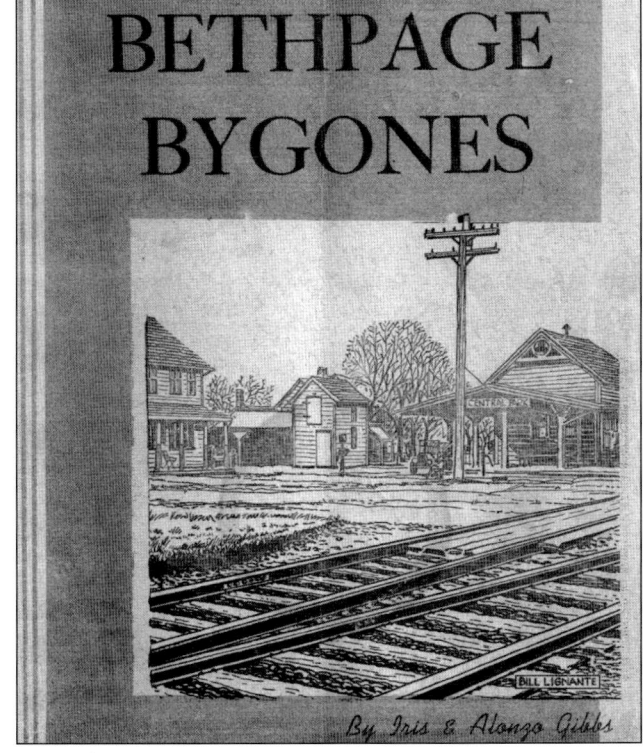

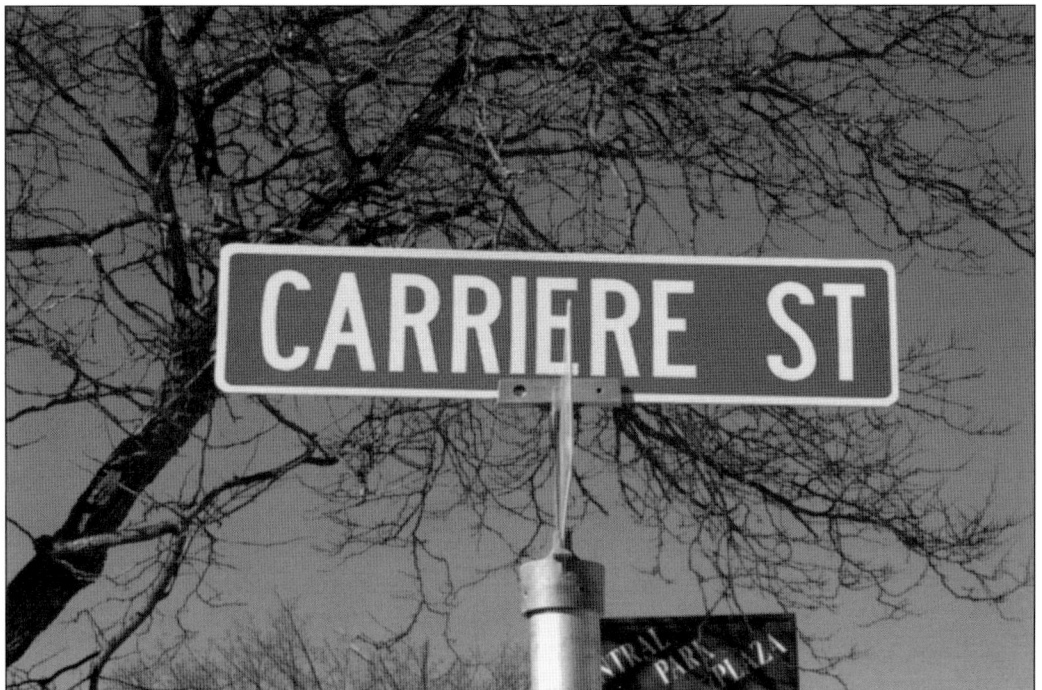

There are a number of streets named for influential families and individuals: Alice Court (named for Alice K. Hosford), Anderson Street (for the florist family), Baldwin Place (a blacksmith shop), Burkhardt Avenue, Gerhard Road, Kramer Lane, Lauman Lane, Leslie Street, McCord Place, Nibbe Lane, Ott Street, Powell Avenue (founding family of the area), Romscho Street, Scherer Street, Schneider Lane (owned a pickle factory), Seaman Avenue, Seitz Drive, Silber Lane (local developer), Stokes Avenue, Stymus Avenue, Thorne Drive, Totten Street, Wilford Street, and Wilson Lane. (Courtesy of Alec Logerfo.)

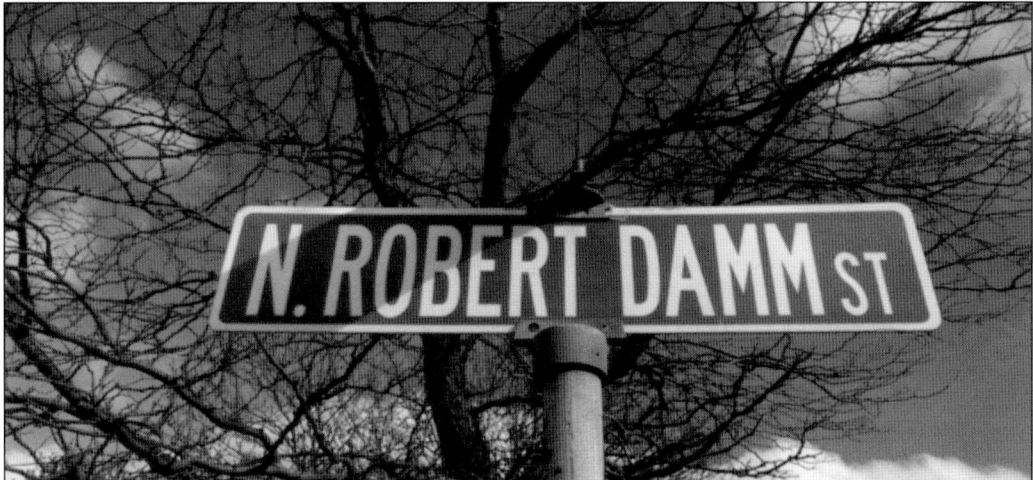

There are also streets named as a tribute to people killed in wars: Benkert Street, in honor of George Jr., killed in World War I; Butehorn Street, in honor of Joseph and Charles, killed in World War II; Caffrey Avenue, in honor of Raymond Caffrey, killed in World War II; Carriere Street, in honor of Raymond Carriere, killed in World War II; and Robert Damm Street, named in honor of Robert Damm, killed in World War II. (Courtesy of Jason Logerfo.)

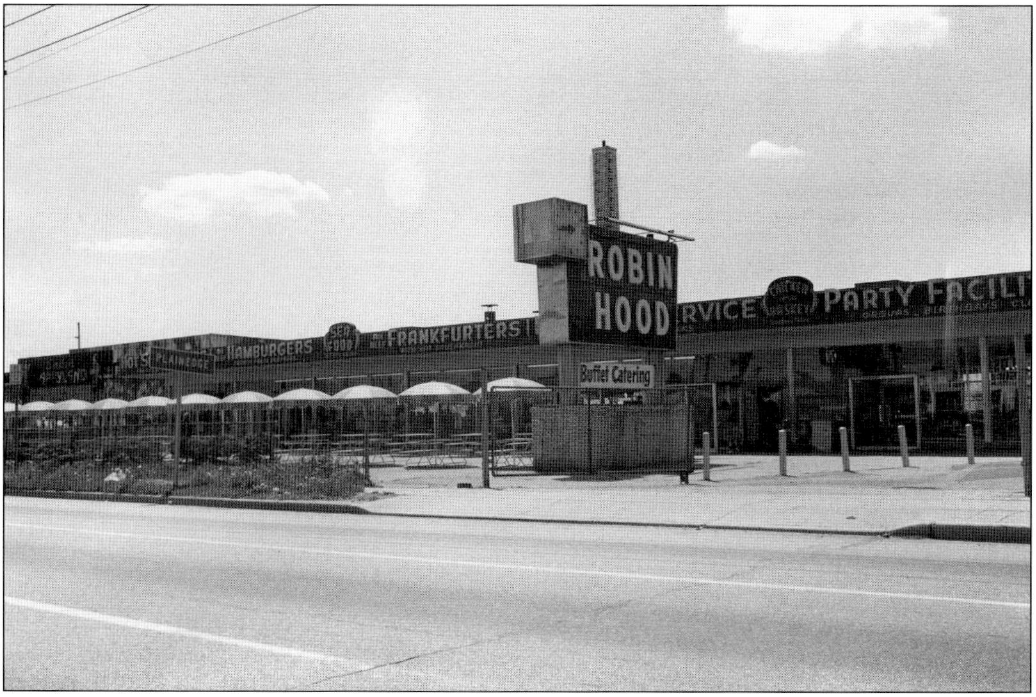

In 1951, William Nunley opened the largest year-round park in Bethpage, on the corner of Hicksville Road and Hempstead Turnpike. It was a 5.5-acre amusement park and restaurant. Removable glass doors, from the 1939 New York World's Fair French Pavilion, allowed for the flow of people from the restaurant, Jolly Roger's, to the rides outside. In 1964, the park changed hands, after the death of Miriam Nunley, and Smiley's Happyland expanded on Nunley's park and added a miniature-golf course and a batting cage. A miniature railroad took the children for a ride around the course. Times changed, and reduced patronage caused the park to shut down in 1978. (Courtesy of Plainedge Public Library.)

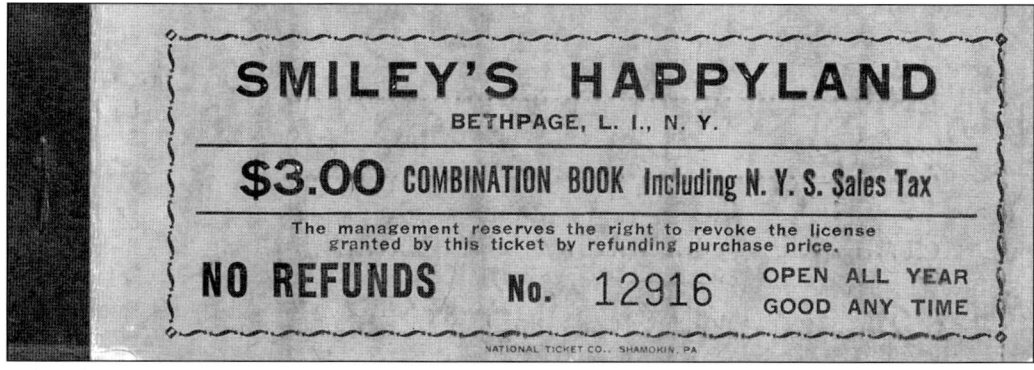

After the Nunley family sold the original Nunley's Happyland in 1964, it was renamed Smiley's Happyland. This coupon booklet contained tickets for the rides at the park. Ride tickets were 10¢ each in the 1950s and the 1960s. In the 1970s, the tickets cost 80¢ each.

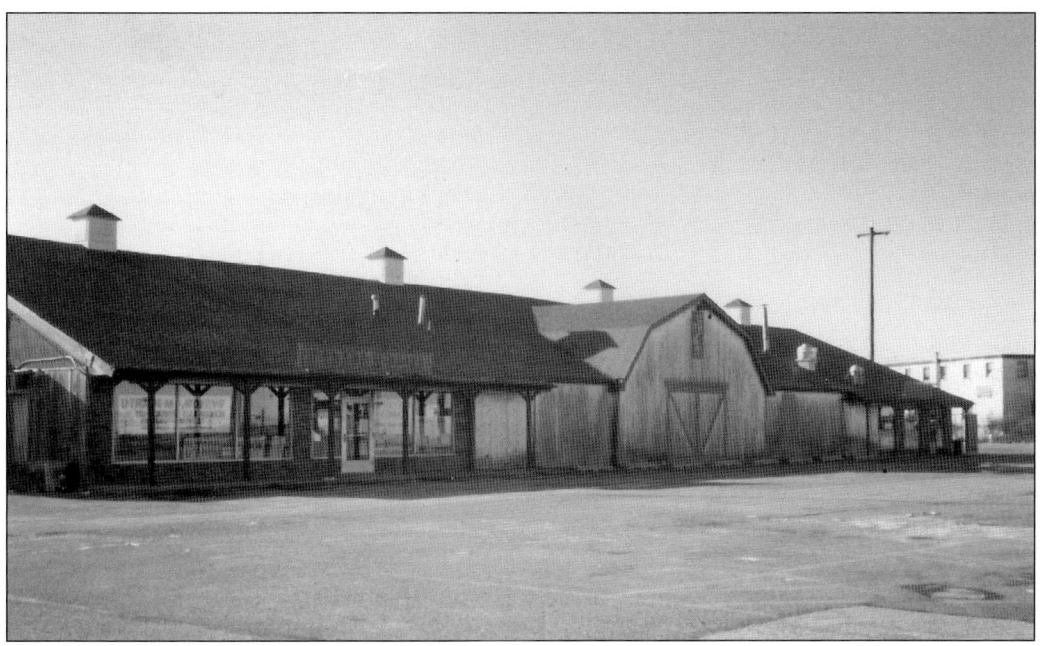

In 1954, the Nassau Farmers' Market opened on Hicksville Road on the present site of Lowes Home Improvement. The 600-foot-long shed-like building had 400 stalls selling everything from produce to clothing and furniture. It attracted as many as 40,000 shoppers a week. The merry-go-round was a big attraction for the children, as was a small movie theater. Residents remember the fresh vegetables, fruit, and bread on Friday and Saturdays. Strolling the stalls in the evening became a night out for the family.

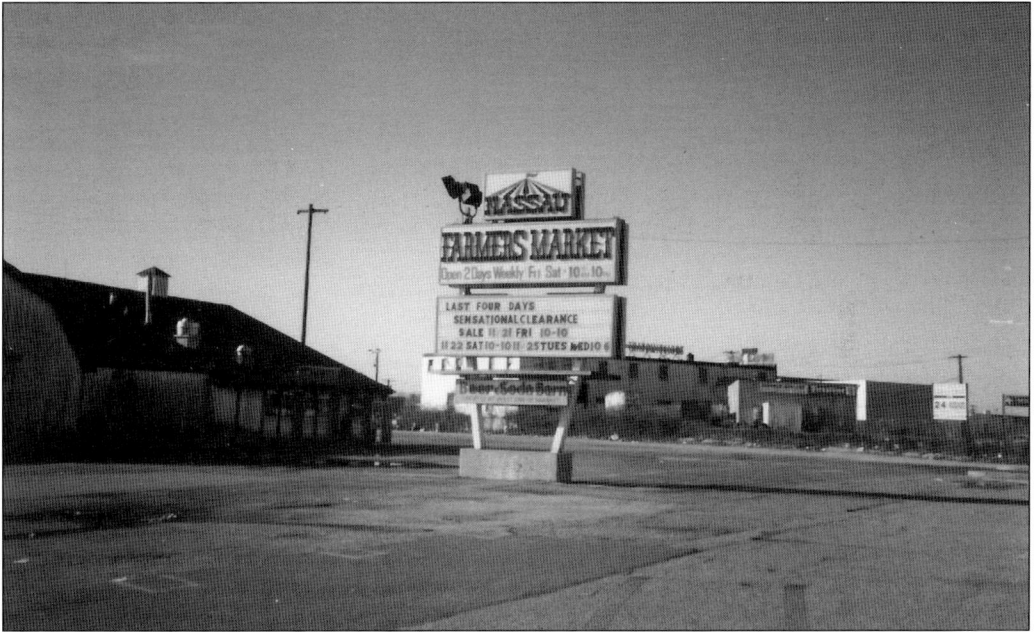

Unfortunately, a suspicious fire destroyed the entire market on June 1987. It was one of the first in the New York metropolitan area to provide such innovations as babysitters for shoppers. It also offered roving musicians during holiday celebrations.

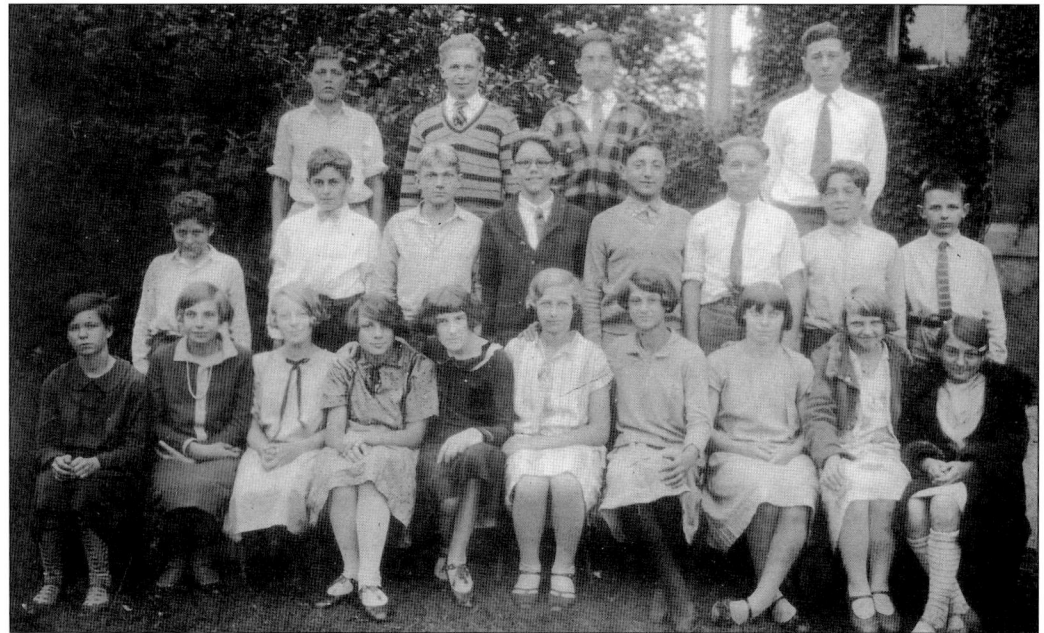

Population growth in the early 1920s made it necessary to add to the original Powell Avenue School. Eight rooms were added in back of the original, now totaling 12 classrooms. A two-room wood annex was built, which took care of the overcrowded school until the addition was finished. In 1923, the new structure was completed. Pictured here is the Powell Avenue School class of 1927. (Courtesy of Joyce Calo.)

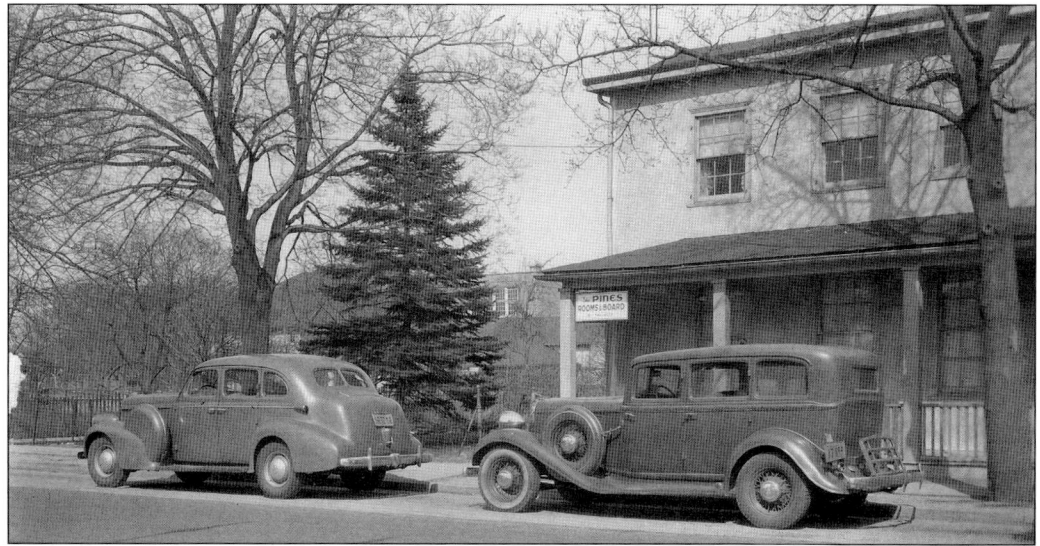

In 1948, the district was forced by the ever-increasing population to make plans for a new school. The Broadway School building with its 23 classrooms was built in 1951 for kindergarten through eighth grade. That year, the Powell Avenue school was vacant. In September 1952, it was necessary to reopen the Powell Avenue School because Farmingdale could no longer take Bethpage's high school children, and for the first time, the ninth grade students were being educated in Bethpage. Pictured here is Broadway and Washington Street with the Powell Avenue School and Annex in the background in 1944.

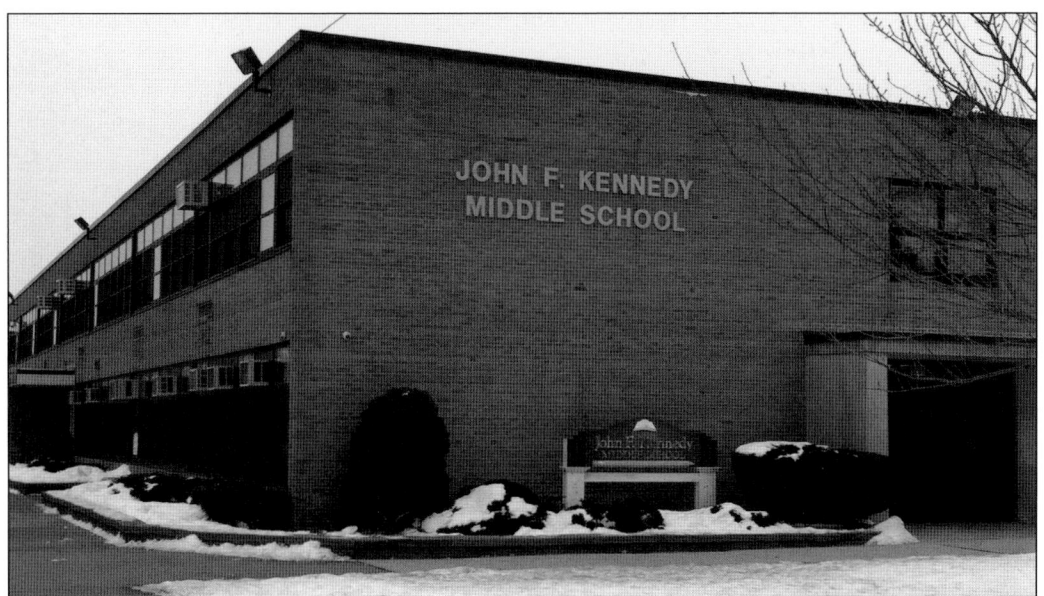

In 1953, the district voted for a new school in the north, where new homes were being built. In 1954, the Pine Avenue School opened with its 22 classrooms. Later that year, plans were being made for a school in the south. Central Boulevard School with 33 classrooms opened in 1955. With increasing high school enrollment at the Broadway School, another school needed to be built. The proposed Kramer Lane Elementary School with 22 classrooms and additions to the Broadway School was before the voters. In September 1955, a complete junior-senior high school program was in operation, and the first graduation took place in June 1956, with 219 graduates. These new structures opened in 1957. (Courtesy of Amanda Laikin.)

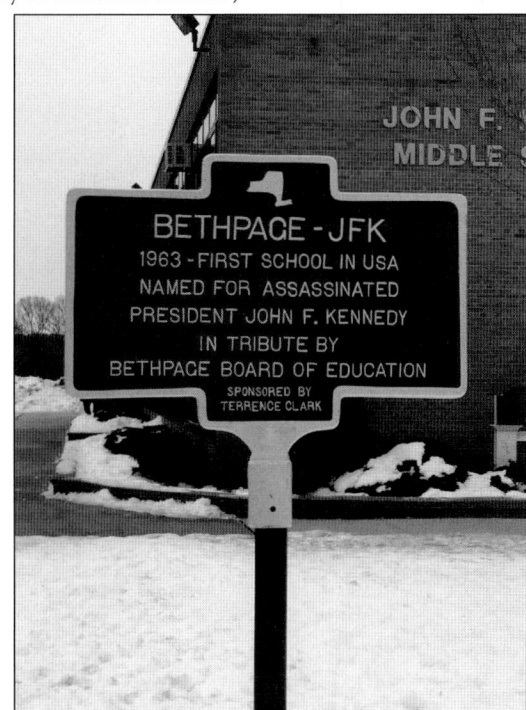

On November 22, 1963, John F. Kennedy's assassination stunned the nation, and the community of Bethpage came together to have the Bethpage Junior High School, now known as the Bethpage Middle School, named to honor President Kennedy. It became the first school in the country to claim this distinction. (Courtesy of Amanda Laikin.)

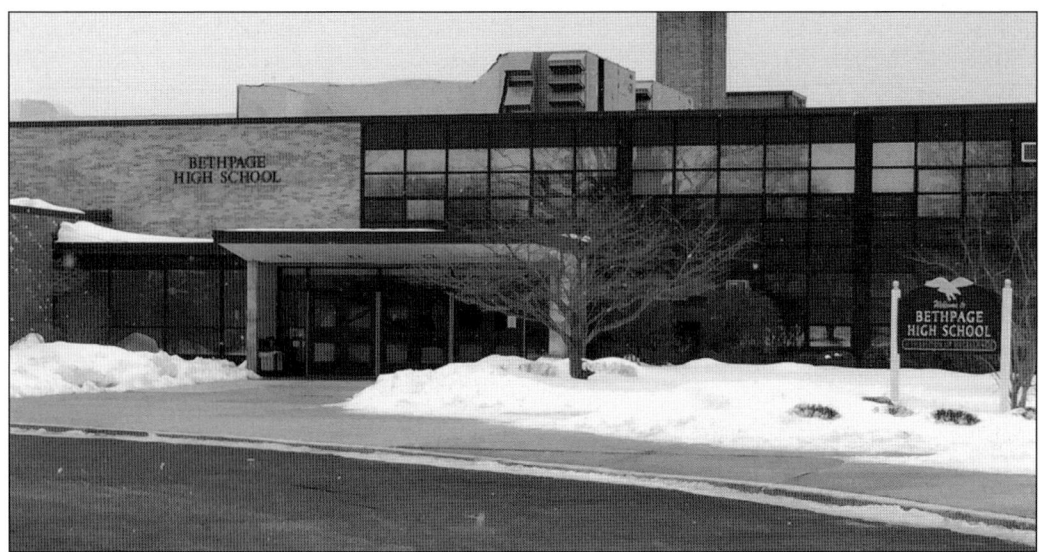

In 1955, New York University made a survey of the educational needs of Bethpage. The exponential growth of the district had caused previous calculations to fall far short of the actual figures. It indicated that 6,806 children would ultimately live in the Bethpage School District in 1963 and would require educational facilities sufficient to care for their needs. In 1959, Bethpage High School was built on Cherry and Stewart Avenues and formally dedicated in 1960. On June 25, 1961, the first full class graduated from the new high school. (Courtesy of Amanda Laikin.)

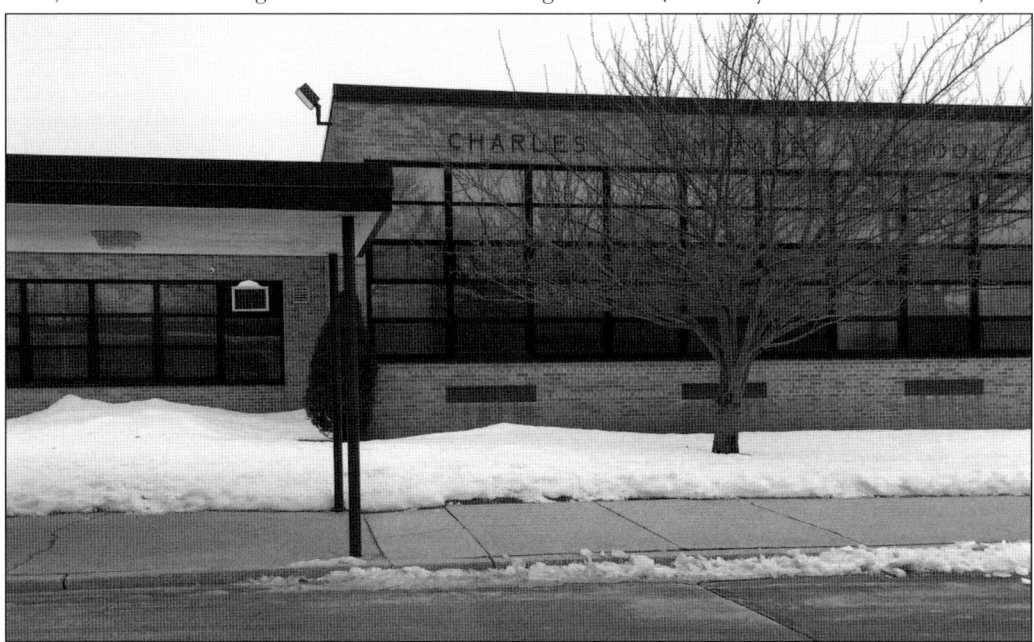

The 14-room Bloomingdale Elementary School opened in 1959, and the Broadway School now became a junior high school, grades seven and eight. In 1962, Charles Campagne Elementary School was built on Plainview Road near where the original Bedell School was built in 1858. Due to declining enrollment, Bloomingdale Elementary was closed in 1972, and Pine Avenue Elementary School closed in 1980. Pictured here is the Charles Campagne School, as it appears today. (Courtesy of Amanda Laikin.)

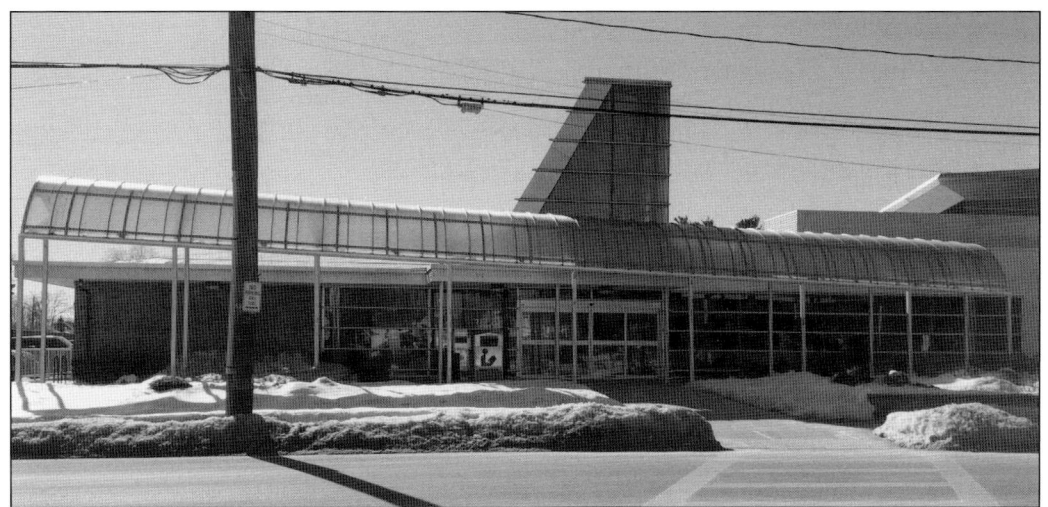

In 1926, the Central Park Free Library was organized as an association library housed in a store near the railroad station. In 1929, the library closed temporarily due to financial difficulties, but it reopened after $2,500 in tax support was approved by voters. In 1931, the library became a school-district library, and the name changed to the Central Park Public Library. In 1936, Central Park became Bethpage, the regents amended the library's charter to read Bethpage Public Library in 1942, and it moved to larger rented quarters on Broadway. In 1949, the library moved to the fire department on Broadway. (Photograph by the author)

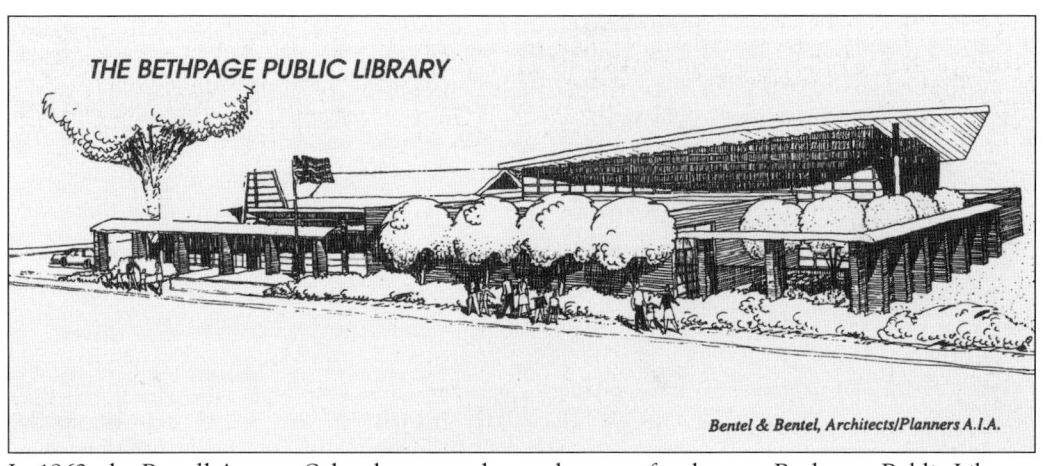

In 1962, the Powell Avenue School was razed to make room for the new Bethpage Public Library, which opened on July 29, 1963. At the time of the dedication, the library board's trustees were Joseph G. Brennan, Leon C. Carlen, Robert J. Glasser, Victor L. Miller, Jacob Schaaf, and Louis A. Sisia. Bethpage was one of the original 38 members to join the Nassau Library System. This is an artist's rendering of the renovated library in 1995, with the addition of the auditorium.

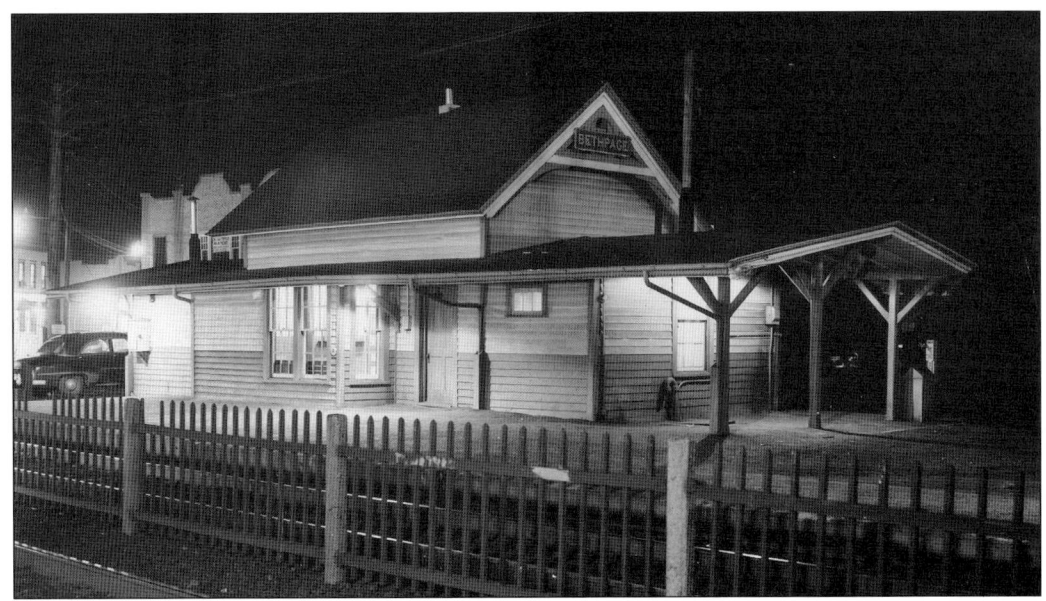

In 1841, the Central Railroad of Long Island was extended through Bethpage. By 1854, the trains stopped at a local station called Jerusalem Station. In 1867, the residents voted to change the name of the station to Central Park. A one-story combination passenger and freight depot was built sometime between 1874 and 1879. A new station was built in 1884, and it was renamed Bethpage in 1936. In 1957, the station was torn down, and a cinder-block station was built on the northeast side of the tracks. In 1984, an elevated platform was added west of Stewart Avenue. Service became electrified, and the first electric train passed through on April 30, 1987. Pictured here is the Bethpage Train Station in 1954.

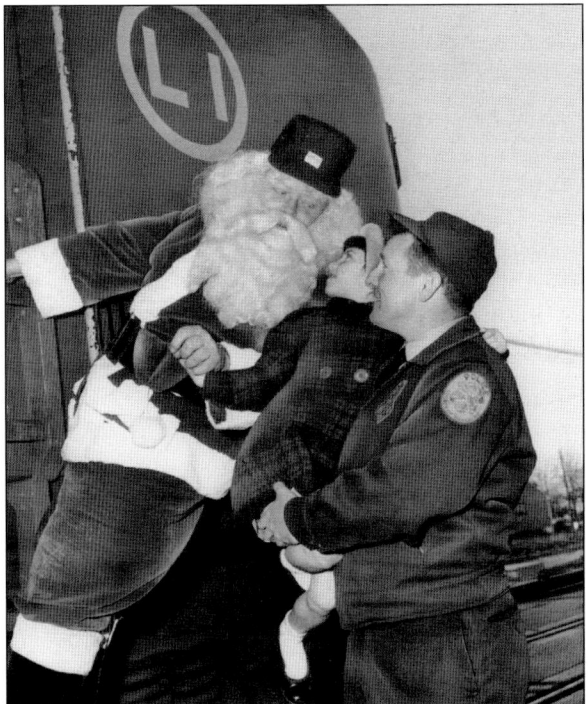

Santa arrives in Bethpage by the Long Island Rail Road to join the Christmas Party organized by the Bethpage unit of the Police Boys Club in 1957 and is greeted by six-year old Regina Doriman with patrolman Walter Scholl. The Police Boys Club is now known as the Police Athletic League, and Scholl was director for 24 years.

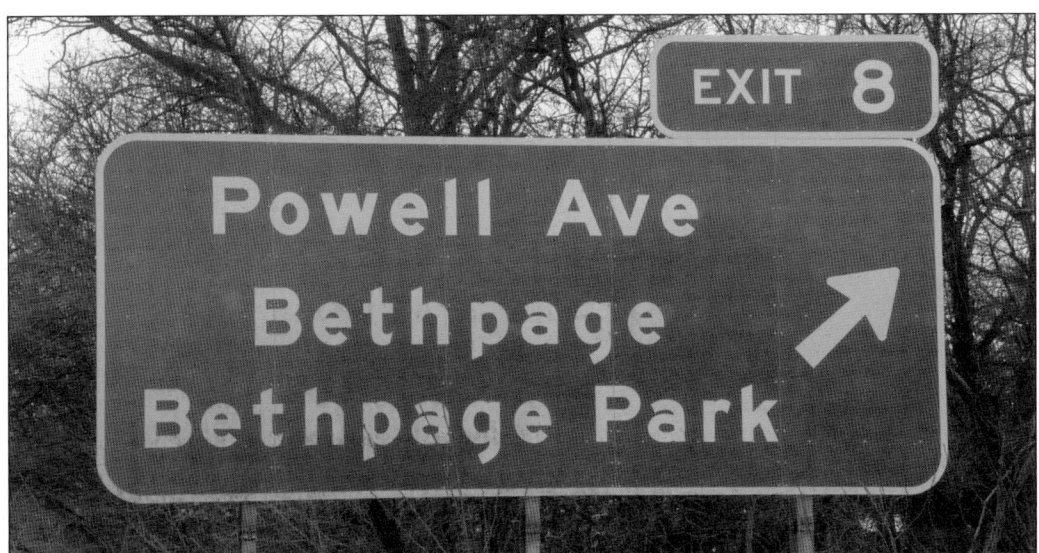

In 1954, the New York State drew plans to build a six-lane, north-south expressway between the Wantagh State Parkway in Wantagh and NY 106 in Oyster Bay. Communities along the proposed path opposed its construction because it divided each community that it passed through and was met by protests. Lewis Waters, the Oyster Bay town supervisor, addressed their concerns and proposed a different direction for the expressway. Waters proposed that it begin at Ocean Parkway in Tobay Beach, cross the Great South Bay and enter West Amityville, then turn to the northeast near the Sunrise Mall and progress its way through Massapequa and Farmingdale into Bethpage State Park. (Courtesy of Mike Tamborrino.)

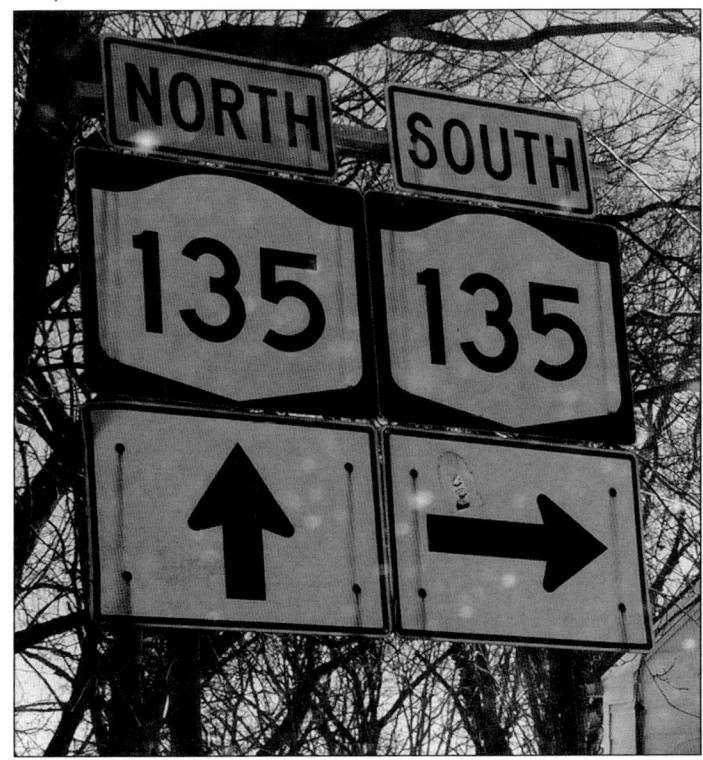

The highway was to cross through Bethpage State Park using the old right-of-way for the Bethpage State Parkway through Old Bethpage and Plainview. Robert Moses won the grant and the right-of-way in 1958, and construction began in 1959. Powell Avenue Exit 8 was completed in 1962. The entire project cost $49 million and totaled 10.8 miles. In 1967, the name of the expressway was renamed to Seaford–Oyster Bay Expressway. (Photograph by the author.)

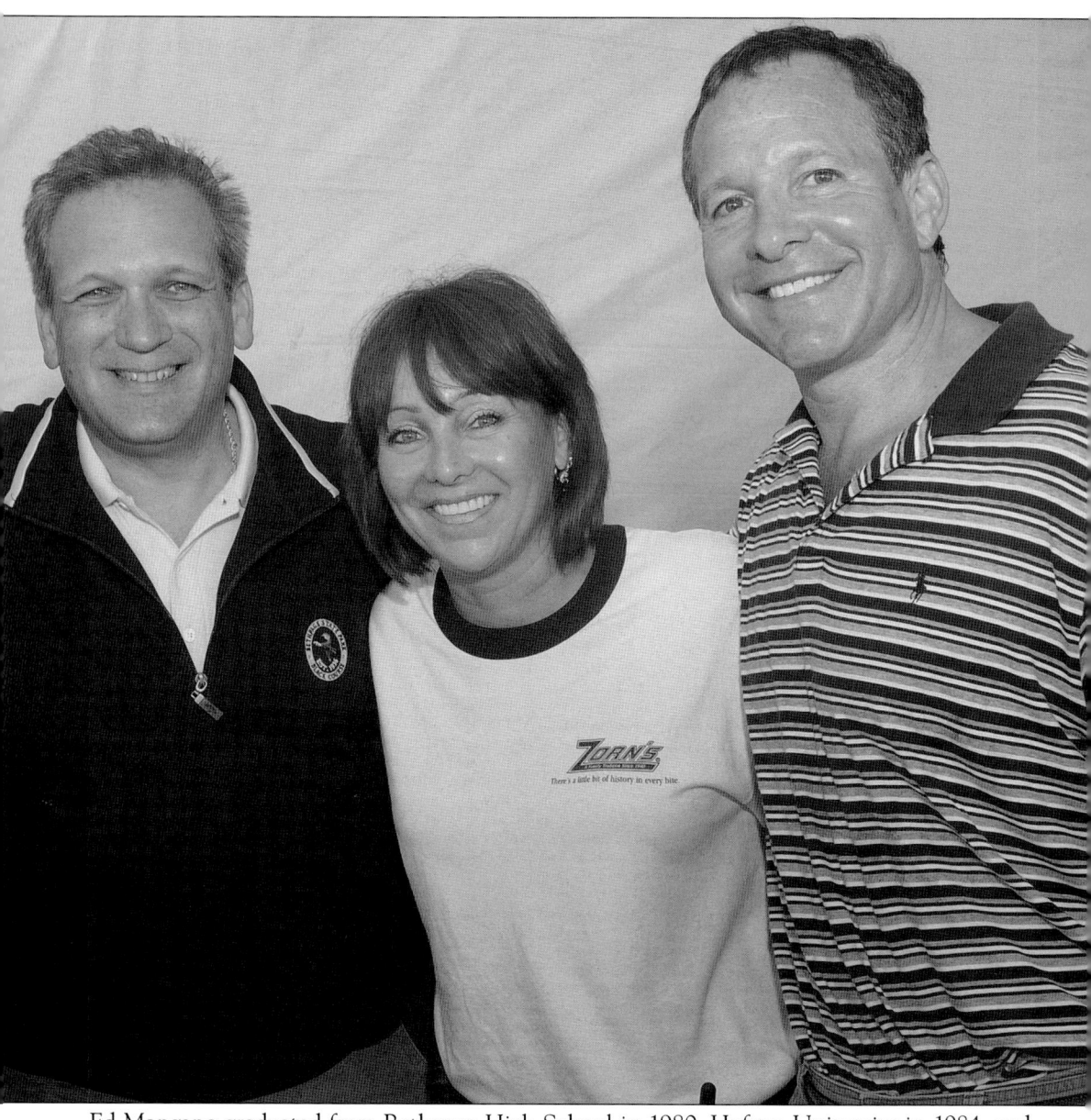

Ed Mangano graduated from Bethpage High School in 1980, Hofstra University in 1984, and Hofstra Law School in 1987 before entering a private law practice. He was elected to the Nassau County Legislature in 1995. As a legislator, he accomplished the redevelopment of the former Grumman Property and established a senior citizen and community center. He preserved land and open space for future generations. As Nassau County legislator, he was the ranking member of the public works, recreation, and parks committee and served on the rules committee, procedures committee, and economic, community development and labor committee. He served the 17th Legislative District for seven terms, until 2009, when he became county executive. Mangano was sworn in on January 1, 2010, at Bethpage High School and reelected on November 5, 2013. Mangano resides in Bethpage with his wife, Linda, and two sons, Salvatore and Alexander. Pictured here from left to right are County Executive Ed Mangano; Merrill Zorn, owner of Zorn's Caterers; and Plainedge High School graduate and actor Steve Guttenberg. (Courtesy of Mike Tamborrino.)

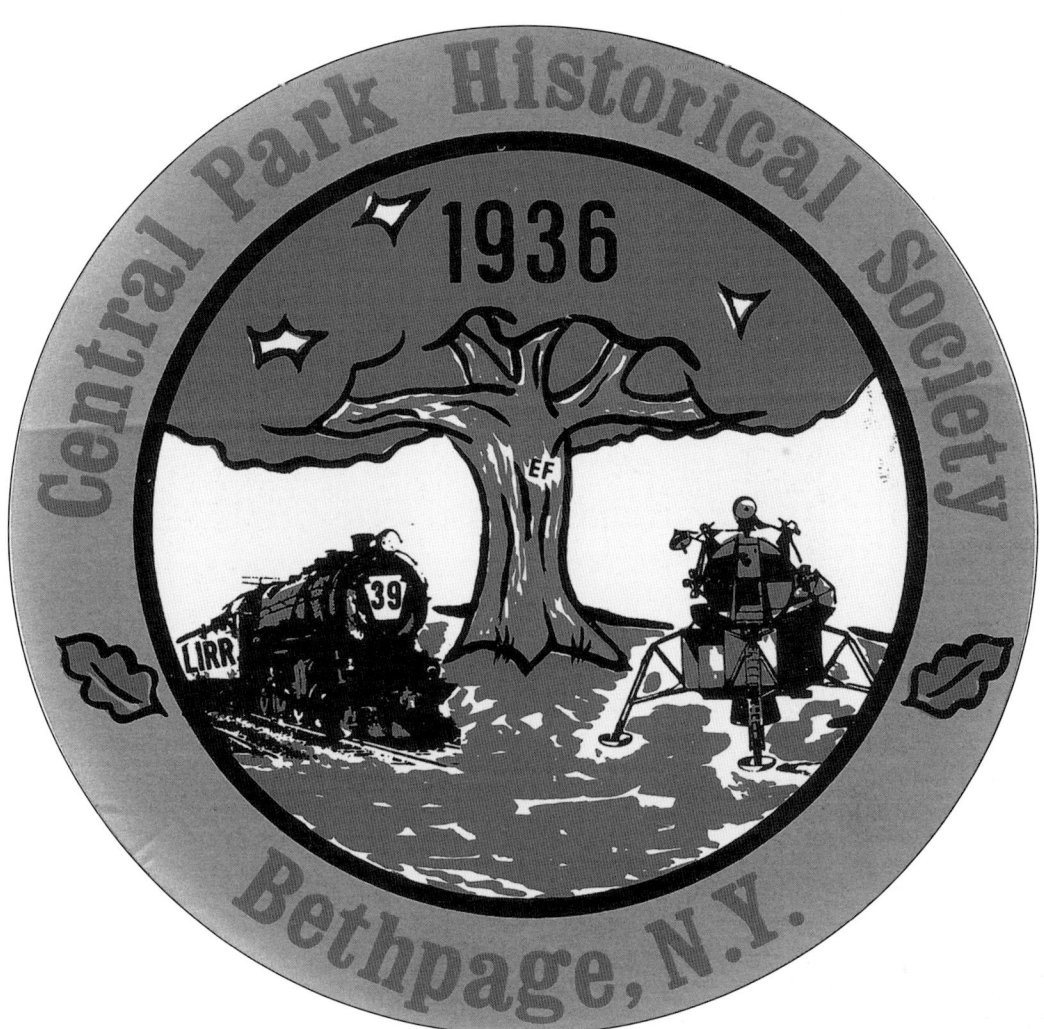

The Central Park Historical Society was founded in 1986, and a provisional charter was granted on February 16, 1990. Their purpose is to promote and encourage historical research through the process of gathering, preserving, displaying, and making available for study artifacts, relics, books, manuscripts, papers, photographs, and other records relating to Bethpage. The CPHS sought a logo that would depict the history of Bethpage at a glance. Progressing along the name circle, one approaches the present name of the community, Bethpage, which was renamed in 1936, as noted on the tree. The tree represents how deeply religious the early settlers of the Bethpage Purchase were. It is symbolic of a fig tree located in the Biblical town of Bethphage located on the Mount of Olives as related in the Gospels. Engine 39, the last steam locomotive to pass through Bethpage, symbolizes the importance of the LIRR to Bethpage, which at one time was a frontier in the eastward movement of people on Long Island. The lunar expedition module (LEM) designed and constructed by the Grumman Aerospace Corporation established a new frontier. Just as the railroad reached eastward in the 1880s, the LEM reached for the moon in achieving a giant step for mankind. As summarized by Daniel Schiavetta, the first president of the Central Park Historical Society, "No place in the world is there a country or village which can claim the only structure on the moon but Bethpage."

DISCOVER THOUSANDS OF LOCAL HISTORY BOOKS FEATURING MILLIONS OF VINTAGE IMAGES

Arcadia Publishing, the leading local history publisher in the United States, is committed to making history accessible and meaningful through publishing books that celebrate and preserve the heritage of America's people and places.

Find more books like this at
www.arcadiapublishing.com

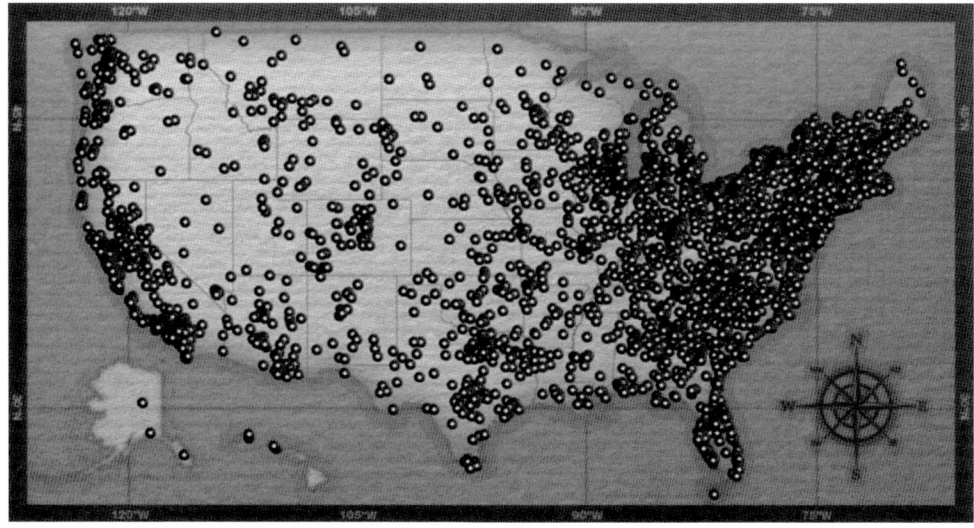

Search for your hometown history, your old stomping grounds, and even your favorite sports team.

Consistent with our mission to preserve history on a local level, this book was printed in South Carolina on American-made paper and manufactured entirely in the United States. Products carrying the accredited Forest Stewardship Council (FSC) label are printed on 100 percent FSC-certified paper.

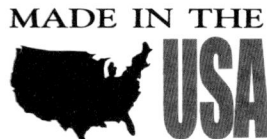